Hands-on Data Analytics for Business gives comprehensive insights covering theoretical frameworks, practical analytics skills, real-world case studies and analytics project management to tackle business challenges effectively. It builds a strong foundation for readers to understand the analytics process for solving diverse business problems. The step-by-step hands-on approach to analytics demonstrates the practical skills clearly and concisely supported by smart visual illustrations. The case studies from diverse industries provide a global perspective. It also offers practical insights in managing analytics projects. This analytics book is a valuable resource to professionals and university students for careers in business, consulting or academia.

Professor Patrick Y.K. CHAU
Provost and Chair Professor in Information Systems and Business Analytics
Beijing Normal-Hong Kong Baptist University

Advancements in data analytics and the widespread use of large-scale data are driving a golden age of evidence-based management. This timely publication addresses limitations in traditional business school curricula. The book serves as an essential guide, equipping students to master diverse data analytics techniques, apply them across business domains, and generate creative analytical solutions for novel problems.

Professor Xu HUANG
Associate Dean (Research and Impact) and Chair Professor in Management,
School of Business, Hong Kong Baptist University

I highly recommend *Hands-on Data Analytics for Business* by Dr. Monica W.M. Tang. This expertly crafted textbook provides a comprehensive, step-by-step guide to mastering the essential data analytics skills that every business student and professional needs. It skillfully integrates practical instruction on using SPSS and Excel with real-world case studies spanning human resources, marketing, and supply chain management. The clarity and accessibility of the content, along with its actionable insights, make this an invaluable resource for anyone looking to understand and apply data analytics to solve complex business challenges. Whether you are a postgraduate student or a business professional, this book offers a hands-on, engaging approach to developing critical analytical capabilities.

Dr. Catherine K. LAM
Associate Professor of Organizational Behavior and Human Resource Management,
Wilfrid Laurier University

Dr. Monica Tang's *Hands-on Data Analytics for Business* is an invaluable resource for understanding and applying data analytics in today's business world. As Programme Director for the MSc Business Management at HKBU, I have seen firsthand how her teaching of "HR Analytics" is praised by students for its clarity and practical focus – qualities reflected in this book. Covering key areas like HR, marketing, supply chain, and future trends, it equips readers with actionable insights for data-driven decision-making. Highly recommended!

Professor Monique WAN
Associate Dean (Taught Postgraduate Studies), School of Business,
Hong Kong Baptist University (HKBU)

Hands-on Data Analytics for Business is an essential guide for students navigating the data-driven business world. With big data transforming decision-making across industries, this book equips learners with practical skills through real-world company cases, bridging theory and application. I commend Monica for crafting such a timely and practical resource, for anyone preparing to harness data for strategic insights!

Professor Kalok CHAN
Chair Professor of Finance, City University of Hong Kong

Hands-on Data Analytics for Business is an excellent guide that combines theory, practical applications, and real-world case studies in the field of analytics. Through its well-structured content and engaging style, the book skillfully demonstrates how analytics can be applied across various business areas to solve problems through evidence-based decision-making. Comprehensive yet approachable, this book is highly relevant for business professionals, as well as undergraduate and postgraduate students in the analytics field.

Professor Muammer OZER
Professor of Management, City University of Hong Kong

Data is no longer just a resource for specialists – it's a vital asset that everyone must harness to stay competitive in the digital age. A data-driven mindset and analytics skills are essential across industries, shaping how decisions are made, innovation unfolds, and value is created.

Hands-on Data Analytics for Business is a practical guide that bridges theory and application. Covering core concepts and real-world examples, it equips individuals and organizations with the knowledge and skills to unlock data-driven opportunities and gain a competitive edge. Empowering readers with data literacy and analytical skills, this book is an essential read for thriving in the AI era.

Dr. Toa CHARM
Founding Chairman, Data & AI Literacy Association

Hands-on Data Analytics for Business

The knowledge and skills of data analytics enable business professionals to make evidence-based decisions rather than relying solely on intuition. To appreciate the knowledge and skills, one needs to understand the theory, hands-on statistical operations using computer software, business application case studies and the analytics project maturity roadmap.

Hands-on Data Analytics for Business is a concise, all-in-one analytics textbook for business professionals and university students who want to:

- Understand the essential theories and concepts of data analytics
- Grasp hands-on, practical, statistical and analytics skills step by step using SPSS and Excel
- Appreciate real-world, well-known case studies in human resources, marketing and supply chain that show how data analytics is applied in business.

This book is for business professionals or university students seeking to master data analytics knowledge and technical skills to a level that allows them to practice data analytics hands-on and manage data analytics projects at scale. For business professionals, the book is written to help them learn statistical skills concisely, with practical, real-world examples that inspire business applications. For students, the book is organized in a sequence readily deliverable for a university course, with classes combining theory or concepts, hands-on practice and case studies. For all readers, the book is an essential guide to using data analytics to tackle modern complex activities that enable companies to gain a competitive edge.

Dr. Monica W.M. Tang is Adjunct Associate Professor at Hong Kong Baptist University School of Business. She also teaches at The University of Hong Kong and other universities. She has been teaching different courses in data analytics for business since earning her doctor of business administration from City University of Hong Kong in 2019. She received the "Outstanding

Teacher Award" from The University of Hong Kong School of Professional and Continuing Education in 2024.

Dr. Tang is also a seasoned information technology (IT) management professional. She has more than 25 years of working experience with a demonstrated history of successful IT projects in public sectors, universities and consulting companies. She is now a senior IT manager at The University of Hong Kong. Her areas of expertise include data analytics, digital transformation and project management in different business areas such as human resources, finance and manufacturing.

Dr. Tang has a vision of bringing measurable benefits to organizations and employees through data analytics in IT. She aims to make a positive impact on the professional community by sharing knowledge and skills in data analytics through different publications. She is a frequent speaker in seminars on analytics, artificial intelligence, management and leadership. She also received the "Contribution to the Society Award" from City University of Hong Kong in 2017.

Hands-on Data Analytics for Business

Monica W.M. Tang

CRC Press
Taylor & Francis Group
Boca Raton London New York

CRC Press is an imprint of the
Taylor & Francis Group, an **informa** business
AN AUERBACH BOOK

Designed cover image: Shutterstock

First edition published 2026
2385 NW Executive Center Drive, Suite 320, Boca Raton FL 33431

and by CRC Press
4 Park Square, Milton Park, Abingdon, Oxon, OX14 4RN

CRC Press is an imprint of Taylor & Francis Group, LLC

ISBN: 978-1-032-62736-6 (hbk)
ISBN: 978-1-032-61999-6 (pbk)
ISBN: 978-1-032-64230-7 (ebk)

DOI: 10.1201/9781032642307

Typeset in Garamond
by Apex CoVantage, LLC

Access the Reader Resources: https://www.routledge.com/Hands-on-Data-Analytics-for-Business/Tang/p/book/9781032627366

To my husband, Kenneth, and my sons, Douglas and Hector.

Contents

Preface

Data analytics is an emerging and important field for different business areas. The knowledge and skills of data analytics enable business professionals to make evidence-based decisions rather than relying only on intuition. To appreciate the knowledge and skills, one needs to understand the theory, hands-on statistical operations using computer software, business application case studies and the analytics project maturity roadmap. This book covers all these essential areas, while most other books cover only some parts of them.

This is a concise all-in-one analytics textbook for business professionals and university students who want to understand the essential theories and concepts of data analytics, grasp hands-on practical statistical and analytics skills step by step using SPSS and Excel, and appreciate real-world, well-known case studies in human resources, marketing and supply chain on how data analytics is applied in business. This book differentiates itself with its well-balanced contents covering the fundamental data analytics theory, hands-on practical examples using SPSS and Excel, real-world case studies in different business areas and the project management roadmap in organizations yet remains concise in volume. It narrates in an engaging way, connecting theory with hands-on practice, which thus unfolds the technical details of the real-world case studies.

WHO SHOULD READ THIS BOOK

This book is for business professionals or university students to grasp data analytics knowledge and technical skills to a level that allows them to practice data analytics hands-on and manage data analytics projects at scale.

For business professionals, this book is written to help them learn statistical skills in a concise way with practical, real-world examples to inspire business applications. It would be more beneficial to use the data files provided with this book and follow the instructed steps for hands-on computer practice. For academia and students, this book is organized in a sequence readily deliverable for a university course with classes combining theory or concepts, hands-on practice and case studies. Computer workshops can be included in the course to strengthen students' hands-on practical skills using the data files provided with this book.

HOW TO USE THIS BOOK

Part One of the book has two chapters. This part introduces the fundamental concepts and the process of data analytics, the data collection activities and the statistical techniques required for modeling in data analytics for business.

Chapter 1 examines the meaning of data analytics and its different types, reviews the literature on the development of the field, introduces the process of data analytics and elaborates on the types of real-world business questions that can be answered by data analytics.

Chapter 2 starts by giving an overview of the analytics process, describing how analytics practitioners apply scientific analysis to solve business problems. Following this, the content will delve into how data are collected, what modeling is, how business hypotheses can be formed and how different statistical analysis methods can be adopted.

Part Two consists of three chapters that examine the applications of the data analytics process with SPSS and Excel in different business areas, including human resources, marketing and supply chain. Specific analytics skills, although illustrated in one specific business area, can, in fact, be applied across different areas. Human resources, marketing and supply chain are chosen as examples because they can illustrate different statistical methods. Readers can practice these analytics skills using the example SPSS and Excel data files provided with this book. The details for preparing SPSS and Excel to use these files are described in the following sections. Case studies will also be discussed.

Chapter 3 starts a discussion on human resources (HR) issues that can be addressed through data analytics. Following this, the chapter delves into using metrics and descriptive analytics to help visualize data patterns, demonstrating how to use SPSS and Excel step by step for HR-related issues such as predicting performance and retention, identifying areas of bias, and introducing the use of organizational network analysis.

Chapter 4 reviews different marketing questions that can be solved by data analytics. Following this introduction, the content will cover metrics and descriptive analytics applied in marketing to discover data patterns, using SPSS and Excel to do analytics to predict marketing-related matters such as customers' lifetime value, up-selling and cross-selling.

Chapter 5 continues the discussion of issues in the supply chain that can be solved by data analytics. Key metrics will be introduced. Data analytics related to the supply chain, such as forecasting demands, predicting delays and identifying bottlenecks, will be discussed.

Part Three has one chapter, which serves as a summary and examines future trends in analytics. This chapter also discusses how to build analytics capabilities and manage analytics projects in organizations. The book concludes with a discussion on the future developments of data analytics for business.

Chapter 6 outlines the directions for building analytics capabilities and the roadmap for analytics projects in organizations. Future trends and developments in analytics are also discussed.

This book uses many walkthrough-like figures to clearly illustrate the steps in running the statistical processes in SPSS and Excel. By following the numbers labeled in these figures, you will find the sequence of clicks and the locations of the buttons or links as described in the text. These figures will also help you interpret the statistical results by highlighting the key numbers to read alongside the text in this book. I encourage you to learn by using the SPSS and Excel files provided with this book to practice your hands-on analytics skills. The data files are prepared in a way that illustrates different cases within a single example. You may want to practice a few times with the same example to strengthen your memory and understanding.

GETTING SPSS READY AND USING THE EXAMPLE SPSS FILES WITH THIS BOOK

This book shows example SPSS files for your hands-on practice. You can download these files from https://www.routledge.com/Hands-on-Data-Analytics-for-Business/Tang/p/book/9781032627366. The SPSS images in this book come from SPSS Version 29. Different SPSS versions may have some differences in their layout. If you are new to SPSS, here is a quick introduction to help you get SPSS ready.

An *SPSS file* ends with the file extension ".sav" (i.e., the suffix at the end of the file name). The SPSS analysis result will be shown in the *Output Viewer*, which is another file with the extension ".spv." Open an SPSS file (e.g., Ch2_Job_Satisfaction_and_Sales_Volume.sav). First, as shown in Figure 0.1, you can see that there are two view pages: (1) Data View and (2) Variable View. The *Data View* simply shows the data. The *Variable View* contains the metadata (i.e., the description of the data). Second, in the *Variable View*, you can see two columns, Name and Label. *Name* is a code representing that variable, while *Label* is a long description of that variable. Third, if you want to know the values of that variable, you can click the three-dot button in the column *Values*, and it will show the description for each of the values in

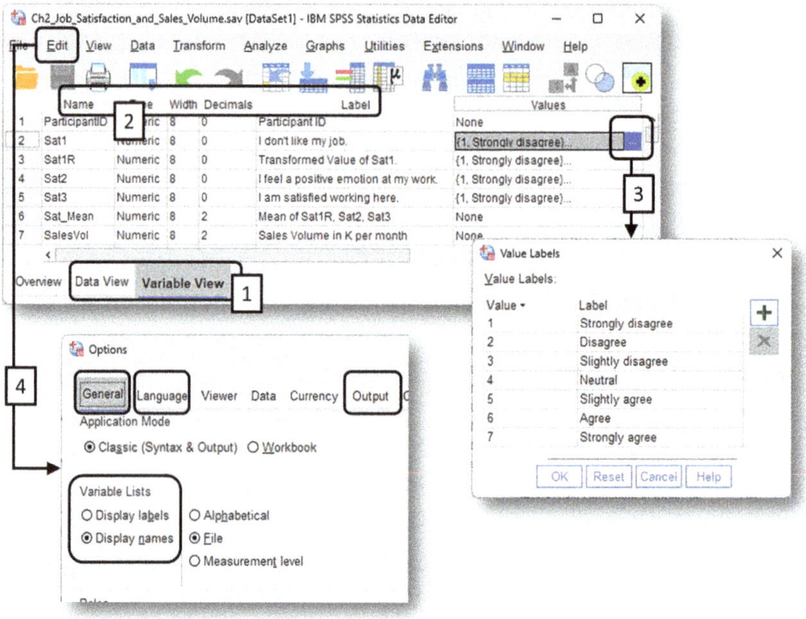

FIGURE 0.1
Getting SPSS Ready

the "Value Labels" pop-up dialog box. Fourth, when running the statistical tests in SPSS, you may want to show the Name of the variables instead of the Label, which is the long description. You can choose by clicking *Edit* > *Options*. Choose correspondingly in the tab pages *General* and *Output* in the "Options" pop-up dialog box. You can also choose the language for your SPSS in the *Language* tab page. Make sure you click "Apply" and then "OK" to save your settings. Now your SPSS is ready.

GETTING EXCEL READY AND USING THE EXAMPLE EXCEL FILES WITH THIS BOOK

This book also shows example Excel files for your hands-on practice. You can download these files from https://www.routledge.com/Hands-on-Data-Analytics-for-Business/Tang/p/book/9781032627366. To run the statistical analyses in this book using Excel, you need to install four add-ins, including (1) **Analysis ToolPak**, (2) **Analysis ToolPak – VBA,** (3) **Solver Add-in** and (4) **Real Statistics (Xrealstats)**.

Real Statistics (Xrealstats) is a free Excel add-in from the website "Real Statistics Using Excel" (https://real-statistics.com/) by Dr. Charles Zaiontz. Read the license agreement on the website before you download it. This add-in supports both Windows and Macintosh, though their installation steps are slightly different. Do *not* open or double-click the downloaded add-in file. Please go to the website and follow the instructions for Windows or Macintosh to install it accordingly. The Excel figures in this book are from Excel on Windows.

You can also use the following steps to install these four add-ins.

For Excel on Windows, follow the numbers in Figure 0.2 to install these add-ins. Go to *File* > *Options*. In the "Excel Options" pop-up dialog box, click *Add-ins* > *Manage: Excel Add-ins* > click *Go*. In the "Add-ins" pop-up dialog box, click *Browse* to choose the Real Statistics Excel add-in (i.e., the file **Xrealstats.xlam** or **XrealstatsX.xlam)** you have downloaded, and tick the four add-ins: (1) **Analysis ToolPak**, (2) **Analysis TookPak – VBA,** (3) **Solver Add-in,** and (4) **Xrealstats**. Click *OK*. Go to the *Add-ins* ribbon; if you see *Real Statistics* > *Data Analysis Tools*, you have installed the Real Statistics add-in successfully. Go to the *Data* ribbon; if you see *Data Analysis* and *Solver*, you have installed the other three add-ins successfully. If you cannot install the Real Statistics add-in, it is most likely because the file location where you placed your file Xrealstats.xlam has not yet been trusted by Excel. You can go to the *Trust Center* in the "Excel Options" pop-up dialog box to add the file path where your add-in file is located. Due to space limitations, I recommend you visit the "Real Statistics Using Excel" website (https://real-statistics.com/) for other detailed troubleshooting illustrations.

For Excel on Macintosh, to install the four add-ins, go to *Tools* > *Excel Add-ins*, or you can press Alt-TI (i.e., press the keys "Alt," "T," and "I" together). Apart from this very first step, the selections in the "Excel Options" and "Add-ins" dialog boxes are similar to those for Windows installation. You may refer to the previous paragraph or Figure 0.2. For Macintosh, install (1) **Analysis ToolPak**, (2) **Analysis TookPak – VBA**, (3) **Solver Add-in** first and click *OK*. Then repeat to install (4) **Real Statistics Excel Add-in** and click *OK*. For more detailed instructions on installing this Excel add-in on Macintosh, please visit the website "Real Statistics Using Excel" at https://real-statistics.com/.

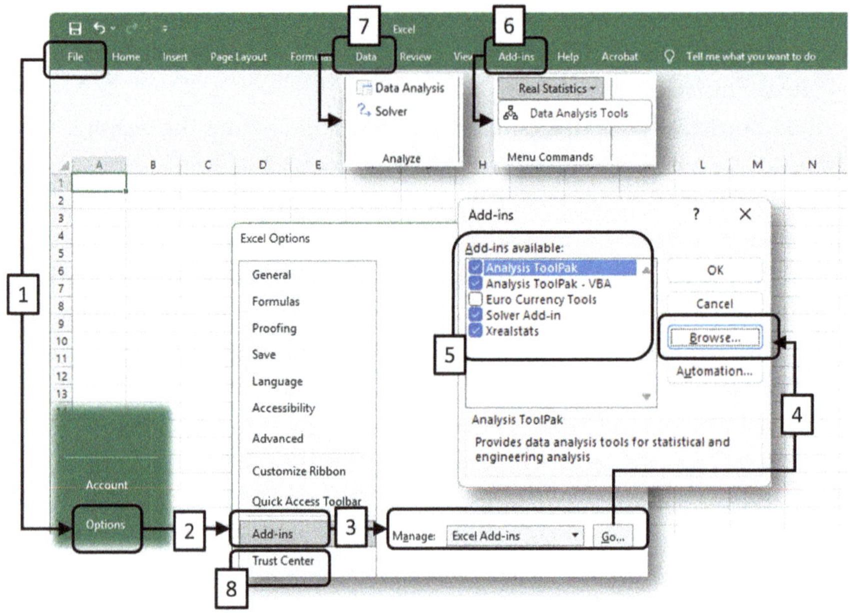

FIGURE 0.2
Getting Excel Add-in Ready on Windows

After you have installed the Real Statistics Excel add-in, in addition to launching this add-in from *Add-ins > Real Statistics > Data Analysis Tools*, you can also press *Ctrl+m* or *Control-m* (i.e., press both the "Ctrl"/"Control" key and the "m" key together) to have the "Real Statistics" dialog box appear.

Open an example Excel file (e.g., Ch2_Job_Satisfaction_and_Sales_Volume.xlsx). In this book, you will usually find a worksheet called "Meta Data," as shown in Figure 0.3. In this "Meta Data" worksheet, you will see the descriptions of the dataset, including the *Variable*, *Description*, and its *Values*. Another worksheet, "Data," simply shows the data. Let us take a look to see how these two worksheets function together. If you see that the value of the variable *Sat2* equals 7 in the worksheet "Data," you can check the values of the variable *Sat2* in the worksheet "Meta Data" and find that 7 means "Strongly agree," and the description of the variable *Sat2* shows that it is a survey item: "I feel a positive emotion at my work." Depending on the demonstration purpose, there may be different worksheets in these Excel

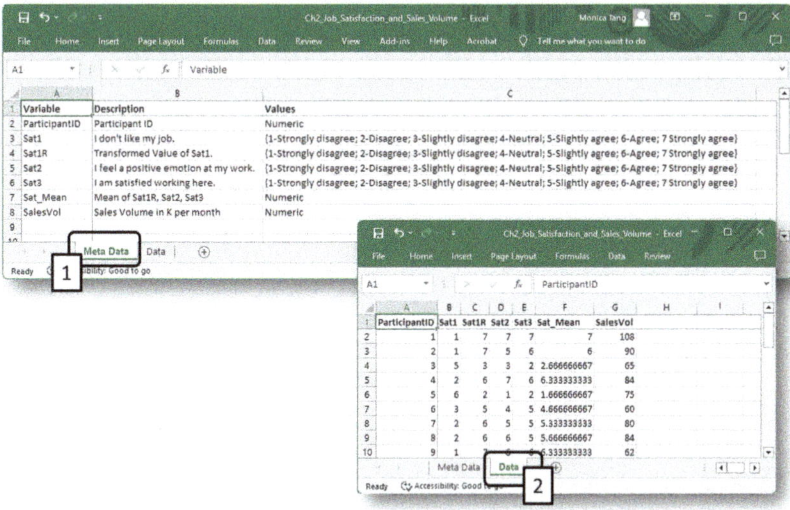

FIGURE 0.3
Using the Example Excel Files

files. Clear instructions and figures will guide you through each example in the book.

Now, we are all set. Let us start the journey of hands-on data analytics for business.

Acknowledgments

I would like to thank the deans, department heads, program directors and coordinators of different universities who have entrusted me to develop and teach courses on data analytics. I would also like to thank my students, who are also business professionals. They have asked good and relevant questions and have shown enthusiasm in learning and applying data analytics. Their questions inspire me to enrich the content of this book, which will be beneficial and of interest to readers. Their enthusiasm motivates me to improve my courses continuously and strengthen my determination to write this book to help students and business professionals learn more effectively.

I would like to thank my editor, Dr. John Wyzalek, for providing me with prompt, clear and effective feedback that kept me on pace to finish this book alongside my professional career in the information technology industry and my teaching assignments at different universities. Thanks also go to my colleagues at Taylor and Francis for their support in the production of this book.

I would also like to thank all the individuals who have kindly provided endorsements for this book.

1

Introduction to Data Analytics

The volume of data we produce every day is truly enormous. According to Marr (2018b), we generate 2.5 quintillion bytes (i.e., 2.5 billion gigabytes) of data every day, which is roughly equivalent to 2.5 billion 2-hour movies. If we can make good use of these data, they can provide amazing opportunities. These opportunities include new angles to better understand our employees, customers and suppliers. For example, managers may predict employees' job performance and act properly to sustain high performance. Marketers can find factors that predict customer satisfaction and better manage sales volume. Suppliers can predict delivery timeliness and manage the supply chain to avoid delays. These new points of view offer insights for businesses to make better decisions. These insights were not obtainable before we had useful and sufficient data. Before then, managers made business decisions based on their own intuition and experience rather than on evidence. Making informed decisions has been shown to improve employee engagement, customer satisfaction and financial performance. Therefore, in order to make data-driven and informed decisions, many organizations turn to applying data analytics in their business.

This chapter will start by introducing what data analytics is and illustrating its four types through simple examples. A brief history and related theories and concepts about data analytics in the literature will follow. The chapter will end with a description of an analytics process using different business examples.

1.1 WHAT IS DATA ANALYTICS FOR BUSINESS?

Data are individual facts or items of information. After data are analyzed and viewed in context, they are transformed into information. Data analytics uses this information to inform decisions.

DOI: 10.1201/9781032642307-1

Data analytics is an important emerging field. There is not yet a common definition of this topic. Here are a few definitions from analytics scholars and advocates. Davenport and Harris (2017) proposed, "By analytics, we mean the extensive use of data, statistical and quantitative analysis, explanatory and predictive models, and fact-based management to drive decisions and actions" (p. 25). Schniederjans et al. (2015) stated, "[analytics is] a process beginning with business-related data collection and consisting of sequential application of descriptive, predictive and prescriptive major analytics components, the outcome of which supports and demonstrates business decision-making and organizational performance" (p. 5). Marr (2018a) has suggested that analytics builds on "traditionally focused" business domain knowledge and turns organizations into becoming more data driven. Agostini and Spano (2021) have added, "modern digital technologies provide an unprecedented capacity to analyze data at a magnificent speed" (p. 110). What is common in these definitions of today's data analytics for business is that it is a process that turns data into insights for better business decision-making. Modern data analytics builds on business domain knowledge and makes use of technologies to speed up this process. To summarize, this definition is proposed:

> Data Analytics for Business is a process for discovering patterns in data and turning data into insights to improve decision-making and make actionable recommendations by using statistical techniques, computer programming skills and business domain knowledge.

Based on this definition, we can identify four characteristics of data analytics for business.

1.2 FOUR CHARACTERISTICS OF DATA ANALYTICS

Data analytics first builds on reliable and valid data, as shown in Figure 1.1, building from the bottom up. Data collection is a fundamental element of data analytics. Business data are collected and cleansed to provide reliable and valid sources for further analysis. Second, these data are analyzed using proper statistical techniques supported by computer software based on business domain knowledge. Third, these analyzed data are turned into insights through the interpretation of results. Fourth, these insights

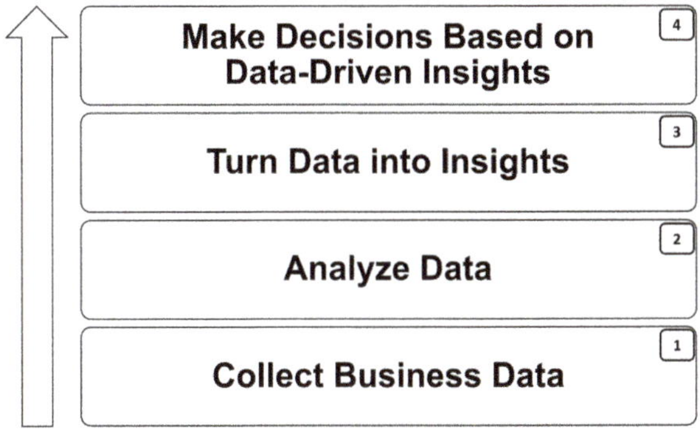

FIGURE 1.1
Four Characteristics of Data Analytics for Business

must guide data-driven decisions and provide actionable recommendations to improve business outcomes.

1.3 FOUR TYPES OF ANALYTICS

There are four types of data analytics, ranging from descriptive analytics and diagnostic analytics to predictive analytics and prescriptive analytics. They increase in complexity while simultaneously increasing the values created.

To understand how the four types of data analytics differ from each other and help solve organizational problems, you can imagine the process of how a doctor prescribes medication to cure a patient. In this process, the patient starts by describing the symptoms of the health situation, that is, *what happened*. Based on the symptoms described, the doctor performs further tests (e.g., measuring blood pressure, examining the level of pain) to find out the possible causes and diseases and give diagnosis, that is, *why it happened*. The doctor will analyze the situation and give the prognosis, considering the benefits and drawbacks of different medication plans, that is, *what is going to happen*. After explaining the diagnosis and prognosis to the patient, with the patient's personalized situation considered (e.g., whether the patient is pregnant or taking other medicines at the moment), the doctor will prescribe a suitable treatment or medication plan, that is, *what actions can be taken*.

Similar to the metaphor in which a doctor prescribes medication to cure a patient, analytics helps organizations solve problems through four types of analytics, each answering one question about a specific organizational situation (Figure 1.2):

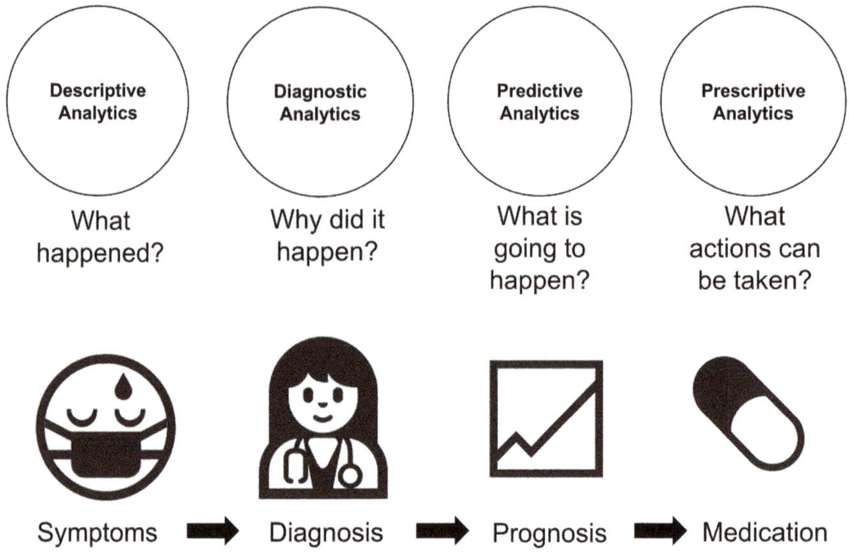

FIGURE 1.2
A Metaphor of the Four Types of Data Analytics

1. Descriptive analytics – What happened?
2. Diagnostic analytics – Why did it happen?
3. Predictive analytics – What is going to happen?
4. Prescriptive analytics – What actions can be taken?

Let us go through each type of analytics one by one, starting with descriptive analytics.

Descriptive analytics describes *what happened in the organization* using data. It is a summary of past data. Some examples of descriptive analytics include a table of employee engagement rates across departments, a chart of customer satisfaction growth rates across services and a graph of revenue growth rates across years (Figure 1.3). From these examples, you can see that they are basically reports that use past data to describe the situation the organization is currently going through. Most companies are already producing these reports regularly to understand how well or poorly the organization is performing.

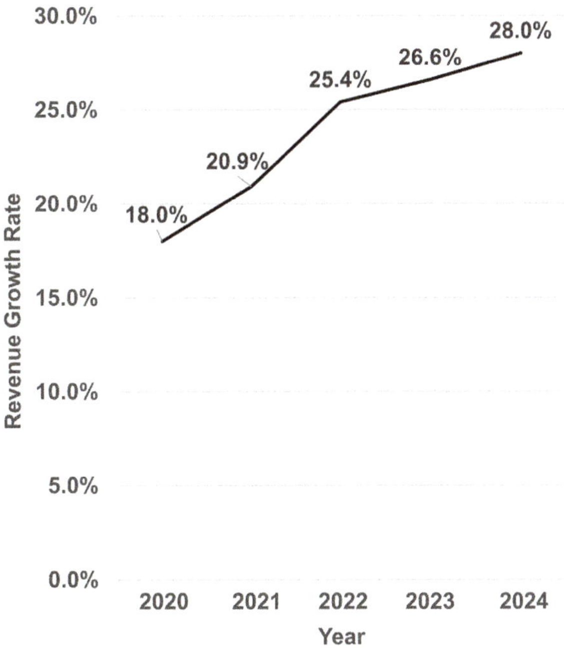

FIGURE 1.3
Revenue Growth Rate across Years

Figure 1.3 shows that there is a growing trend in the revenue growth rate. If the company does not know the possible reasons behind this growth rate, it cannot be certain how to sustain the growth. These reports may reflect the trend of how the organization is performing. Yet it does not answer an important question of *why* such a trend may occur. Thus, this limits the values that descriptive analytics creates. Therefore, a more in-depth type of analytics, which tells more about the reasons behind the trend, is required. This is where diagnostic analytics comes in.

Diagnostic analytics finds out potential reasons *why a situation occurred in the organization*. Explaining why a certain situation happened requires diagnosing the possible reasons or factors. Thus, the first step is to test if there is any possible relationship between what happened and the corresponding potential factors. Potential factors can be identified based on business knowledge, experience or observations. Once these potential factors are identified, the second step is to visualize these possible factor-consequence relationships with graphs and test them using statistical methods (e.g., correlation tests).

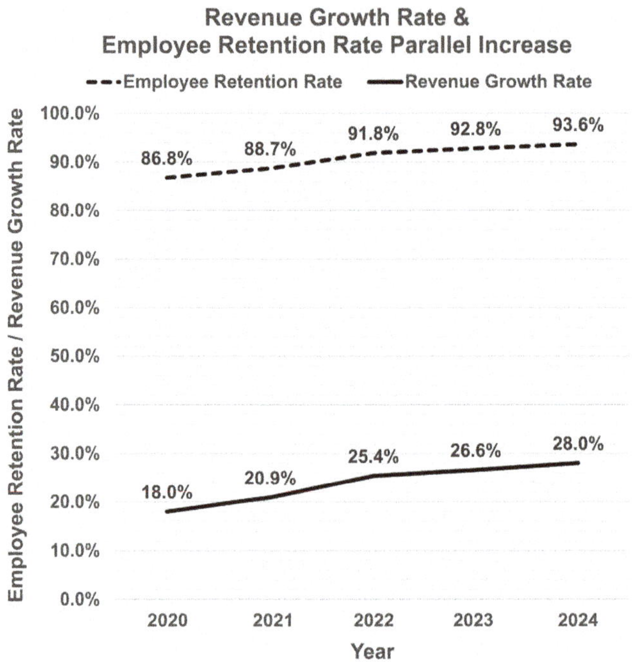

FIGURE 1.4
Revenue Growth Rate Increases alongside Employee Retention Rate

For example, if we diagnose and consider the potential factor that the increasing revenue growth rate may be due to the growing employee retention rate, we can plot the revenue growth rate and employee retention rate (which we call *variables*) in the same graph and visualize their trends (Figure 1.4).

Figure 1.4 shows a pattern in which the revenue growth rate increases in parallel with the employee retention rate over 5 consecutive years. This pattern gives us some support to hypothesize that there is a relationship between these two variables. We can put this hypothesis to statistical tests like correlation test – in this case to test whether this relationship is significant or happens just by chance (the modeling techniques and different statistical tests will be introduced in Chapter 2, and their applications will be illustrated with case studies in Chapters 3 to 5). After identifying the potential factors for this phenomenon, we would like to know if these factors can significantly predict it in the future or whether this happens just by chance alone. To do this, we turn to predictive analytics.

Predictive analytics describes *what is going to happen* by using modeling techniques and statistical tools. Significant statistical results provide proof to support the factors or predictors of a certain phenomenon.

The statistical results being significant means:

1. The pattern of results can be relied upon;
2. It is robust enough to make assumptions about what is going on in this set of data (i.e., the population or the sample);
3. It is not due to chance alone (i.e., it is not just a coincidence).

Let us use our example of the relationship between employee retention growth rate and revenue growth rate to illustrate the use of predictive analytics. After formulating a model in which employee retention growth rate positively predicts revenue growth rate, we can run a regression test (the process of how to carry out a regression test will be discussed in detail in Chapter 2) to find out whether this relationship is significant. If the result shows that employee retention growth rate positively predicts revenue growth rate, we can support the conclusion that this is not due to chance alone and that employee retention growth rate is a significant predictor of revenue growth rate.

As mentioned earlier, one of the characteristics of data analytics is linking data-driven business decisions to business outcomes. Now we have found significant evidence that the employee retention growth rate positively predicts the revenue growth rate, which is our business outcome. The next step is to put this evidence into actions with business impact. This is where prescriptive analytics comes in.

Prescriptive analytics describes *what actions can be taken* based on the evidence found from predictive analytics. Data-driven business decisions mean the decisions made are based on evidence collected from data. In our example, the evidence shows that employee retention is one of the best ways to sustain revenue growth. Therefore, we will implement solutions (e.g., improving organizational support, fostering a positive workplace culture) that can improve the employee retention rate, which in turn will improve the revenue growth rate.

So now you may ask which solutions are effective in improving the employee retention rate. This is a very good question. This leads us to the next round of the analytics process: finding the most effective solution to improve employee retention rate. Similar to many other important business processes, this process is continuously executed and refined. Data analytics is not a one-off process. It is a practical research process that continuously helps organizations understand the underlying factors of their business and identify new predictors of different business phenomena. Therefore, businesses can monitor not only the *performance indicators* but also the *predictors* before issues occur. This will definitely help organizations gain competitive advantages.

After an introduction to the different types of data analytics, you may have wondered how data analytics has gained attention and why now is a great time to learn about it. In the following section, a brief history along with related theories and concepts will be introduced. These will help answer the question of why data analytics is so important today.

1.4 A BRIEF HISTORY, THEORIES AND CONCEPTS AROUND DATA ANALYTICS

Following the rapid growth of data and the improvement of computing power, the demand for prediction using data in business is also increasing. In fact, the idea of predicting the future is not new in human history. People have long been curious to know what the future would bring. In ancient Greece, philosophers sought different ways and signs to predict the unforeseen future (Woodard, 2022). In contemporary literature, it is not difficult to find science fiction stories about predicting the future, such as *The Minority Report* by Philip K. Dick, published in *Fantastic Universe* in 1956. This story is about people in the future who have found a way to predict future crimes so that the police can prevent any crimes from happening. This story was also made into a movie starring Tom Cruise in 2002. In business and management, scholars and practitioners have long been seeking ways to measure and predict future trends in different business areas. *The Principles of Scientific Management,* written by Sir Frederick Winslow Taylor and published in 1911, is one of the classics. Jac Fitz-Enz's *How to Measure Human Resources Management*, published in 1984, is another important book that guides measurements in business.

Apart from business measurements, scholars and researchers have identified various predictors for business outcomes using robust research methods, sophisticated statistical techniques, increasingly powerful technologies and growing amounts of data. There are many examples in different academic areas. In management, scholars have found that participative leadership positively predicts work performance (Lam et al., 2015). In information systems, meaningful gamification positively predicts psychological empowerment in self-help systems (Li et al., 2020). In marketing, organizations making use of the metaverse – a digital copy of the physical world where users can have a shopping experience via avatars – as a future marketing platform improves marketing performance (Hollensen et al., 2022). In supply chain, supply chain managers' social capital, human capital and cognition predict supply chain resilience (Nikookar & Yanadori, 2021). I can keep on listing these examples. When these research methods are applied in business practices, they become data analytics applications.

Scholars have viewed analytics from the application and practice perspective. Cascio et al. (2019) proposed the LAMP model for analytics, which is considered a force for strategic change in business. The word "LAMP" is an acronym that stands for the right *logic*, *analytics*, *measures* and *process*. The right *logic* is required when building the vital connections among variables. The right *analytics* reminds us that businesses should make data-driven decisions by finding answers in data instead of relying on intuition. The right *measures* indicate that data should be collected using valid and reliable measures. The right *process* emphasizes making insights actionable.

Scholars have also viewed analytics from the resource distribution perspective, that is, to invest resources in the most pivotal issues to maximize the return. Boudreau (2011) proposed five principles of evidence-based decision-making. The first principle, *logic-driven analytics*, emphasizes identifying and addressing the most pivotal issues through robust analysis. The second principle, *segmentation*, suggests that practitioners discover strategic categories of employees and design unique deals to attract them. The third principle is *risk leverage*, which encourages practitioners to take the right risks to maximize returns, which is as important as avoiding the wrong ones. The fourth principle is *integration and synergy*, which reminds that the decisions must be considered together to make sure they are in concert. The last one is *optimization*, which summarizes identifying investments that bring excess returns while minimizing those that are underperforming.

Although the segmentation idea mentioned by Boudreau (2011) mostly focuses on human resources, it also applies in other business areas. For example, in marketing, Kotler et al. (2021) further elaborated on the four methods of segmentation: *geographic*, *demographic*, *psychographic* and *behavioral*. Analyzing these segments together forms a profile (persona) of a customer. They viewed data-driven marketing from a macroscopic perspective and define the process in three steps: (1) Define the data-driven marketing objectives, (2) Identify data requirements and availability, (3) Build an integrated data ecosystem.

Building on the views from different business fields, we may find common ground for the data analytics process.

1.5 THE PROCESS OF DATA ANALYTICS

This data analytics process improves the robustness of business decision-making by applying skills that have long been used in academic research. Academics use the research process to discover new knowledge. When applying research skills in business, organizations can uncover insights they did not yet know, improving business performance.

Sir Karl Popper (1972) advanced a research cycle that starts by formulating the research question and building the hypothesis, continues through collecting and analyzing data to build a model, and culminates in forming a solution and presenting the solution. Creswell and Guetterman (2021) define research as "a process of steps used to collect and analyze information to increase our understanding of a topic or issue" (p. 27). It consists of three steps: pose a question, collect data to answer the question and present an answer to the question. To summarize from different views:

Data analytics is a research process that includes five key steps:

1. identify the problem and formulate the research question,
2. build hypotheses and models,
3. collect data,
4. analyze the data using robust analysis techniques, and
5. give actionable recommendations.

Identifying the problem and formulating the research question is the first and most important step in the analytics process because the problem and the research question direct the analytics approach, characterize the stakeholders who may be affected by the analytics process and prescribe the impacts of the analytics project. Following the formulation of the research question, hypotheses and models can be built corresponding to the research questions based on business knowledge and observations. According to the hypotheses and models, data collection is the next step, providing the sources for data analytics. The availability of valid and reliable data (more about validity and reliability will be discussed in Chapter 2) always decides whether the analytics project is feasible. Using the appropriate statistical techniques with proper interpretation of the results is a crucial step because actions are recommended based on the results of the statistical tests. If incorrect statistical techniques are applied or the results are misinterpreted, not only may the business problems remain unsolved, but the recommended actions may even worsen the situation. To ensure proper statistical techniques are applied, the objectives and usage of the statistical test applications must be carefully observed.

In Chapter 2, the techniques for the research process described earlier and different statistical techniques will be discussed in detail and elaborated with practical examples.

1.6 WHAT REAL-WORLD PROBLEMS CAN BE SOLVED BY DATA ANALYTICS?

Now that you have an essential understanding of data analytics, you may want to know what real-world problems can be solved using it. In this section, I will list some potential problems that can be addressed, along with examples.

In human resources (HR): Which HR areas have the greatest business impact? Can we develop measures to ensure our managers are accountable for these HR management areas?

A real-world analytics example is from Lowe's Company, a retail company specializing in home improvement (Coco et al., 2011). The company carried out an analytics project to identify the HR areas that contribute to the greatest business impact. No company would have enough resources to invest in every possible factor that may influence business results. In Lowe's project, they use data analytics to identify the most effective factor for investment. They collected over 600 variables across different functional departments across finance, market research and operations in order to identify the factors that most impact business outcomes. By applying statistical and analytical techniques, they identified one important factor that positively and significantly influences store financial performance – employee engagement. The company can then focus its resources on the most impactful factor to improve business performance.

In marketing: Can we better predict the factors that improve customer satisfaction? Can we identify which products are suitable for cross-selling and up-selling to improve business profit?

A marketing analytics example is from Royal Bank of Scotland (Marr, 2016a). The bank initiated a big data strategy called "personology," providing personalized banking services in order to reconnect with its customers. The bank adopted data-driven marketing, including audience segmentation instead of mass mailing. They developed an 800-person strong analytics department to identify the product that is most beneficial to the customers. These personalized services help the bank increase customer satisfaction and retain its customers. Without analytics, it is not possible to identify these personalized products for different customer segments.

In supply chain: Can we find predictors of demands in the supply chain?

A supply chain analytics example comes from Walmart, a retail company operating a chain of supermarkets, discount department stores and grocery stores (Marr, 2016b). When the company attempted to forecast the demand for emergency supplies when Hurricane Sandy hit the United States in 2004, they found some surprising statistics: bad weather also led to an increase in the sales of strawberry Pop-Tarts. Based on this finding, when Hurricane Frances approached in 2012, extra supplies of strawberry Pop-Tarts were dispatched to stores and sold extremely well. There are thousands of products in any single retail store; without analytics, it is difficult to visualize which products significantly predict sales at a certain time. This example illustrates one of the applications of data analytics.

These are some examples of the amazing applications of analytics. In Chapter 2, detailed analytics and statistical techniques will be demonstrated in the analytics process. In Chapter 3, practical analytics applications in HR will illustrate hands-on statistical skills and computer usage in SPSS and Excel. In Chapter 4, practical applications in marketing will be demonstrated. In Chapter 5, practical applications in supply chain will illustrate further examples. Chapter 6, the final chapter, will discuss how to build analytics capabilities and describe future trends in analytics with advancing technologies such as artificial intelligence.

REFERENCES

Agostini, M., & Spano, A. (2021). Big data and business analytics: definitions and implications in the business environment. In *Intellectual Capital, Smart Technologies and Digitalization* (pp. 107–117). Springer International Publishing.

Boudreau, J. (2011). *Transformative HR: How Great Companies Use Evidence-based Change for Sustainable Advantage.* New York: Wiley.

Cascio, W. F., Boudreau, J. W., & Fink, A. A. (2019). *Investing in People: Financial Impact of Human Resource Initiatives* (3rd ed.). Society for Human Resource Management.

Coco, C. T., Jamison, F., & Black, H. (2011). Connecting people investments and business outcomes at Lowe's: using value linkage analytics to link employee engagement to business performance. *People and Strategy, 34*(2), 28–33.

Creswell, J. W., & Guetterman, T. C. (2021). *Educational Research: Planning, Conducting, and Evaluating Quantitative and Qualitative Research* (6th ed.). Pearson Education Limited.

Davenport, T. H., & Harris, J. G. (2017). *Competing on Analytics: Updated, with a New Introduction: The New Science of Winning.* Harvard Business Review Press.

Hollensen, S., Kotler, P., & Opresnik, M. O. (2022). Metaverse – the new marketing universe. *Journal of Business Strategy, 44*(3), 119–125.

Kotler, P., Kartajaya, H., & Setiawan, I. (2021). *Marketing 5.0: Technology for Humanity.* Wiley.

Lam, C. K., Huang, X., & Chan, S. C. H. (2015). The threshold effect of participative leadership and the role of leader information sharing. *Academy of Management Journal, 58*(3), 836–855.

Li, M., Chau, P. Y. K., & Ge, L. (2020). Meaningful gamification for psychological empowerment: exploring user affective experience mirroring in a psychological self-help system. *Internet Research*, *31*(1), 11–58.

Marr, B. (2016a). Royal Bank of Scotland: using big data to make customer service more personal. In B. Marr (Ed.), *Big Data in Practice: How 45 Successful Companies Used Big Data Analytics to Deliver Extraordinary Results* (pp. 81–85). West Sussex, United Kingdom: John Wiley and Sons Ltd.

Marr, B. (2016b). Walmart: how big data is used to drive supermarket performance. In B. Marr (Ed.), *Big Data in Practice: How 45 Successful Companies Used Big Data Analytics to Deliver Extraordinary Results* (pp. 5–10). West Sussex, United Kingdom: John Wiley and Sons Ltd.

Marr, B. (2018a). *Data-driven HR: How to Use Analytics and Metrics to Drive Performance*. New York: Kogan Page.

Marr, B. (2018b, May 21). *How much data do we create every day? The mind-blowing stats everyone should read.* Forbes. https://www.forbes.com/sites/bernardmarr/2018/05/21/how-much-data-do-we-create-every-day-the-mind-blowing-stats-everyone-should-read/?sh=6cb29f8160ba

Nikookar, E., & Yanadori, Y. (2021). Preparing supply chain for the next disruption beyond COVID-19: managerial antecedents of supply chain resilience. *International Journal of Operations & Production Management*, *42*(1), 59–90.

Popper, K. R. (1972). *Objective Knowledge: An Evolutionary Approach*. Clarendon Press.

Schniederjans, M. J., Schniederjans, D. G., & Starkey, C. M. (2015). *Business Analytics Principles, Concepts, and Applications with SAS. What, Why, and How.* Pearson Education Inc.

Woodard, R. D. (2022). *Divination and Prophecy in the Ancient Greek World.* Cambridge University Press.

2

The Data Analytics Process

Chapter 1 has identified the basic concepts of data analytics and has introduced the idea that data analytics is a process to turn data into insights. In this chapter, the process of data analytics will be illustrated step by step with some hands-on analyses. You can have your SPSS and Excel Add-in (Zaiontz, 2025) ready (as mentioned in the Preface) to go through these examples together. I will use a business situation to demonstrate this analytics process.

Imagine the business in a hypothetical toy manufacturing and retail company called Best Toy Company. In this company, there are different departments, including human resources (HR), finance, information technology (IT), marketing, manufacturing and logistics. This company manufactures toys and distributes and sells them in physical and online retail shops.

In this chapter, the analytics process will be explained in detail and illustrated through a situation in this toy company. The company reviews the sales volume of the salespersons and finds that some salespersons perform better than others. They would like to know the factors affecting their sales volume so that they can act to improve the salespersons' performance. You may think that there could be many different possibilities that affect the sales volume of a salesperson, for example, personality, sales skills and job satisfaction. It is not possible to invest in all possible factors. How do we find out which factor is more impactful than the others? This is a good question. To find the factor that is significant and does not happen just by chance alone, we can use the analytics process. By the end of this process, the company will be able to find out the significant factor to act on and make evidence-based decisions.

Data analytics is a business research process to turn data into insights that lead to evidence-based, actionable recommendations. It includes five key steps:

1. identify the problem and formulate the research question,
2. build hypotheses and models,

 DOI: 10.1201/9781032642307-2

3. collect data,
4. analyze the data using robust analysis techniques, and
5. give actionable recommendations.

2.1 IDENTIFY THE PROBLEM AND FORMULATE THE RESEARCH QUESTION

The objective of business data analytics is to solve business problems. Therefore, the first step in a business data analytics process is to identify what problem to solve. No single tool can solve every problem in the business world. To make the best use of a data analytics tool, we need to understand what problems it can solve. So, what problems can data analytics solve? Table 2.1 shows a list of major problems with examples to illustrate the use of data analytics.

One of the best uses of data analytics is to identify whether two phenomena have significant **correlations**. This is especially important if we want to make evidence-based decisions rather than relying just on intuition. For example, in the case of Walmart mentioned in Chapter 1, if they had not applied data analytics to analyze the relationship between the sales volume of individual products and specific weather conditions, they might never have discovered the relationship between the increase in sales of strawberry Pop-Tarts and approaching bad weather.

TABLE 2.1

Major Problems Which Can Be Solved by Data Analytics

	Problem Type	Examples
1	Understanding if two phenomena have **correlations**	Does it happen by chance, or is there a significant correlation that a certain product sells better on Mondays?
2	Finding the **factors** of a phenomenon	What are the factors that may sustain revenue growth?
3	Predicting the **consequence** of a phenomenon	What are the consequences for the sales volume of increasing the price of a product?
4	Identifying if there are significant **differences** in a variable for different groups	Are there significant differences in employee satisfaction levels among different offices?

Another good function of data analytics is to find the **factors** of a phenomenon. When certain situations happen in business, whether good or bad, we need to know the factors or antecedents such that we can help sustain the positive outcomes or prevent negative situations from occurring again. For example, when we observe continuous revenue growth over the past few years, we need to know the factors (i.e., the competitive advantages) behind this growth rate to help sustain it.

Data analytics can also help predict the **consequences** of a phenomenon. When making business decisions, we have a better basis for predicting results when supported by data evidence. For example, when we make pricing decisions for a product, we are better able to understand its impact on sales volume to predict overall revenue.

When we come to measuring the impacts of an intervention like a training seminar or an organization-wide cultural change program, data analytics can help find out whether there are **significant differences** in a variable either among different groups or within the same group collected at different times. For example, when a company launches a staff engagement program aimed at increasing staff engagement levels, the company would like to know if the engagement level of the staff has significantly increased after the program to determine its effectiveness. We can apply data analytics to do this. The staff engagement level before and after the program can be compared using a statistical method to show if there are significant differences. Another example is that the company can compare if the sales volumes of different markets have significant differences so that the resources can be focused on the markets that need improvement.

Recall the situation of our hypothetical company, Best Toy Company. The company observes that some salespersons have higher sales volume than others from descriptive analytics. Figure 2.1 is a bar chart that shows that, out of a total of 30 salespersons, only 8 of them achieved high sales volume, while the rest achieved only medium or low sales volume. In this chart, you can see that the two bars representing medium and low sales volumes are highlighted in dark colors showing the high proportion of the less-performing salespersons. Using color strategically in your charts, rather than just for categorization purposes, can draw the attention of your audience at the first sight when they read your chart (Knaflic, 2015).

As one of the tasks of HR is performance management, the HR manager is tasked with addressing this **business problem**:

How can the company improve the sales volume of the less performing salespersons?

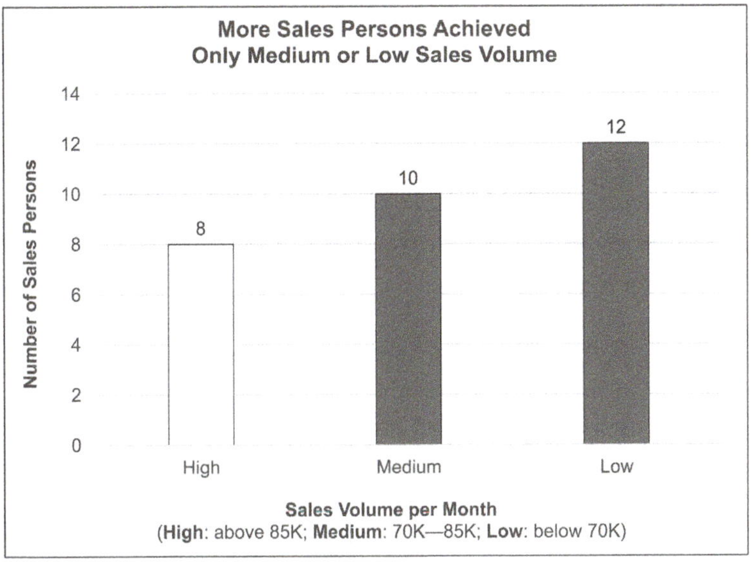

FIGURE 2.1
More Sales Persons Achieved Only Medium or Low Sales Volume

One of the ways to effectively improve the sales performance of the salespersons may be to understand which activities correlate with and positively influence the sales volume. The HR manager discusses this with the line managers. The line managers observe that some salespersons seem to have lower job satisfaction recently. The HR manager suspects that the salespersons' lowered job satisfaction may be reflected in their sales volume. So, he poses the following **research question**:

> **Does job satisfaction of the salespersons positively influence their sales volume?**

Now, we have a well-defined problem and a clear research question, which will guide our way to the next step of the analytics process: building a hypothesis and a model.

2.2 BUILD HYPOTHESES AND MODELS

Data analytics is a scientific method used to test whether an observation shown in descriptives is significant. Before conducting statistical tests, we first build our hypotheses from our observations or literature review. The hypotheses should correspond to the research question. In our example, the HR manager of Best Toy Company thinks that the salespersons with higher job satisfaction will improve their sales volume; thus, we have our hypotheses here:

H_1: Salespersons' job satisfaction positively influences their sales volume.
H_0: Salespersons' job satisfaction does not positively influence their sales volume.

When the hypothesis passes the statistical tests, which will be discussed in a later section of this chapter, hypothesis H_1 will be accepted while the null hypothesis H_0 will be rejected, and vice versa.

To visualize the hypothesis, we can present it in a model. In a basic model, we put our hypothesized factor or antecedent on the left-hand side and our hypothesized consequence on the right-hand side, connecting them with a single arrow pointing from the hypothesized factor to the hypothesized consequence. To indicate a positive (negative) relationship, we place a plus (minus) sign near the arrow. A positive relationship means that when the value of the variable indicating the hypothesized factor increases (decreases), the value of the variable indicating the hypothesized consequence also increases (decreases). A negative relationship means that when the value of one variable increases (decreases), the value of the other variable decreases (increases). We will also refer to the hypothesized factor as the **independent variable (IV, also called the predictor variable)** and the hypothesized consequence as the **dependent variable (DV, also called the outcome variable)**. Whether a variable is the independent variable or the dependent variable depends on whether it is the predictor or the outcome in that specific model. For example, job performance is the independent variable when it is in a model hypothesizing that job performance predicts revenue. On the other hand, job performance is the dependent variable when it is in a model hypothesizing that job satisfaction predicts job performance. For our example in Best Toy Company, we have our hypothesized model shown in Figure 2.2.

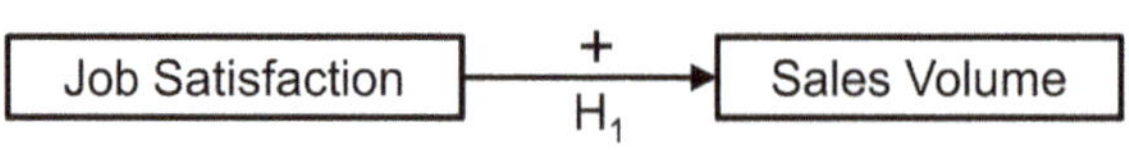

FIGURE 2.2
The Hypothesized Model

With the hypothesis and the model ready, we can collect the necessary data to prepare for the statistical tests.

2.3 COLLECT DATA

Data collected by ourselves via surveys, interviews or observations are called **primary data,** while data collected by others, such as statistics from governments, are called **secondary data**. In the data analytics process, some of the data, such as location, gender and age, can likely be found in the organization's databases. Other data may be collected via surveys.

2.3.1 Prepare a Survey

In preparing the survey items, we may refer to the literature for the definition of the data we need to collect. In our example of Best Toy Company, the HR manager tries to collect the job satisfaction of the salespersons using a survey. Understanding that job satisfaction is defined as "a pleasurable or positive emotional state resulting from the appraisal of one's job or job experiences" (Locke, 1976, p. 1300), he has prepared the following three **survey items** to measure the job satisfaction of the salesperson:

1. I don't like my job.
2. I feel a positive emotion at my work.
3. I am satisfied working here.

Here, we call "job satisfaction" a **construct**, which includes three survey items in this example. These survey items are measured on a 7-point Likert scale (1 – Strongly disagree; 2 – Disagree; 3 – Slightly disagree; 4 – Neutral; 5 – Slightly agree; 6 – Agree; 7 – Strongly agree).

Not all surveys can be collected anonymously. For example, in our model, which hypothesizes that the salespersons' job satisfaction predicts their sales volume, we need to link the job satisfaction data collected from the survey with the individual salesperson's sales volume, which is retrieved from the organization's database. Therefore, the survey form must be able to identify which salesperson each piece of data belongs to. Although the data may not be collected anonymously, we should always keep the collected data safe and confidential.

Apart from preparing the survey items, preparing a proper **survey cover letter** is also an important part because the survey participants will decide whether to complete the survey based on this cover letter. A survey cover letter basically contains the following information:

1. the objectives of the survey;
2. administrative arrangements:
   - the expected time to complete the survey,
   - how participants should fill in the survey,
   - how participants should submit the completed survey,
   - voluntary participation;
3. confidentiality and data protection measures;
4. contact information for questions.

2.3.2 Validity and Reliability of the Measures

Imagine that we use a measuring tool (e.g., a ruler) to measure the length of physical objects. We would need this measuring tool to actually measure the length, not something else. We would also need this measuring tool to be reliable in measuring the length of different objects on the same scale. Similarly, for our survey measure, we would need it to actually measure the intended construct (i.e., **validity**). We would need it to be reliable in measuring across different participants (i.e., **reliability**).

Validity here covers two common types: face validity and construct validity (Edwards et al., 2024). **Face validity** relies on the subjective view of a professional who understands the construct well to determine whether the survey items are good measures of the construct. **Construct validity** refers to using **factor analysis** to analyze whether the survey items are measuring the same construct. When the **factor loading** of each survey item is **greater than 0.6**, the measure is said to be valid.

Reliability refers to the survey responses which follow a similar pattern across the respondents (Edwards et al., 2024). When the reliability test results in a **Cronbach's alpha greater than 0.7**, it indicates that the measure is reliable.

In our Best Toy Company situation, the HR manager has collected 30 survey forms with job satisfaction survey items from all the salespersons via an **online form**. The advantage of using an online form to collect data is that it can make the inputs mandatory to avoid missing data. However, if your participants are usually not able to be online, you may need to choose pen-and-paper survey forms. When there are **missing data**, you may choose to remove the survey form with missing data or replace the missing piece of data with the mean value of that variable.

The HR manager now needs to check the validity and reliability of this job satisfaction variable.

The HR manager reviews the wording of the following three survey items on job satisfaction and compares them with the definition of job satisfaction. Based on his HR expertise and literature review (Cammann et al., 1983), the following survey items appear to measure job satisfaction. They pass face validity.

1. I don't like my job.
2. I feel a positive emotion at work.
3. I am satisfied working here.

In these three survey items measuring job satisfaction, you may be aware that item 1 ("I don't like my job") is asking the question in an opposite way. That is, if the participant answers "1 – Strongly disagree," it means that they like their job very much. We call this a **reverse item**.

When there are reverse items in the survey, we need to transform their values according to the number of points on the Likert scale. In our example, we are using a 7-point Likert scale. If a participant inputs 1, we transform this value to 7. If another participant inputs 2, we transform this value to 6, and so on.

After we have transformed the values of the reverse item, we can then find the **factor loadings** of the three items (i.e., the transformed value of item 1, the original values of items 2 and 3) to check the construct validity of job satisfaction.

To check the **construct validity in SPSS**, open the file "*Ch2_Job_Satisfaction_and_Sales_Volume.sav.*" Go to *Analyze > Dimension Reduction > Factor.* Select Sat1R, Sat2 and Sat3 as the *Variables.* Click the *Rotation* button and choose the radio-button *Varimax* as the *Method.* Click *Continue* and *OK.* The result is in the output viewer. Look for the table "Component Matrix." It shows that the factor loadings for all three items (0.949, 0.952 and 0.928, respectively) are greater than 0.6, indicating the measure is valid. To try it yourself, follow the numbers (which are the steps) in Figure 2.3. The result is shown in this figure as well.

To check the **construct validity in Excel**, open the file "*Ch2_Job_Satisfaction_and_Sales_Volume.xlsx.*" Go to the worksheet "Data." Go to *Add-ins > Real Statistics > Data Analysis Tools.* In the pop-up dialog box, click the tab page *Multivar,* click *Factor Analysis* and click *OK.* In the "Factor Analysis" pop-up dialog box, select cells C1 to E31 (which contain the values of the

File: *Ch2_Job_Satisfaction_and_Sales_Volume.sav*
Analyze > Dimension Reduction > Factor

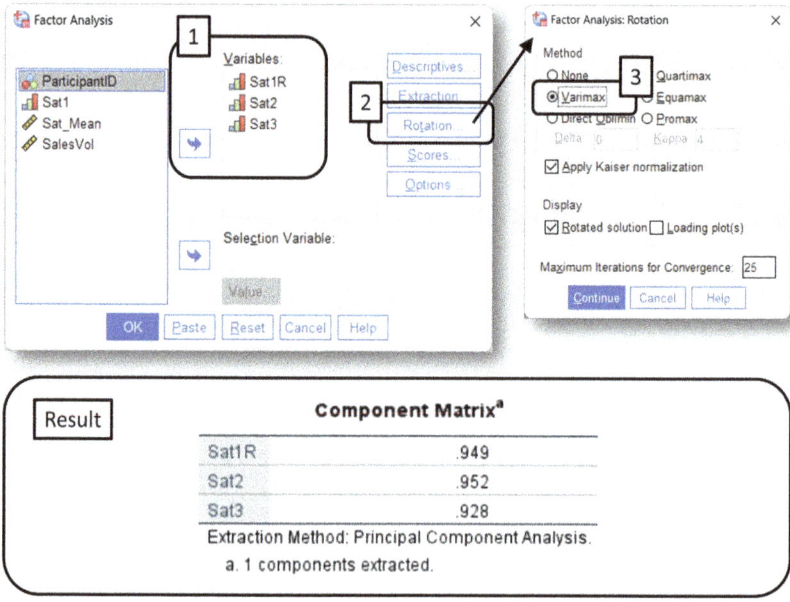

Component Matrix[a]

Sat1R	.949
Sat2	.952
Sat3	.928

Extraction Method: Principal Component Analysis.
a. 1 components extracted.

FIGURE 2.3
Factor Analysis in SPSS

three survey items Sat1R, Sat2 and Sat3) on the worksheet "Data" as the *Input Range*. Make sure the checkbox *Varimax* is ticked. Leave the *Output Range* field blank to have the result shown on a new worksheet. Click *OK*. In the result worksheet, look for the table "Factor Matrix (rotated Varimax)." It shows that the factor loadings for all three items (0.949, 0.952 and 0.928, respectively) are bigger than 0.6, indicating the measure is valid. To try it yourself in Excel, follow the numbers (which are the steps) in Figure 2.4. The result is also shown in this figure.

After checking the face validity and construct validity of "job satisfaction," the HR manager will check its reliability.

To check the **reliability in SPSS**, open the file "*Ch2_Job_Satisfaction_and_Sales_Volume.sav.*" Go to *Analyze > Scale > Reliability Analysis*. Select Sat1R, Sat2 and Sat3 as *Items*. Enter "Job Satisfaction" as the *Scale Label*. Click *OK*. The result is in the output viewer. Look for the table "Reliability Statistics." It shows that Cronbach's alpha equals 0.935, which is bigger than 0.7, indicating the measure is reliable. To try it yourself, follow the numbers (which are the steps) in Figure 2.5. The result is in the same figure.

File: *Ch2_Job_Satisfaction_and_Sales_Volume.xlsx (Worksheet: Data)*
Add-ins > Real Statistics > Data Analysis Tools (Multivar > Factor Analysis)

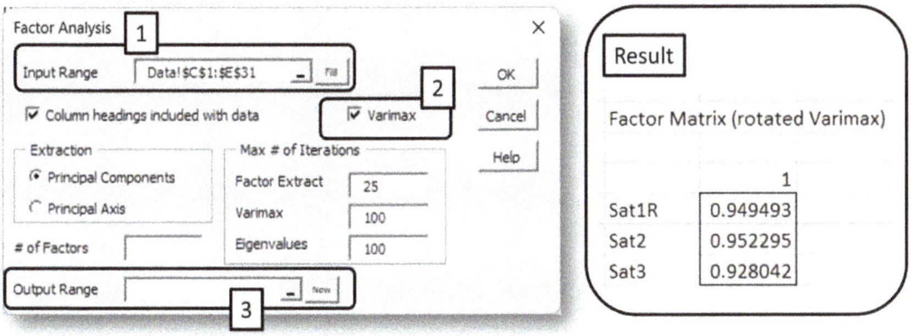

FIGURE 2.4
Factor Analysis in Excel

File: *Ch2_Job_Satisfaction_and_Sales_Volume.sav*
Analyze > Scale > Reliability Analysis

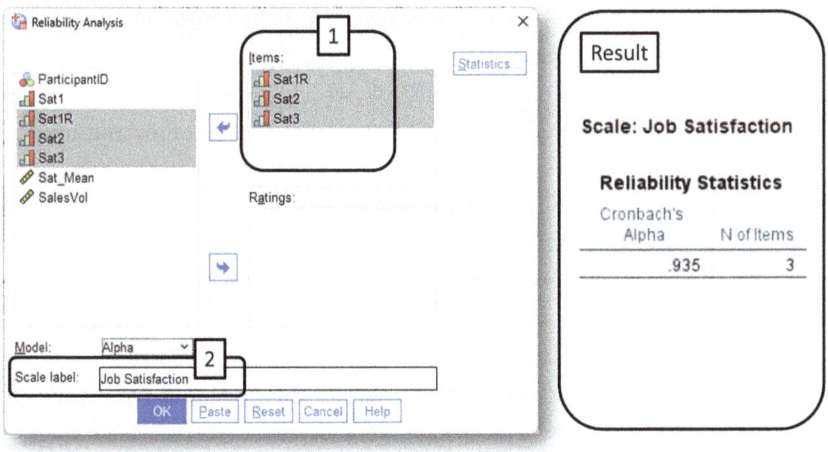

FIGURE 2.5
Reliability Test in SPSS

To check the **reliability in Excel**, open the file "*Ch2_Job_Satisfaction_and_Sales_Volume.xlsx.*" Go to the worksheet "Data." Go to *Add-ins* > *Real Statistics* > *Data Analysis Tools*. In the pop-up dialog box, click the tab page *Corr*, then click *Internal Consistency Reliability* and *OK*. In the "Internal Consistency Reliability" pop-up dialog box, select cells C1 to E31 (which are the values of the three survey items Sat1R, Sat2 and Sat3) on the worksheet "Data" as the *Input Range*. Make sure the radio-button *Cronbach's alpha* is selected. Leave

File: *Ch2_Job_Satisfaction_and_Sales_Volume.xlsx (Worksheet: Data)*
Add-ins > Real Statistics > Data Analysis Tools (Corr > Internal Consistency Reliability)

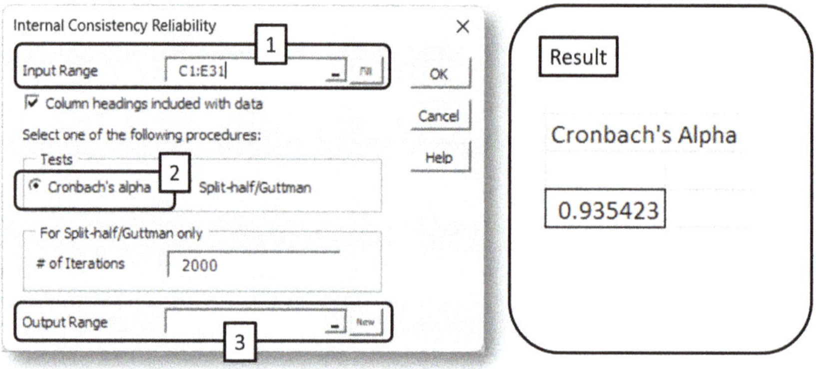

FIGURE 2.6
Reliability Test in Excel

the field *Output Range* blank to have the result shown on a new worksheet. Click *OK*. In the result worksheet, look for the table "Cronbach's Alpha." It shows that Cronbach's alpha equals 0.935, which is greater than 0.7, indicating the measure is reliable. To try it yourself in Excel, follow the numbers (which are the steps) in Figure 2.6. You can find the result in the same figure.

Recall that our model has two variables: job satisfaction and sales volume. We have checked the validity and reliability of job satisfaction. Let us check these for the variable "sales volume." This variable contains one piece of data retrieved from the organization's database, and there is only one question item for it. As construct validity and reliability tests are only possible for measures with multiple question or survey items, we can only conduct face validity for the variable "sales volume." The HR manager checks with the finance manager that this value represents the salespersons' monthly sales volume, so it passes the face validity test.

Now, the HR manager has the valid and reliable data ready for testing the hypothesis.

2.4 ANALYZE THE DATA USING ROBUST ANALYSIS TECHNIQUES

There are different statistical tests for different purposes. Apart from addressing these purposes, to determine which statistical test to use, we also need to understand the **data type** of the variables to be tested. There are basically two data types: **categorical** and **continuous**.

Differentiating whether a variable is of categorical or continuous data type depends on the values you can select for that variable. For example, we have a variable "gender" with two values to choose from: male and female. The two values are basically categories and have no specific order. That is, we can either list the values as (1) male and (2) female or (1) female and (2) male. So, we call "gender" a categorical variable. On the other hand, let us take a look at the variable "job satisfaction" in our example. The values available to choose are on a 7-point Likert scale ranging from (1) Strongly disagree through (4) Neutral up to (7) Strongly agree. There are seven different values, but they have an order, moving from strongly disagree gradually to strongly agree. So, we call "job satisfaction" a continuous variable. We have another variable, "sales volume," in our example. This variable allows any numbers as input. There are no categories in the values, so we also call "sales volume" a continuous variable.

As introduced at the beginning of this chapter, there are major types of problems that data analytics can solve or objectives that data analytics can achieve. Considering the problem types or objectives, and depending on the data types of the dependent variables, we can identify which statistical test to use. Here, different statistical tests are introduced (Table 2.2), and there will be examples in Chapters 3 to 5 to illustrate their practical applications.

When we examine the results of different statistical tests, we aim to determine whether the model points to a **statistically significant** result. A statistically significant result means that:

1. The pattern of the result can be relied upon;
2. The result is robust enough to make assumptions about this dataset;
3. The result is not by chance alone.

If the result is statistically significant at a **95% confidence interval**, we will accept the hypothesis and reject the null hypothesis. Most statistical software will indicate it as $p < 0.05$. That is, there is less than a 5% probability that this pattern of results occurred completely by chance.

In our example, the HR manager has the following hypotheses:

H_1: Salespersons' job satisfaction positively influences their sales volume.

H_0: Salespersons' job satisfaction does not positively influence their sales volume.

TABLE 2.2

Major Problems and the Related Statistical Tests

	Problem Type	Independent Variable (IV)	Dependent Variable (DV)	Statistical Tests
1	Understanding if two phenomena have **correlations**	Categorical/ continuous	Categorical/ continuous	Correlation test
2	Finding the **factors** of a phenomenon	Categorical/ continuous	Continuous	Simple linear regression (for 1 IV) Multiple linear regression (for multiple IVs)
		Continuous	Categorical	Logistic regression
3	Predicting the **consequence** of a phenomenon	Categorical/ continuous	Continuous	Simple linear regression (for 1 IV) Multiple linear regression (for multiple IVs)
		Continuous	Categorical	Logistic regression
4	Identifying whether there are significant **differences** in a variable	Categorical	Categorical	Chi-square test
		Categorical	Continuous	Independent-samples *t* test (for two different groups) Paired-samples *t* test (for the same group at two different instances) One-way ANOVA (for 3+ different groups with one factor) Two-way ANOVA (for 3+ different groups with two factors)

He will first test if the variables "job satisfaction" and "sales volume" have any correlations. **Correlation** means the strength of the linear relationship between the two variables by measuring how closely the data lie on a straight line (Francis & Mousley, 2014). We usually measure correlation using **Pearson's coefficient (*r*)**. Pearson's coefficient lies between –1 and 1. If *r* equals 1, it means the two variables have a positive relationship and the data points lie completely on a straight line. If *r* equals –1, it means the two variables have a negative relationship and the data points lie completely on a straight line. If *r* equals 0, it means the two variables have no relationship and the data points are scattered. Figure 2.7 plots the graphs for different values of Pearson's coefficient.

To test the **correlation of the two variables in SPSS**, open the file "*Ch2_Job_Satisfaction_and_Sales_Volume.sav.*" Go to *Analyze* > *Correlate* > *Bivariate.* Select Sat_Mean and SalesVol as the *Variables.* Tick the checkbox for *Pearson* for the *Correlation Coefficients.* Click *OK.* The result is in the output

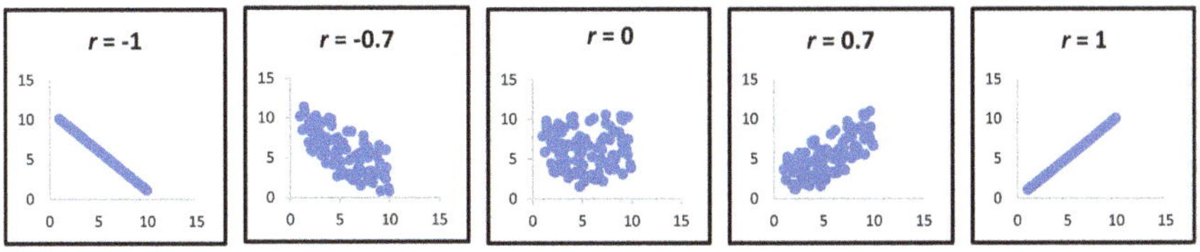

FIGURE 2.7
Visualizing Correlation

File: *Ch2_Job_Satisfaction_and_Sales_Volume.sav*
Analyze > Correlate > Bivariate

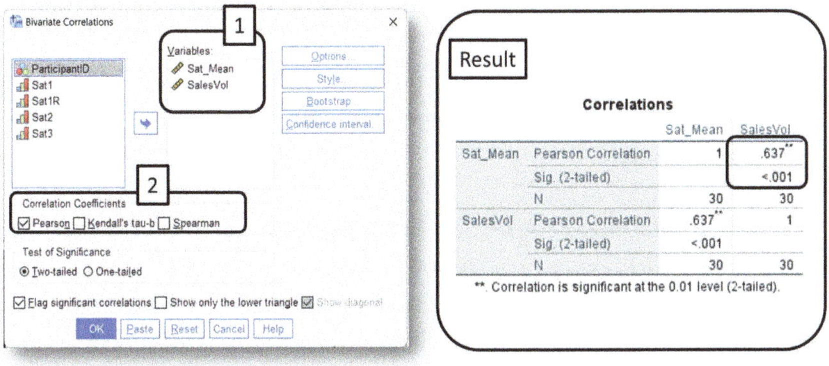

FIGURE 2.8
Correlation Test in SPSS

viewer. It shows that the Pearson's coefficient equals 0.637, meaning that there is a positive relationship, and this relationship is significant with $p < 0.001$, which is less than 0.05 ($r = 0.637, p < 0.001$). To try it yourself, follow the steps indicated by the numbers in Figure 2.8. The result is shown in the same figure.

To test the **correlation of the two variables in Excel**, open the file "*Ch2_Job_Satisfaction_and_Sales_Volume.xlsx.*" Go to the worksheet "Data." Go to *Add-ins > Real Statistics > Data Analysis Tools*. In the pop-up dialog box, click the tab page *Corr*, click *Correlation Tests* and then click *OK*. In the "One-sample Correlation" pop-up dialog box, select cells F1 to F31 (which are the values of the mean of the three items of job satisfaction) for the field *Input Range 1* and cells G1 to G31 (which are the values of sales volume) for the field *Input Range 2*. Make sure the radio-button *Pearson's* is selected for the *Test Type*. Leave the field *Output Range* blank to have the result shown on a new worksheet. Click *OK*. In the result worksheet, it shows that Pearson's coefficient equals 0.637 (rounded to three decimal places), meaning that there is a positive relationship, and this relationship is significant with p = 0.000154, which is less than 0.05 ($r = 0.637, p < 0.001$). To try it yourself in Excel, follow the numbers (which are the steps) in Figure 2.9. The result is also shown in this figure.

Now, the HR manager is certain that there is a significant positive relationship between job satisfaction and sales volume. He proceeds to test if job satisfaction positively influences sales volume. This is to test if job satisfaction is a factor influencing sales volume. In this model, job satisfaction is a continuous independent variable, and sales volume is a continuous dependent variable. Referring to Table 2.2, he will use simple linear regression to test the hypotheses.

H_1: Salespersons' job satisfaction positively influences their sales volume.
H_0: Salespersons' job satisfaction does not positively influence their sales volume.

To run **simple linear regression in SPSS**, open the file "*Ch2_Job_Satisfaction_and_Sales_Volume.sav.*" Go to *Analyze* > *Regression* > *Linear.* Select SalesVol as the *Dependent* variable and Sat_Mean as the *Independent* Variable. Click the *Statistics* button. In the "Statistics" pop-up dialog box, make sure that the checkboxes *Estimates* and *Model fit* are ticked. Click *Continue*

File: *Ch2_Job_Satisfaction_and_Sales_Volume.xlsx (Worksheet: Data)*
Add-ins > Real Statistics > Data Analysis Tools (Corr > Correlation Tests)

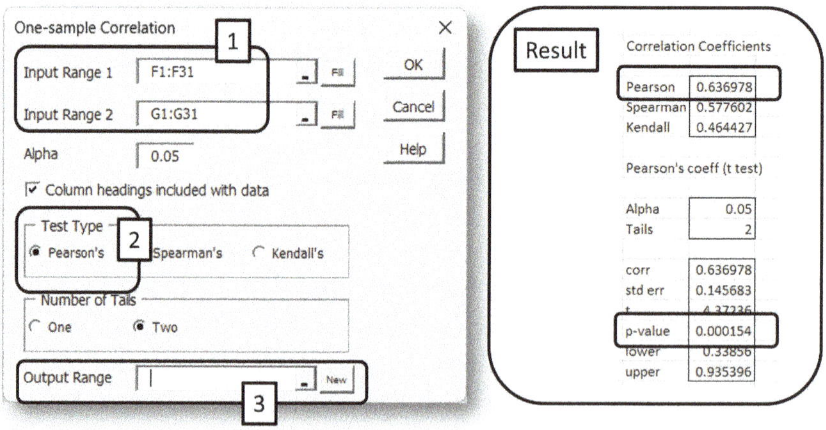

FIGURE 2.9
Correlation Test in Excel

and then *OK*. The result is shown in the output viewer. First, check the table "Model Summary." R Square equals 0.406, meaning 40.6% of the variance in the variable "Sales Volume" is accounted for by its relationship with the variable "Job Satisfaction" in the model. Next, check the table "ANOVA." The model significance is less than 0.001 (which is less than 0.05), indicating that the model is significant. In the table "Coefficients," the variable "Job Satisfaction" is positively and significantly related to the variable "Sales Volume" (B = 6.208, p < 0.001), meaning that every 1-unit increment in job satisfaction increases sales volume by 6.208K per month. To try it yourself, follow the numbers (which indicate the steps) in Figure 2.10. The result is also shown in the figure, with the key results highlighted in boxes.

To run **simple linear regression in Excel**, open the file "*Ch2_Job_Satisfaction_and_Sales_Volume.xlsx.*" Go to the worksheet "Data." Go to *Add-ins* > *Real Statistics* > *Data Analysis Tools*. In the pop-up dialog box, click the tab page "*Reg*," click *Multiple Linear Regression* and click *OK*. In the pop-up dialog box *Linear Regression*, select cells F1 to F31 (which are the values of the mean of the three items of job satisfaction) in the worksheet "Data" for the field

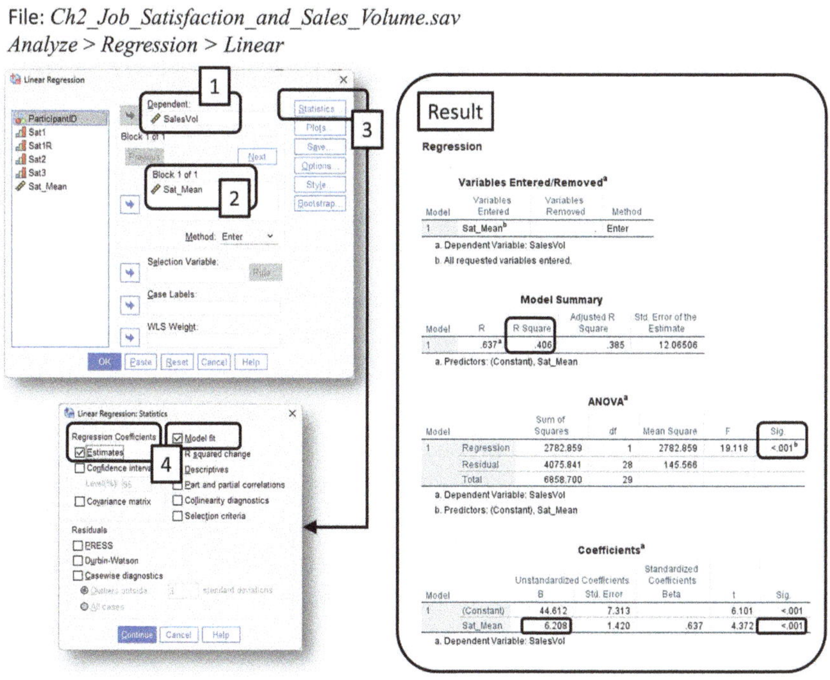

FIGURE 2.10
Simple Linear Regression in SPSS

File: *Ch2_Job_Satisfaction_and_Sales_Volume.xlsx (Worksheet: Data)*
Add-ins > Real Statistics > Data Analysis Tools (Reg > Multiple Linear Regression)

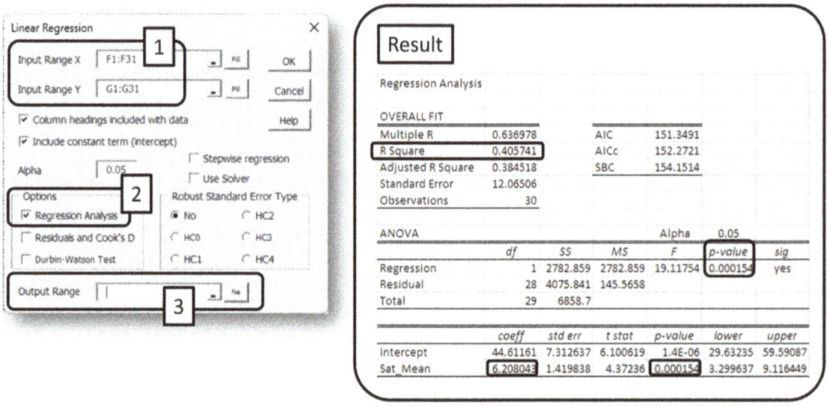

FIGURE 2.11
Simple Linear Regression in Excel

Input Range X, and cells G1 to G31 (which are the values of Sales Volume) for *Input Range Y*. Make sure the checkbox *Regression Analysis* is ticked. Leave the field *Output Range* blank to have the results shown on a new worksheet. Click *OK*. In the result worksheet, first check the table "OVERALL FIT." R Square equals 0.406 (rounded to three decimal places), meaning 40.6% of the variance in the variable "Sales Volume" is accounted for by its relationship with the variable "Job Satisfaction" in the model. Next, check the table "ANOVA." The model significance is 0.000154 (which is less than 0.05), indicating that the model is significant. In the table at the bottom, the variable "Job Satisfaction" is positively and significantly related to the variable "Sales Volume" ($B = 6.208$, $p < 0.001$), meaning that every 1-unit increment of job satisfaction increases sales volume by 6.208K per month. To try it yourself, follow the numbers (which are the steps) in Figure 2.11. The result is also shown in the figure, with the key figures highlighted in boxes.

In Excel, we can also visualize the result of simple linear regression in a chart (Figure 2.12). To do this, go to the worksheet "Data." Select cells F1 to G31, which are the two columns of data for the variables "Job Satisfaction" and "Sales Volume." Go to *Insert > Charts > Scatter*. Click the chart and then click the *Chart Elements* button (i.e., the green "+" button at the top right-hand corner of the chart). Tick the checkbox for *Trendline*, click *More Options . . .* and tick the checkbox for *Display Equation on chart*. You can see the equation shown on the chart: **y** = 6.208x + 44.612. Sales Volume in K

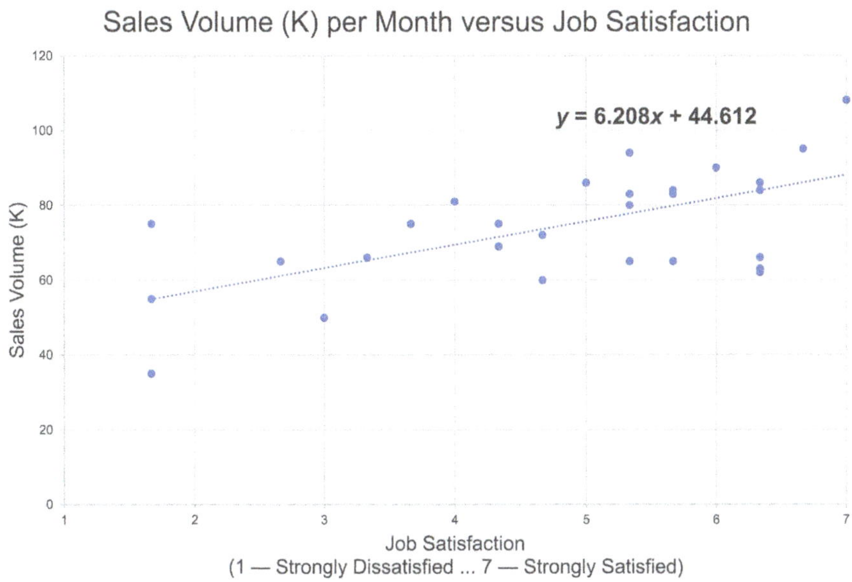

FIGURE 2.12
Visualizing the Result of Simple Linear Regression in Excel

is the *y*-axis, and Job Satisfaction is the *x*-axis in the chart. From the equation, we know that every 1-unit increment in job satisfaction increases sales volume by 6.208K per month, and the y-intercept is 44.612.

Review the result of our simple linear regression in Figure 2.10 or Figure 2.11. We can find that the coefficient of the variable "Job Satisfaction" is 6.208 and the coefficient of the intercept is 44.612. This means we can have the prediction formula for sales volume in K as 6.208 multiplied by the salesperson's job satisfaction, plus the intercept 44.612. That is why we call it predictive analytics because, as this example shows, we can predict the sales volume if we know the salesperson's job satisfaction using this formula.

The HR manager can now accept hypothesis H_1 and reject the null hypothesis H_0. That is, he is certain that salespersons' job satisfaction positively influences their sales volume ($B = 6.208$, $p < 0.001$).

2.5 GIVE ACTIONABLE RECOMMENDATIONS

One of the most important parts of the data analytics process is to drive for actions. Only when the recommendations are actionable can changes for improvement be made in an organization. The power of predictive analytics is that we do not only observe the consequence; we also observe the factor (or the predictor) so that we can act to increase the chance of a positive consequence or take preventive measures before a negative one occurs.

In our example, given the significant result that job satisfaction positively influences sales volume, the HR manager can focus on improving the salespersons' job satisfaction (i.e., the factor) in order to improve their sales volume (i.e., the consequence). The HR manager has reviewed the literature and, based on his HR knowledge, he believes that instilling participative leadership skills in the line managers (Tang & Lam, 2020) and adding a sense of fun to the working environment (Chan, 2019) will improve the salespersons' job satisfaction.

To find support for his thoughts on improving job satisfaction, he organizes some focus group discussion sessions with the salespersons about how to improve their job satisfaction. During the sessions, the HR manager also invites the salespersons to complete a survey collecting quantitative data on their supervisors' participative leadership behaviors and the sense of fun in the work environment, as well as qualitative data through an open-ended question about how job satisfaction can be improved. The HR manager jots down the discussion contents, which are also qualitative data.

While this book mainly focuses on quantitative analysis using statistical tests, I would like to introduce here one common method to analyze qualitative data: **Tesch's eight-step coding process** (Creswell & Creswell, 2022). First, get a sense of the qualitative materials. In our example, the qualitative materials include the focus group discussion contents and the answers to the open-ended questions in the survey. Second, pick several of the most interesting documents and write down your thoughts in the margin. Third, make a list of major and unique topics. Our HR manager finds that leadership, benefit, and fun are mentioned as major topics in the materials. Fourth, abbreviate the topics as codes. He abbreviates LEAD for leadership, BENE for benefit and FUN for fun. Fifth, find descriptive wordings for each topic. Sixth, finalize the abbreviations of the codes. Seventh, assemble the qualitative materials for each code. The HR manager counts the occurrence of wordings mentioned in these qualitative documents. Eighth, recode if necessary.

The HR manager has another HR officer perform the same coding process independently and check the results. Both of them agree that participative leadership is ranked as the top factor influencing the salespersons' job satisfaction. The HR manager decides to propose leadership training for the line managers as an improvement intervention.

Data Analytics is not a one-off process. Instead, it is a continuous cycle. After the HR manager has implemented the leadership training intervention, he continues to monitor the improvements in salespersons' job satisfaction and the line managers' leadership skills by collecting data and continuing the analytics process.

This chapter has detailed and demonstrated the data analytics process using a hypothetical example from Best Toy Company. Upon understanding the process and practicing the statistical steps, the following chapters will illustrate its applications in different business areas, starting with HR and marketing, followed by supply chain. In these coming chapters, more statistical tests and their applications will be demonstrated in detail.

REFERENCES

Cammann, C., Fichman, M., Jenkins, G. D., & Klesh, J. (1983). Michigan organizational assessment questionnaire. In S. E. Seashore, E. E. Lawler, P. H. Mirvis, & C. Cammann (Eds.), *Assessing Organizational Change: A Guide to Methods, Measures, and Practices* (pp. 71–138). New York: Wiley-Interscience.

Chan, S. C. H. (2019). Participative leadership and job satisfaction. *Leadership & Organization Development Journal, 40*(3), 319–333.

Creswell, J. W., & Creswell, J. D. (2022). *Research Design: Qualitative, Quantitative, and Mixed Methods Approaches* (6th ed.). SAGE Publications, Inc.

Edwards, M. R., Edwards, K., & Jang D. (2024). *Predictive HR Analytics: Mastering the HR Metric* (3rd ed.). Kogan Page Limited.

Francis, A., & Mousley, B. (2014). *Business Mathematics and Statistics* (7th ed.). Cengage Learning.

Knaflic, C. N. (2015). *Storytelling with Data: A Data Visualization Guide for Business Professionals*. Hoboken, New Jersey: Wiley.

Locke, E. A. (1976). The nature and causes of job satisfaction. In M. D. Dunnette (Ed.), *Handbook of Industrial and Organizational Psychology* (pp. 1297–349). Chicago: Rand McNally.

Tang, M. W. M., & Lam, C. K. (2020, April 23–25). Skip-level participation and helping behavior: the role of leader-leader exchange [Poster session]. *35th Annual Conference of the Society for Industrial and Organizational Psychology (SIOP 2020)*, Austin, TX, United States.

Zaiontz, C. (2025). *Real statistics using Excel.* Real Statistics Using Excel. https://real-statistics.com/

3

Data Analytics in Human Resources

3.1 AN INTRODUCTION TO DATA ANALYTICS IN HUMAN RESOURCES

In Chapter 2, the five-step analytics process was introduced with a simple practical example of finding one significant factor influencing the salespersons' sales volume in our hypothetical Best Toy Company. In this chapter, the focus is on the data analytics applications in human resources (HR). By using the hypothetical data and real-world case studies, we will know how data analytics can be applied in solving different HR problems in an employee life cycle.

An employee life cycle starts with the recruitment process. When an applicant becomes aware of a suitable position under recruitment, gets interested and decides to apply for the job, the company begins to engage with a prospective employee. The recruitment process selects and appoints suitable employees. The onboarding process follows. This process, if done right, helps the newly appointed employees familiarize with the company and pick up speed to perform well. After the onboarding period, a series of HR processes continue. These processes include performance reviews to manage performance, salary adjustments to better compensate the employees, and providing training to continuously develop them. With well-performed and well-trained employees, HR targets to retain them by enhancing the employee experience, for example, by providing a better working environment, increasing employee satisfaction, improving employee well-being and providing mobility opportunities like a promotion or a lateral move. Even if one day the employee chooses to leave the company, HR would like to maintain the good impression till the last moment of offboarding.

Throughout the process of providing a good employee experience in the employee life cycle, in addition to the traditional wisdom and intuition, HR needs to make evidence-based decisions to maintain their competitiveness

DOI: 10.1201/9781032642307-3

and, at the same time, to fulfill the new roles and tasks which organizations now expect HR to perform. HR needs to prove their contributions to the organization on top of demonstrating the HR activities performed. HR is also a strategic partner with the leadership team, providing evidence-based recommendations to improve business results. Moreover, the workforce is now more diverse and demanding. HR needs to act fast by monitoring not only the outcomes of the workforce but also their factors, so that HR can enhance a positive outcome or prevent a negative one. To do all these, HR has to apply data analytics to provide evidence for actionable recommendations.

In this chapter, using the hypothetical data from our Best Toy Company together with real-world case studies, different analytics statistical tests will be demonstrated to solve different HR problems. The chapter will start by listing the most popularly used metrics, which serve as quick indicators to highlight the areas HR needs to monitor. To solve different problems like high turnover, improving performance and enhancing employee engagement, HR analytics will be able to find significant factors so that HR can focus resources on them. After implementing interventions, like trainings or cultural change programs, HR analytics will be able to provide support to measure their outcomes. To provide evidence for diversity and gender balance, HR analytics will also be able to play a role. A new trend in understanding the relationships among the employees using organizational network analysis (ONA) for planning a more effective workforce will also be discussed.

3.2 METRICS

Metrics are indicators which help others gain a quick understanding of the situation. Metrics are also one type of descriptive analytics. They describe the situations, usually in the form of a number or a status. Imagine that we usually watch the weather report every morning, especially when we plan to go outdoors. The first thing we may want to know is the current temperature, which helps us decide the suitable clothes that day, for example, we need to wear a jacket if it is cold. The next thing we may want to know is whether it is going to be sunny or rainy. It helps us to decide whether to bring an umbrella. The current temperature and the sunny/rainy status are metrics and indicators which help us make evidence-based decisions.

In HR, there are also metrics to help HR professionals understand the healthiness of HR situations in an organization (Boudreau et al., 2019).

Some popular HR metrics are **cost per hire**, **time to hire**, **absenteeism rate**, **employee retention rate,** and **employee turnover rate**. Let us go through them one by one.

Cost per hire is the average cost for hiring a new employee in a certain period of time, for example, a year. It is the sum of internal recruiting costs and external recruiting costs divided by the number of new hires over that period, as shown in Equation 3–1.

$$Cost\ per\ Hire = \frac{(Internal\ Recruiting\ Costs + External\ Recruiting\ Costs)}{Number\ of\ New\ Hires} \quad (3\text{–}1)$$

The components of internal recruiting costs and external recruiting costs vary from organization to organization in practice. Here are some examples of these costs. **Internal recruiting costs** are the costs of the internal resources used for recruitment, which may cover administrative costs (e.g., a proportion of administrative expenses like rent and office equipment), hiring manager costs (i.e., the hours the hiring managers spent doing screening and interviewing candidates multiplied by their hourly salary), and onboarding and training costs (i.e., the training costs spent to upskill the new hires). **External recruiting costs** are the costs of the external resources used during the recruitment process, which may cover job fairs and promotion costs, job advertisement and sourcing expenses, travel expenses if the candidates or the hiring managers need to travel for the interviews. Although different organizations may calculate these costs differently, for comparison purposes, it is recommended to calculate them in a consistent way within the same organization. Similarly, this consistency practice should also be applied to the rest of the metrics we are going to discuss.

Time to hire is the average duration from the time the organization starts to engage the prospective employee (e.g., when that prospective employee submits a job application) to the time that they accept the job offer, as shown in Equation 3–2.

$$Time\ to\ Hire = \frac{\Sigma(Duration\ from\ a\ Job\ Application\ to\ an\ Offer\ Acceptance)}{Number\ of\ New\ Hires} \quad (3\text{–}2)$$

Time to hire reflects the efficiency of the hiring process. The activities in a hiring process differ across organizations. They may include resume screening, aptitude tests, phone and in-person interviews. Analyzing this duration helps organizations understand which activities have spent most time and can be improved. For example, Cathay Pacific, an airline company, replacing their phone interview of their flight attendant applicants with an on-demand online interview, effectively shortening the hiring process (HireVue, 2020). This process refinement reduces the difficulty of finding a common interview time slot for the interviewer and the applicant. The applicants can do the interview online anytime, anywhere, which is convenient for them. There are a lot of examples that technologies help to improve the efficiency and effectiveness in the hiring process. Yet technology is not a silver bullet for all problems. Blindly computerizing a series of manual processes is not likely to make a successful project. Without identifying the bottleneck of a process and finding a proper solution, it will likely fail to meet the expected results. More about achieving analytics project objectives in different stages will be discussed in Chapter 6.

Absenteeism rate is the percentage of time lost due to absences like sickness, medical appointments, emergencies, or accidents, divided by the total working hours multiplied by the average number of employees, as shown in Equation 3–3. To calculate the average number of employees for a period, one simple way is to add the number of employees on the first day and the last day of the period and then divide the result by 2. In general, the lower the absenteeism rate is the better.

$$Absenteeism\ Rate = \frac{Absent\ Hours}{Average\ Number\ of\ Employees \times Working\ Hours} \times 100\% \quad (3\text{–}3)$$

Does absenteeism incur costs to the organization? It depends on whether that employee is allowed to adjust their working hours. If there is such flexibility – for example, if employees are allowed to finish their job before or after their medical appointment – absenteeism is irrelevant. If the job nature does not allow such flexibility, the cost of absenteeism can be calculated as the employee's hourly salary rate multiplies by the number of absent hours.

Employee retention rate is the percentage of the number of employees who are in the organization on the first day of the period and also stay until the last day of the period, divided by the number of employees on the first day of that period, as shown in Equation 3–4. In general, the higher this rate, the better.

$$Employee\ Retention\ Rate = \frac{\begin{array}{c}Number\ of\ Employees\ Stay\\ from\ the\ First\ Day\ until\ the\ Last\ Day\\ of\ the\ period\end{array}}{\begin{array}{c}Number\ of\ Employees\\ on\ the\ First\ Day\ of\ the\ Period\end{array}} \times 100\% \quad (3\text{–}4)$$

Employee turnover rate of a period is the percentage of the number of employees who left divided by the average number of employees in that period, as shown in Equation 3–5. For simplicity, one way to calculate the average number of employees in a period is to add the number of employees on the first day and the last day of the period and then divide the result by 2. The employee turnover rate differs from industry to industry and from company to company. In general, a low employee turnover rate indicates that the organization is doing something right in terms of employee management.

$$Employee\ Turnover\ Rate = \frac{Number\ of\ Employees\ Left}{Average\ Number\ of\ Employees} \times 100\% \quad (3\text{–}5)$$

Employee turnover rate, arguably, is the most important HR metric due to the impacts of employee turnover on workforce productivity and its costs. The costs incurred include separation costs, replacement costs and training costs. **Separation costs** cover the costs spent on the exit interview and administrative procedures with the leaving employee, separation benefits paid to the leaving employee, decline in productivity (e.g., reassigning representatives for the clients), overtime or temporary personnel costs for the vacancy. **Replacement costs** include costs in job advertisements and administrative work (like interviews for the replacement employees), relocation and medical examination of the new replacement employee. **Training costs** cover the costs in formal and on-the-job training and productivity reduction while the new employee is picking up the job.

Given that the employee turnover rate is an important quick indicator to reflect how the organization is managing its employees, organizations may need a handy way (e.g., a dashboard) to monitor and visualize the changes of this number across different periods, down to different departments or even teams. In the coming section, I will use the data from our hypothetical company, Best Toy Company, to demonstrate some key features of a dashboard using Excel. Excel is a common tool in most offices. Once you master the skills for building a dashboard in Excel, it helps you to pick up other visualization tools more efficiently.

3.3 DASHBOARD

A **dashboard** is a quick visualization tool to report key indicators, highlight changes and provide drill-down details, trends or forecasts of important business figures. Its objective is to provide a quick update on the business situation in a readily understandable manner.

Recall our example of watching a weather report. We first look for key indicators, including temperature and eye-catching symbols like sunny, cloudy or rainy. Next, we would like to know the changes of these indicators compared to the past few days such that we can make quick decisions about our clothing options for that day. If there are big changes, for example, a sharp drop in temperature, we would like to know more details to understand the reason, whether it is due to a typhoon or seasonal changes. We would like to know the weather forecast for the coming few days as well to better prepare ourselves to adapt to the weather changes. A weather report is an effective and efficient way to show us the weather. Similarly, we would like a business dashboard to have these characteristics: showing important **metrics**, highlighting **changes using symbols** and providing **details or trends** on request. Keep the design simple such that the dashboard readers will not be burdened with too many details unless they want to know it by clicking the drill-down buttons.

Now, let us use the data from Best Toy Company to demonstrate an HR dashboard showing the employee turnover information. We will build a dashboard with the employee turnover rate and the headcount of the current period, their changes compared with those in the same period last year, and the trend for these two years as shown in Figure 3.1.

To build this **dashboard in Excel**, open the file "*Ch3_HR_Dashboard.xlsx.*" Go to the worksheet "Data" and let us read the data. This worksheet contains four columns: period, average headcount, leaver count, and turnover rate. We are going to use these data to prepare this dashboard with (1) the **key indicators,** turnover rate and headcount, (2) the **symbols** highlighting the changes by comparing these two indicators with the same period last year, (3) a **chart with details** including the turnover rate, the average headcount and the leaver count over the 2-year period. Go to the worksheet "Dashboard." The dashboard is already prepared. By analyzing it, you will learn how it is built.

We will now analyze how to add the **key indicators** in the worksheet "Dashboard." Follow the numbers in Figure 3.2, which highlight the steps in the following text. First, we will look at the two drop-down boxes in cells C3 and H3, which allow the dashboard reader to choose the periods to compare the turnover rates and the headcounts. Click cell C3. Go to *Data > Data Validation.* In the "Data

FIGURE 3.1
An HR Dashboard about Employee Turnover

File: *Ch3_HR_Dashboard.xlsx*

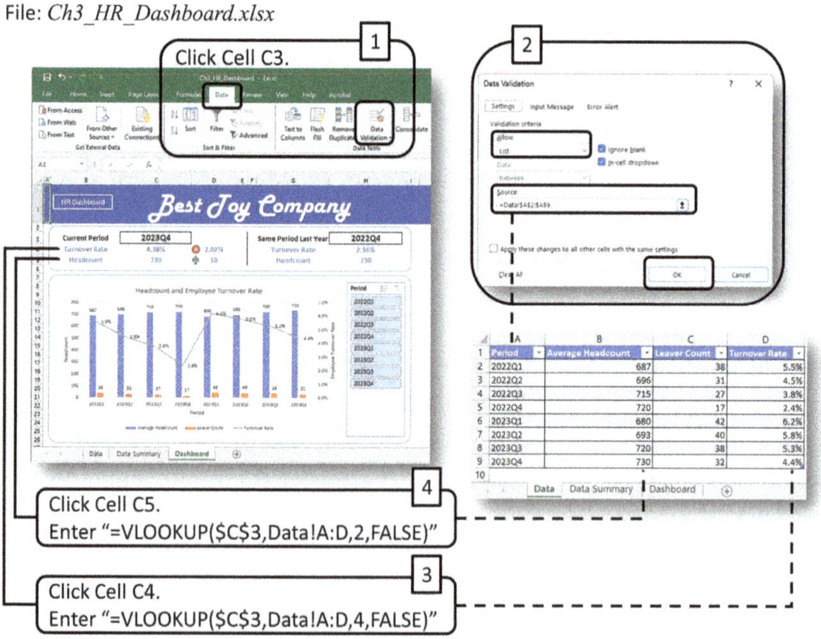

FIGURE 3.2
HR Dashboard: Add Key Indicators

Validation" pop-up dialog box, click the *Settings* tab. Select "List" for *Allow* and select cells A2 to A9 (which are the selectable periods) from the worksheet "Data" as the *Source*. Click *OK*. Click cell H3 and repeat the steps to add the drop-down box with the periods as selections. Next, we will show the indicators of employee turnover rate and headcount in cells C4 and C5 for the current quarter, and cells H4 and H5 for the same quarter last year. Click cell C4 in the worksheet "Dashboard" and enter "=VLOOKUP(C3, Data!A:D, 4, FALSE)," which means to find the corresponding turnover rate according to the period in cell C3 from the fourth column of the data range in columns A to D in the worksheet "Data." Click cell C5 and enter "=VLOOKUP(C3, Data!A:D, 2, FALSE)," which means to find the corresponding headcount from the worksheet "Data" according to the period shown in cell C3 from the second column of the data range in columns A to D in the worksheet "Data." Repeat and adjust the input for cells H4 and H5 for the results of the same quarter last year. One of the best ways of learning is by doing, so try to follow the steps and add these key indicators.

We will now look at how the **symbols** highlighting the changes in employee turnover rate and headcount are prepared in the worksheet "Dashboard." Follow the numbers in Figure 3.3, which highlight the steps in the following

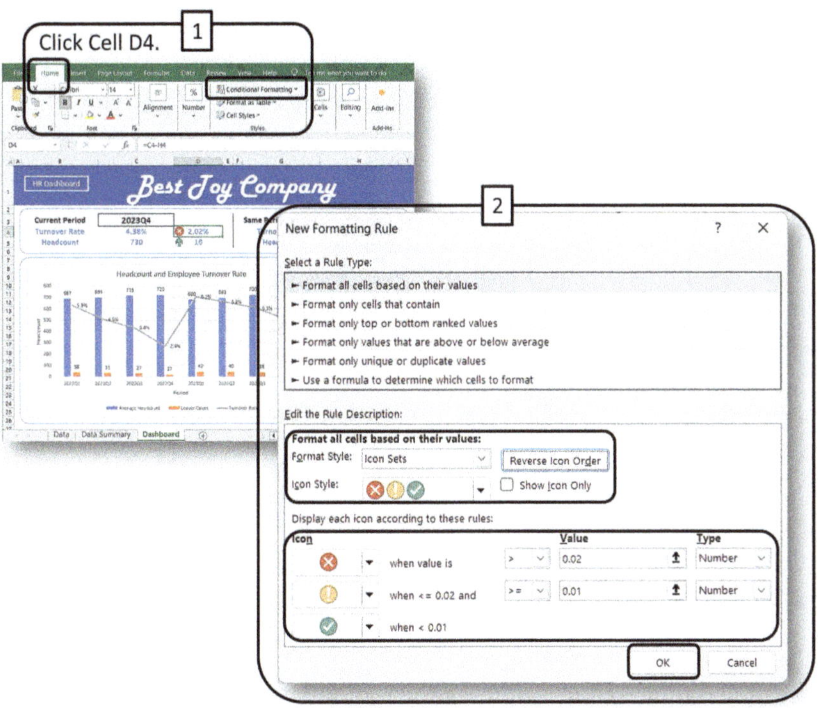

FIGURE 3.3
HR Dashboard: Add Symbols

text. Click cell D4 and enter "=C4-H4," indicating the difference in the employee turnover rate between the current period and the same period last year. It highlights to the reader using a red cross if the increase is greater than 2%. It shows a yellow exclamation mark if it is between 1% and 2% increase. Otherwise, a green tick is shown. To do this, go to *Home* > *Conditional Formatting* > *New Rule.* In the pop-up dialog box "New Formatting Rule," choose "Icon Sets" as *Format Style.* Pick "Cross-Exclamation-Tick" as *Icon Style.* Click the button *Reverse Icon Order* because we want to highlight in a way that the lower the number, the better. Now, enter the rules: when the value is greater than 0.02, show a cross. When the value is between 0.01 and 0.02, show an exclamation mark. When the value is smaller than 0.01, show a tick. Click *OK.* Based on this logic, try to figure out the conditional formatting rule for the symbol of the headcount (i.e., cell D5).

Lastly, we will prepare a **chart** of employee turnover rate, headcount and leaver count for the 2-year period with a slicer. A **slicer** allows the reader to further select the periods to show in the chart. Go to the worksheet "Data." Select the table with cells from A1 to D9. Go to *Table Design.* Give this table the name "HeadCount" in the field *Table Name.* A slicer needs to identify a table by this table name. Follow the numbers in Figure 3.4, which highlight the steps in the following text. To prepare a chart, continue selecting the table with cells from A1 to D9 in the worksheet "Data," go to *Insert* > *Recommended Charts.* Click the recommended "Clustered Column"

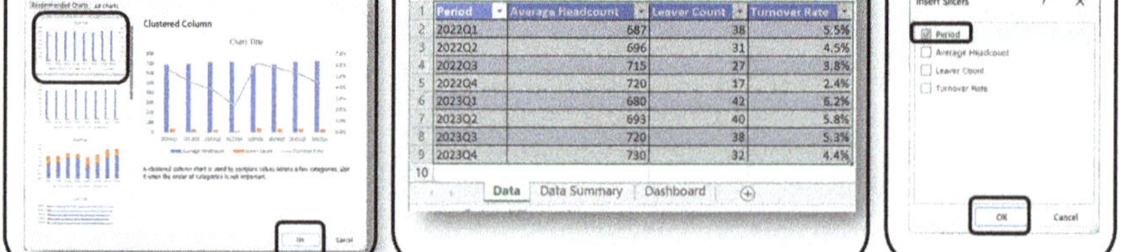

FIGURE 3.4
HR Dashboard: Add a Chart

chart. Click *OK*. Update the chart title and axis titles accordingly. To add a slicer, continue selecting the table with cells from A1 to D9, go to *Insert > Slicer*. In the "Insert Slicers" pop-up dialog box, tick "Period." Click *OK*. You can then copy the chart and the slicer to the worksheet "Dashboard." By holding the *Ctrl* button and clicking different periods in the slicer, you can choose different periods to display in the chart.

A good dashboard which readers find useful and enjoy reading has several criteria: (1) the data are pivotal to the reader's decision-making, (2) the data must be correct and up-to-date, and (3) the dashboard is readily understandable. To achieve these objectives, different areas of professionals are required to contribute their expertise. The **business analyst** needs to understand what matters most to the readers. The **programmer** needs to understand the requirements well to develop the correct program with the correct data. The **designer** needs to create a user-friendly graphical interface. Not being able to achieve any of these criteria, the dashboard will not be able to serve as a quick alert for decisions and actions.

The HR director of Best Toy Company reads the HR dashboard (Figure 3.1). The red cross, indicating a 2.02% increase of employee turnover rate in the 4th quarter this year (4.38%) compared to last year (2.36%), draws her attention. Due to the high costs of turnover to the organization, turnover is an important issue to fix. High turnover is, in fact, not an uncommon problem for different organizations in different industries. **Nielsen**, an international data and research company, faced this problem and applied HR analytics to find the significant factor which could combat turnover. Let us go through this case study in the next section.

3.4 CASE STUDY: NIELSEN'S HR ANALYTICS FOR EMPLOYEE TURNOVER

Nielsen is an American international data, information and market measurement company. They provide marketing research services for their clients. Nielsen has applied data and research not only to their clients but has also applied data analytics to resolve their HR attrition problem (Steiner, 2017).

Many great solutions start with good questions. Piyush Mathur, the head of Nielsen's "people analytics" program at that time, faced a big question from one of the business leaders in the company:

Do you know why people are leaving my team?

This is a simple question. However, to find an evidence-based answer may not be that straightforward. There is an overwhelming large number of possible answers, ranging from the hygiene of the working environment to the people relationships within the organizational network. If you were the head, how would you find the answer? Think of what you have learned in Chapter 2. One of the problems that data analytics is possible to solve is identifying factors of a phenomenon; in this case, it is attrition. Nielsen did use analytics and was able to identify significant factors for this problem within months.

One good practice we may learn from this case study is that they started with the data which were readily available in the organization. They hypothesized that gender, tenure, ethnicity, manager's rating, trainings, commute time and lateral job role movements would influence the attrition phenomenon. They found astonishing results. They made good use of the available data to gain quick wins.

Mathur and Doug Shagam, Nielsen's technologists at that time, presented three important results at Talent Connect 2016. First, gender and ethnicity do not account for the attrition phenomenon. This implies that there is no indication of diversity or gender biases which lead to the high employee turnover. Second, employees working less than 1 year in the organization have a significantly higher likelihood of attrition. Third, employees who have had a lateral move significantly increase the chance of staying within the company.

These results have differentiated the significant factors from the insignificant ones. Therefore, the company could reserve the resources to solve the key problems. The results have also identified the segment of employees with high attrition risks, those working less than 1 year, whom the company could pay special attention to retain. Most importantly, the results also uncovered one solution: lateral moves could help retain employees.

You may recall the last step of the data analytics process is to give actionable recommendations. Nielsen did the same. They did not stop at the point of finding the answers to important questions but also put them into actions. They presented the results as a compelling story. Nielsen then set up a program called "Golden Year" to help first-year employees stay in the company. They empowered the employees to make lateral moves by a "Ready to Rotate" program, which significantly helped to retain the employees.

Data analytics is not a one-off exercise. Nielsen then collects more data and continues its analytics journey.

Isn't this case study amazing? Imagine that if Nielsen did not apply data analytics to find the significant factors, they might have either invested resources in insignificant places or spread the resources too thin across all possible factors, which in turn may not be able to make significant improvements to the attrition situation.

Case studies share experience, no matter whether good or bad, help other companies plan their analytics process. Many companies would replicate (i.e., to repeat other companies' processes) and implement the practice from case studies in their own company.

Now, let us try to replicate Nielsen's analytics process in our hypothetical Best Toy Company to understand *how* Nielsen found these results. Let us have some hands-on practice (Edwards et al., 2024).

3.5 EMPLOYEE TURNOVER AND EMPLOYEE ENGAGEMENT – AN EXAMPLE OF LOGISTIC REGRESSION

Back to our Best Toy Company. The red cross on the HR dashboard (Figure 3.1), indicating a 2.02% increase in the employee turnover rate this quarter (4.38%) compared to that last year (2.36%), draws the HR director's attention. The HR director tasks an HR team, consisting of an HR manager and several HR officers, to further drill down into the employee turnover details. The HR manager identifies that the product design department has the highest turnover rate. There are three product lines in the company with a total of 120 product designers. The HR manager has interviewed the product design managers to understand the attrition situation. The HR team has analyzed the interview data using **Tesch's eight-step coding process** (see Chapter 2) and has figured out that low engagement levels may be the key factor increasing attrition. They have followed the **five-step data analytics process** (see Chapter 2) and have formulated the business problem and research question as follows:

Business Problem: The product design department has a high turnover rate, which negatively impacts the company. The HR department targets to find out the factor behind the high turnover rate.

Research Question: What is the key factor influencing employee turnover?

Following that, they have built the **hypotheses** and the **model**:

H_1: Increasing employee engagement reduces turnover.

H_0: Increasing employee engagement does not reduce turnover.

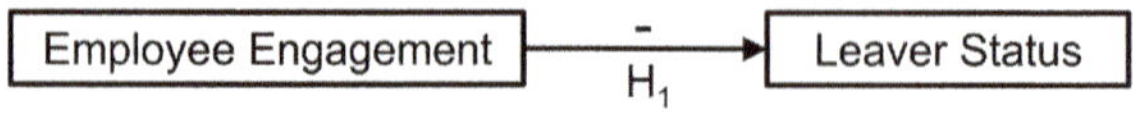

FIGURE 3.5
The Hypothesized Model for the Factor of Turnover

In our hypothesized model, we have employee engagement as the independent variable (IV) and leaver status as the dependent variable (DV), as shown in Figure 3.5. We have hypothesized that increasing employee engagement will retain employees; that is, they are more likely to be a stayer (leaver status = 0) rather than a leaver (leaver status = 1). In other words, when the value of employee engagement increases, a decrease in the value of the leaver status is hypothesized. So, the relationship is a negative one.

The HR team prepares to test the hypotheses by gathering data. The HR department has an HR database keeping track of the employee data and collects annual employee sentiment survey at the beginning of each year. The HR database contains employees' demographic data (e.g., gender, education background, tenure), trainings attended and supervisor-rated performance data (e.g., job performance, helping behavior). The employee sentiment survey gathers employees' engagement levels and their ratings to their supervisor's participative leadership behavior.

The HR officer has extracted the relevant data from the HR database and the survey results into the SPSS file "*Ch3_HR_Data.sav*" and the Excel file "*Ch3_HR_Data.xlsx.*" The two files contain the same set of 120 employees from the product design department. Each row of data represents the data for one employee. Every row contains 34 columns of data. We will go through the corresponding columns of data when the model requires. In this set of data, the variable names have some naming conventions. First, if a variable name ends with "*_Mean,*" it represents the calculated mean value of its survey items. Second, if a variable name starts with "*T1,*" this piece of data was collected at **Time 1,** which is the beginning of last year. If a variable name starts with "*T2,*" this piece of data was collected at **Time 2,** which is the beginning of this year. In the Excel file, the required columns of data for individual statistical tests are copied from the worksheet "Data" to different *worksheets*. Please follow the steps in the specified *worksheet* to run the tests for the rest of this chapter.

Let us now study the variables of our model, which hypothesizes that employee engagement at Time 1 negatively influences the leaver status at Time 2 which is 1 year later.

Employee engagement is a positive state of mind with vigor, dedication and absorption when at work (Schaufeli et al., 2006). An engaged employee feels a high level of energy, has a strong sense of enthusiasm and fully concentrates on his or her work. To measure their employee engagement level, the HR team has referenced to this meaning of employee engagement and prepared the following three survey items, measuring by a 7-point Likert scale (0 – Never; 1 – Almost never; 2 – Rarely; 3 – Sometimes; 4 – Often; 5 – Very often; 6 – Always) in their annual employee survey:

1. I feel like full of energy when I am at work.
2. I have a strong sense of enthusiasm for my work.
3. I feel happy when I concentrate on my work.

The **leaver status** is simply a flag (0 – Stayer; 1 – Leaver) retrieved from the HR database, indicating whether that employee stays or has left the company at Time 2.

Before testing the hypotheses, it needs to make sure the measures are valid and reliable (see Chapter 2). Checking the wordings used in the survey items for employee engagement which reflect the meaning of the employee engagement. So, it passes the **face validity**. The HR team has checked that the values of the leaver status which correctly reflects whether that employee stays or leaves the company. So, it also passes the **face validity**.

Use the SPSS file "*Ch3_HR_Data.sav*" and the Excel file "*Ch3_HR_Data.xlsx*." The leaver status has only 1 question item, so we cannot further test its construct validity and reliability. While for employee engagement for Time 1, there are three survey items, so we will check its construct validity using factor analysis in SPSS (Figure 3.6) or in Excel (Figure 3.7) and its reliability in SPSS (Figure 3.8) or in Excel (Figure 3.9). In the Excel file, the data are copied to the worksheet "Validity and Reliability" for these two tests. To find the details about construct validity and reliability, see Chapter 2 (Section 2.3.2 "Validity and Reliability of the Measures"). Figures 3.6 to 3.9, showing the steps indicated by the numbers and the results of these two tests, serve as a quick memory refresher.

Construct validity test for employee engagement at Time 1 shows that all three factor loadings (0.843, 0.889 and 0.845, respectively) are greater than 0.6, indicating that the measure is valid (Figures 3.6, 3.7).

Reliability test for employee engagement at Time 1 shows that Cronbach's alpha equals 0.819, which is greater than 0.7, indicating that the measure is reliable (Figures 3.8, 3.9).

After we have tested the validity and reliability of both the independent variable (i.e., employee engagement) and the dependent variable (i.e., leaver status), we can now test our hypotheses. In this hypothesized

File: *Ch3_HR_Data.sav*
Analyze > Dimension Reduction > Factor

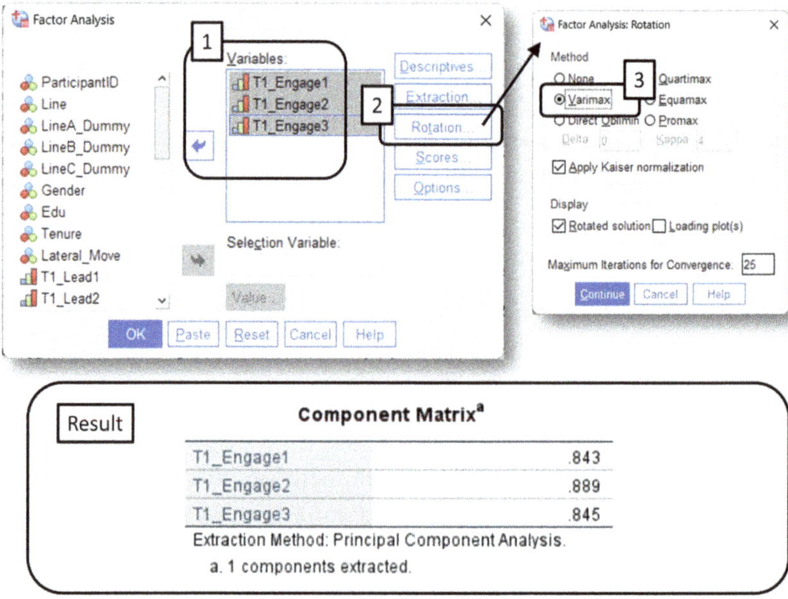

FIGURE 3.6
Factor Analysis for Employee Engagement in SPSS

File: *Ch3_HR_Data.xlsx (Worksheet: Validity & Reliability)*
Add-ins > Real Statistics > Data Analysis Tools (Multivar > Factor Analysis)

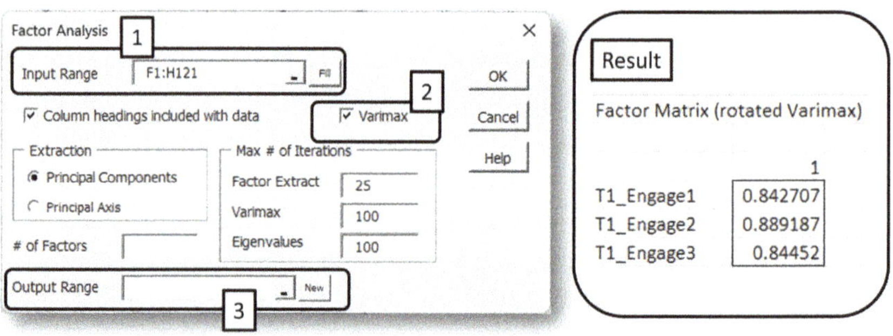

FIGURE 3.7
Factor Analysis for Employee Engagement in Excel

model, we are **finding factors of the leaver status**, a categorical variable. It is categorical because it contains only the values 0 (i.e., stayer) and 1 (i.e., leaver), which are basically categories. So, we will use **logistic regression** (see Chapter 2).

File: *Ch3_HR_Data.sav*
Analyze > Scale > Reliability Analysis

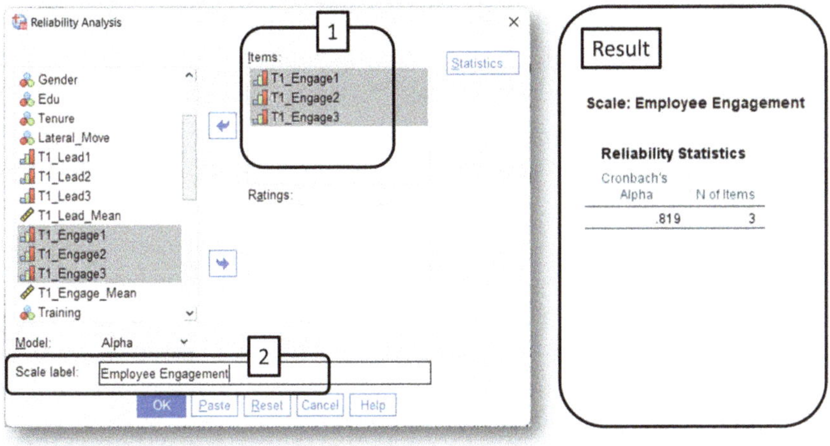

FIGURE 3.8
Reliability Test for Employee Engagement in SPSS

File: *Ch3_HR_Data.xlsx (Worksheet: Validity & Reliability)*
Add-ins > Real Statistics > Data Analysis Tools (Corr > Internal Consistency Reliability)

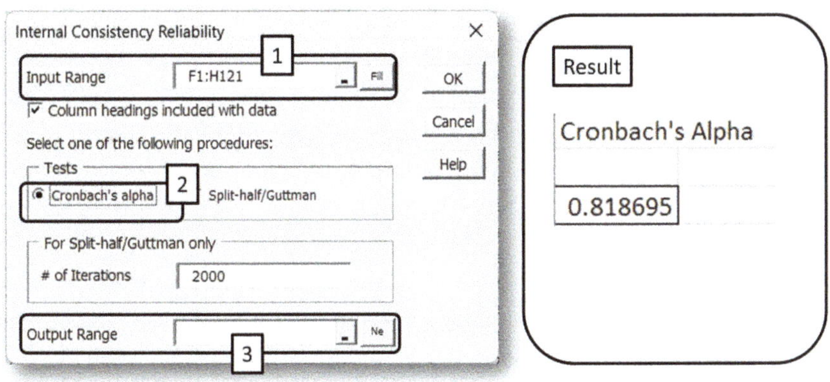

FIGURE 3.9
Reliability Test for Employee Engagement in Excel

In data analytics for HR, when we are finding factors of a phenomenon or predicting the consequence of a phenomenon, we will usually include some control variables like *gender*, *education* and *tenure*. These demographic variables have been shown as some common factors of people phenomena in prior research. Therefore, we will include these control variables as independent variables in the statistical test to show that their effects are considered. As these control variables are not our focus of study, we will usually not draw them in our hypothesized model.

In Best Toy Company, they usually include product line as the control variable to consider its effect as well. The variable *Line* is categorical with three values (1 – Line A; 2 – Line B; 3 – Line C). Logistic regression only accepts continuous independent variables. To include the variable *Line*, we will turn it into **dummy variables**. In the dataset, there are three columns, namely *LineA_Dummy*, *LineB_Dummy* and *LineC_Dummy*. If the value in the variable *Line* is 1 (i.e., Line A), the value of *LineA_Dummy* will be 1, and the values of the other two columns will be 0. If the value in the variable *Line* is 2 (i.e., Line B), the value of *LineB_Dummy* will be 1, and the values of the other two columns will be 0. The same logic applies to *LineC_Dummy*. We will then pick one of the three dummy variables as the reference (I will show you the rationale when we analyze the result). Let us pick *LineA_Dummy* as the reference, and we will NOT include it in the statistical test as the independent variable.

In this **logistic regression** test, we will include *Gender*, *Education*, *Tenure*, *LineB_Dummy* and *LineC_Dummy* as the control variables; the mean of the three employee engagement survey items (i.e., *T1_Engage_Mean*) as the independent variable (IV); and the leaver status (i.e., *T2_Leaver_Status*) as the dependent variable (DV).

To do this **logistic regression in SPSS**, open the file "*Ch3_HR_Data.sav.*" Go to *Analyze* > *Regression* > *Binary Logistic*. Select T2_Leaver_Status as *Dependent*. Select Gender, Edu, Tenure, LineB_Dummy, LineC_Dummy, and T1_Engage_Mean as *Covariates*. Click *OK*. The steps and the result are shown in Figure 3.10.

The result is in the output viewer. In the table "Omnibus Tests of Model Coefficients," it shows that the model is significant ($p < 0.001$). In the table "Model Summary," the Nagelkerke R Square = 0.618, indicating that the control and independent variables account for 61.8% variance in the leaver status. In the table "Variables in the Equation," read columns Exp(B) and Sig. Identify those significant variables (i.e., Sig. < 0.05). We call Exp(B) the **Odds Ratio,** which represents the likelihood of an event occurring. Follow Equation 3–6 to interpret the meaning of the Odds Ratio:

$$Exp(B) = \frac{Probability\ of\ DV = 1}{Probability\ of\ DV = 0}\ when\ IV\ is\ 1\ unit\ higher \qquad (3\text{–}6)$$

File: *Ch3_HR_Data.sav*
Analyze > Regression > Binary Logistic

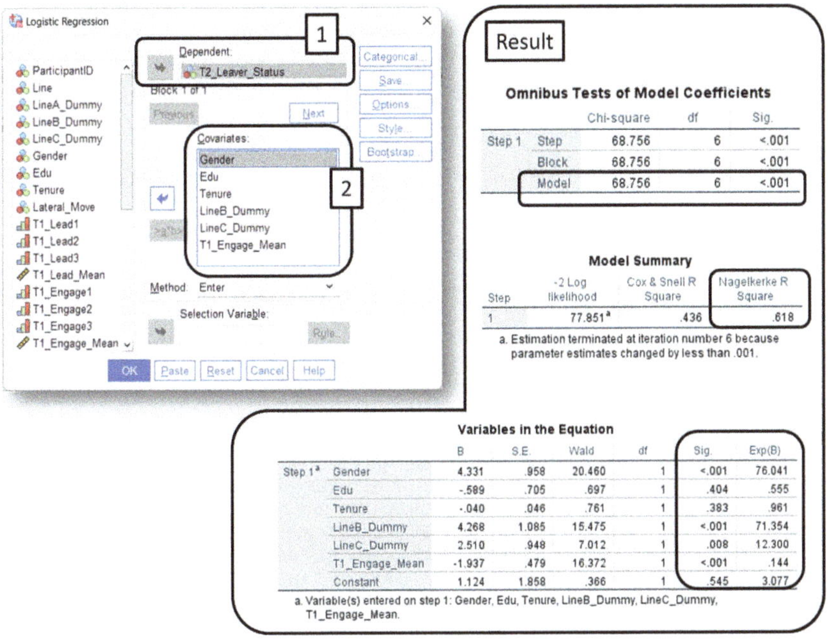

Omnibus Tests of Model Coefficients

		Chi-square	df	Sig.
Step 1	Step	68.756	6	<.001
	Block	68.756	6	<.001
	Model	68.756	6	<.001

Model Summary

Step	-2 Log likelihood	Cox & Snell R Square	Nagelkerke R Square
1	77.851[a]	.436	.618

a. Estimation terminated at iteration number 6 because parameter estimates changed by less than .001.

Variables in the Equation

		B	S.E.	Wald	df	Sig.	Exp(B)
Step 1[a]	Gender	4.331	.958	20.460	1	<.001	76.041
	Edu	-.589	.705	.697	1	.404	.555
	Tenure	-.040	.046	.761	1	.383	.961
	LineB_Dummy	4.268	1.085	15.475	1	<.001	71.354
	LineC_Dummy	2.510	.948	7.012	1	.008	12.300
	T1_Engage_Mean	-1.937	.479	16.372	1	<.001	.144
	Constant	1.124	1.858	.366	1	.545	3.077

a. Variable(s) entered on step 1: Gender, Edu, Tenure, LineB_Dummy, LineC_Dummy, T1_Engage_Mean.

FIGURE 3.10
Logistic Regression in SPSS

The IV *Gender* is significant ($p < 0.001$) and has an odds ratio of 76.041. Follow Equation 3–6 to interpret its meaning. The probability of leaving (i.e., DV = 1) to the probability of staying (i.e., DV = 0), when the employee is a female (i.e., IV = 1) rather than a male (i.e., IV = 0), is 76.041. A more interpretable way of saying this is that a female is 76.041 times more likely to leave than a male.

The IV *LineB_Dummy* is significant ($p < 0.001$) and has an odds ratio of 71.354. It means the probability of leaving (i.e., DV = 1) to the probability of staying (i.e., DV = 0), when the employee is in Line B (i.e., IV = 1) rather than Line A (i.e., the reference product line), is 71.354. We can also say that employees in Line B are 71.354 times more likely to leave than those in Line A. Similarly, *LineC_Dummy* is significant ($p = 0.008$) and has an odds ratio of 12.300. Employees in Line C are 12.300 times more likely to leave than those in Line A. This explains why we need to take one of the values as the reference for categorical variables because we will take this reference category for comparison purpose.

File: *Ch3_HR_Data.xlsx (Worksheet: 1. Logistic Regression)*
Add-ins > Real Statistics > Data Analysis Tools (Reg > Multinomial Logistic Regression)

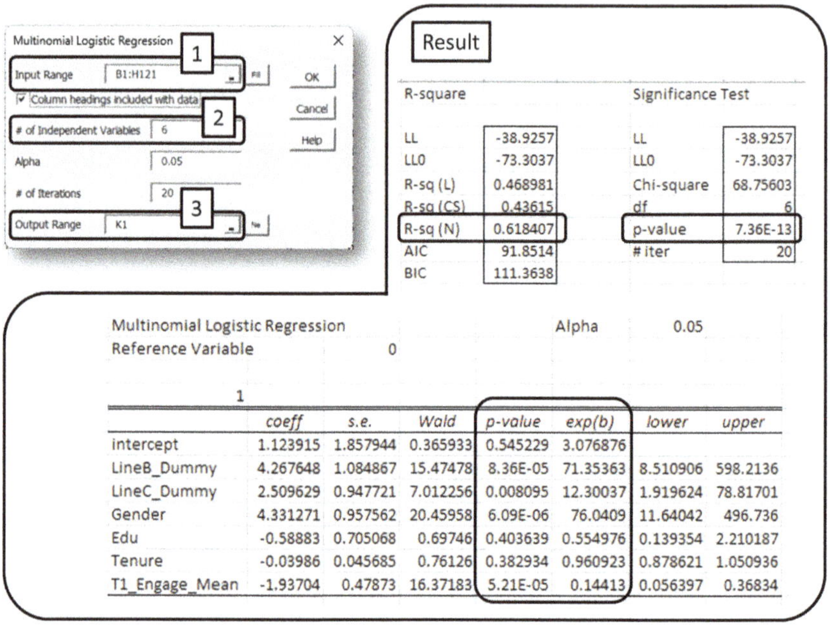

FIGURE 3.11
Logistic Regression in Excel

The IV *T1_Engage_Mean* is significant ($p < 0.001$) and has an odds ratio of 0.144. The probability of leaving (i.e., DV = 1) to the probability of staying (i.e., DV = 0) when the employee has a 1 engagement rating higher is 0.144. The odds ratio is lower than 1. To make the sentence more understandable, we flip the numerator and denominator on both sides of the equation. That is, employee who has 1 engagement rating higher is 6.944 (= 1 ÷ 0.144) times more likely to stay. So, H_1 is accepted, and H_0 is rejected.

To do this **logistic regression in Excel**, open the file "*Ch3_HR_Data.xlsx.*" Go to the worksheet "1. Logistic Regression." Go to *Add-ins > Real Statistics > Data Analysis Tools.* In the pop-up dialog box, click the tab page *Reg*, click *Multinomial Logistic Regression* and *OK.* In the "Multinomial Logistic Regression" pop-up dialog box, select cells B1 to H121 (which are the values of the control variables, the independent variable and the dependent variable, which must be in the last column) as the *Input Range.* Enter "6" in the field *# of Independent Variables.* Enter cell K1 as the *Output Range.* Click *OK.* In the result area, the table "R-square" shows that R-sq (N) = 0.618, meaning Nagelkerke R Square = 0.618, indicating that the control and independent variables account for 61.8% variance in the leaver status. In the table "Significance Test", p-value < 0.001, meaning the model is significant. (In Excel, when you see a number, for example, 8.36E-05, it means 0.0000836, which is smaller than 0.05.) Follow Equation 3–6. The results in the table "Reference Variable" are summarized here. Female is 76.041 times more likely to leave than male. Employees in Line B are 71.354 times more likely to leave than those in Line A. Employees in Line C are 12.300 times more likely to leave than those in Line A. Employee who has 1 engagement rating higher is 6.944 (= 1 ÷ 0.144) times more likely to stay. So, H_1 is accepted, and H_0 is rejected. The steps and the result are in Figure 3.11. The result details are explained in the earlier paragraphs using SPSS, so I am not going to repeat them here.

The last step of an analytics process is to give actionable recommendations based on the statistical results. First, female employees are a lot more likely to leave than male employees, which indicates that there may be some gender bias situations in the company. The gender differences may come from procedural fairness or organizational support for the employees. Some companies will hold focus group discussions to find out more in-depth potential reasons. Second, employees in Line B and Line C are also more likely to leave than those in Line A. Interviews, focus group discussions or on-site observations can provide more details. This could be due to the working environment, different practices in different teams, or employees' relationship with their supervisors. Third, increasing employee engagement level by 1 unit (on its 7-point Likert scale) will help that employee 6.94 times more likely to stay in the company. Some companies will hold employee engagement programs to improve employee engagement. Some companies, like Nielsen, identify certain working arrangements (in their case, lateral moves) to improve employee engagement, which in turn improves employee retention. Data analytics is not a one-off process. Therefore, the HR team in Best Toy Company, after finding that employee engagement improves retention, continues to find evidence to see whether lateral moves improve employee engagement.

3.6 STAFF MOBILITY AND EMPLOYEE ENGAGEMENT – AN EXAMPLE OF MULTIPLE LINEAR REGRESSION

The result shows that employees with 1 unit higher in their engagement level will be almost seven times more likely to stay. This indicates that engagement is an important factor in employee retention. The HR team would further like to know if lateral moves, similar to the case at Nielsen, will help to improve employee engagement, which in turn reduces turnover.

Business Problem: Employee engagement is identified as a factor reducing employee turnover. HR department would like to verify if lateral move will improve employee engagement, which in turn will improve employee retention.
Research Question: Does a lateral move improve employee engagement?

Then, the HR team has built the **hypotheses** and the **model**:

H_1: Employees with a lateral move have higher employee engagement.
H_0: Employees with a lateral move do not have higher employee engagement.

In our hypothesized model, we have lateral move as the independent variable and employee engagement as the dependent variable, as shown in Figure 3.12. We have hypothesized that having a lateral move (i.e., 1), rather than no lateral move (i.e., 0), will increase employee engagement. So, the relationship is a positive one.

Look at the data in the SPSS file "*Ch3_HR_Data.sav*" and the Excel file "*Ch3_HR_Data.xlsx.*" The variable *Lateral_Move* indicates whether an employee had a lateral move in the previous year (1 – yes; 0 – no). The HR team has checked that this value represents the correct meaning of a lateral move. So, it passes the **face validity**. As it only contains one question, construct validity and reliability tests are not required. For employee engagement at Time 1, it was tested in the previous section that it passes the **face validity**, the **construct validity** test in SPSS (Figure 3.6) and in Excel (Figure 3.7), and the **reliability** test in SPSS (Figure 3.8) and in Excel (Figure 3.9).

To test the hypothesis of finding whether a lateral move is **a factor of the continuous variable** which is employee engagement here, we will use **multiple linear regression** (see Chapter 2). We will also include *Gender*,

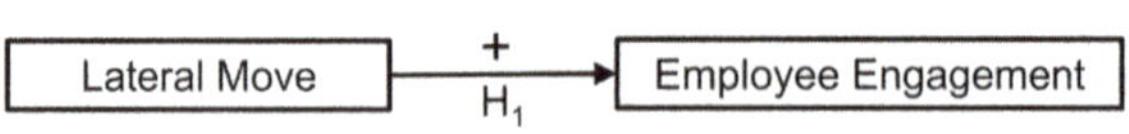

FIGURE 3.12
The Hypothesized Model for the Impact of Lateral Move on Employee Engagement

Education, *Tenure*, *LineB_Dummy* and *LineC_Dummy* as the control variables. Although multiple linear regression allows categorical variables as the independent variables, we will continue to use the dummy variables for product line to have a more meaningful representation.

To do this **multiple linear regression in SPSS**, open the file "*Ch3_HR_Data.sav.*" Go to *Analyze > Regression > Linear.* Select T1_Engage_Mean as *Dependent.* Select LineB_Dummy, LineC_Dummy, Gender, Edu, Tenure, and Lateral_Move as *Independent(s).* Click *OK.* The result is in the output viewer. In the table "Model Summary," R Square = 0.431, indicating that the control and independent variables account for 43.1% variance in employee engagement. In the table "ANOVA," it shows that the model is significant ($p < 0.001$). In the table "Coefficients," read columns Unstandardized B and Sig. Identify those significant variables (i.e., Sig. < 0.05). Tenure is negatively and significantly related to employee engagement ($B = -0.039$, $p < 0.001$), meaning that the longer the tenure, the lower the employee engagement. Lateral move is positively and significantly related to employee engagement ($B = 0.943$, $p < 0.001$), meaning that the employees with a lateral move have higher employee engagement. So, H_1 is accepted, and H_0 is rejected. The steps and results are shown in Figure 3.13.

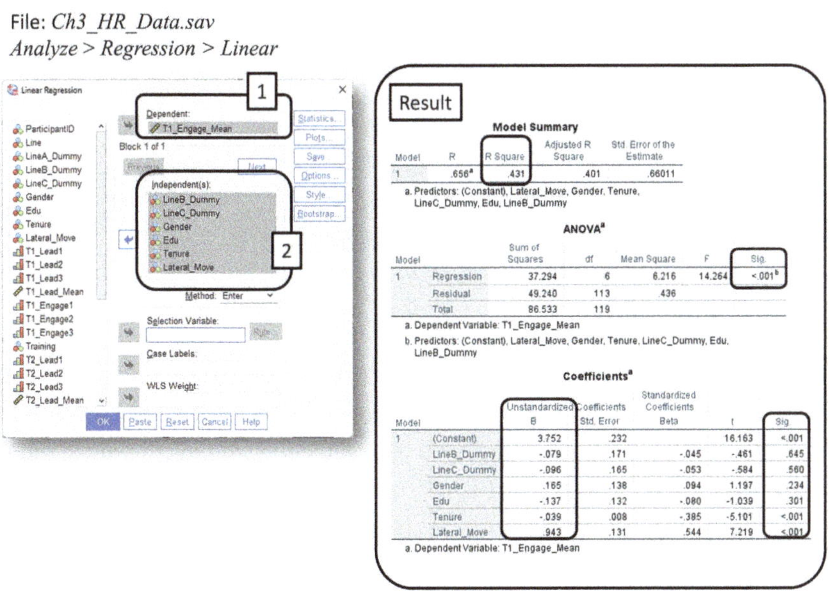

FIGURE 3.13
Multiple Linear Regression in SPSS

To do this **multiple linear regression in Excel**, open the file "*Ch3_HR_Data.xlsx.*" Go to worksheet "2. MLR (Lateral Move)." Go to *Add-ins > Real Statistics > Data Analysis Tools*. In the pop-up dialog box, click the tab page *Reg*, click *Multiple Linear Regression* and *OK*. In the "Linear Regression" pop-up dialog box, select cells B1 to G121 (the control variables and independent variable) as the *Input Range X*. Select cells H1 to H121 (the dependent variable) as the *Input Range Y*. Enter the cell L1 as *Output Range*. Click *OK*. In the result area, the table "OVERALL FIT" shows that R Square = 0.431, indicating that the control and independent variables account for 43.1% of the variance in employee engagement. In the table "ANOVA," it shows that the model is significant ($p < 0.001$). In the coefficient table, identify those significant variables (i.e., Sig. < 0.05). Tenure is negatively and significantly related to employee engagement ($B = -0.039, p < 0.001$), meaning that the longer the tenure, the lower the employee engagement. Lateral move is positively and significantly related to employee engagement ($B = 0.943, p < 0.001$), meaning that the employees with a lateral move have higher employee engagement. So H_1 is accepted, and H_0 is rejected. The steps and the result are in Figure 3.14.

To predict an employee's engagement, we can use the following equation formed from the result of multiple linear regression. Because the model is significant, all the control and independent variables will be included, as shown in Equation 3–7. By substituting the values of the control and independent variables (e.g., if the employee is male, substitute *Gender* with 0), the employee engagement level can be predicted.

$$\begin{aligned} Engagement = 3.752 & \\ & -0.079 \times LineB\_Dummy \\ & -0.096 \times LineC\_Dummy \\ & +0.165 \times Gender \\ & -0.137 \times Edu \\ & -0.039 \times Tenure \\ & +0.943 \times Lateral\_Move \end{aligned} \quad (3\text{–}7)$$

Based on the statistical result, the HR team now has evidence to show that lateral moves will improve employee engagement. Employees with a lateral move improve almost 1 unit (0.943) of employee engagement in a 7-point Likert scale. HR officer plans to suggest a rotation program to help improve employee engagement and hence reduce employee turnover.

In the result, there is an additional finding that an increase in tenure decreases employee engagement. The HR team has interviewed the product design managers. The product design managers reflect their observations

File: *Ch3_HR_Data.xlsx (Worksheet: 2. MLR (Lateral Move))*
Add-ins > Real Statistics > Data Analysis Tools (Reg > Multiple Linear Regression)

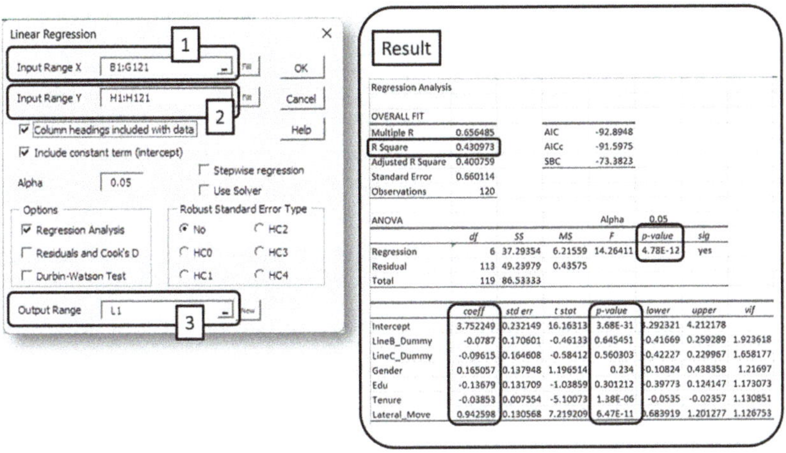

FIGURE 3.14
Multiple Linear Regression in Excel

that designers working more than 10 years seem to be less engaged, perhaps because their salary most likely reaches the top point with no further increment. Based on the interview results, the HR team tries to verify the product design managers' observations from data to see whether designers working more than 10 years are significantly less engaged.

3.7 COMPARING ENGAGEMENT LEVEL – AN EXAMPLE OF INDEPENDENT-SAMPLES T TEST

To find evidence to support if the two groups of designers, those working for 10 years or more and the rest, are significantly different in their employee engagement level, the HR team starts another analytics process.

Business Problem: In the process of finding out why an increase in tenure decreases employee engagement, some product design managers observe that designers working for 10 years or more have lower engagement levels, which may be because of some HR policies. The HR team seeks support for this observation.

Research Question: Do designers working for 10 years or more have lower employee engagement?

Then, the HR team has built the **hypotheses** and the **model** (Figure 3.15):

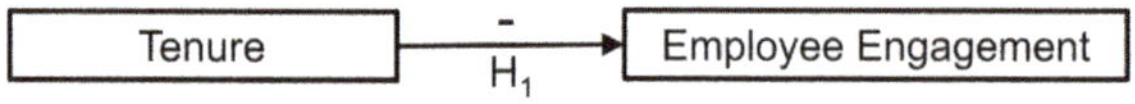

FIGURE 3.15
The Hypothesized Model for the Impact of Tenure on Employee Engagement

H_1: Employees working for 10 years or more have lower employee engagement.
H_0: Employees working for 10 years or more do not have lower employee engagement than the rest.

Look at the data in the SPSS file "*Ch3_HR_Data.sav*" and the Excel file "*Ch3_HR_Data.xlsx.*" Employee engagement for Time 1 has been tested and passed the **face validity** test, the **construct validity** test in SPSS (Figure 3.6) and in Excel (Figure 3.7), and the **reliability** test in SPSS (Figure 3.8) and in Excel (Figure 3.9), as shown in the previous section.

To test the hypothesis of finding whether the two groups of employees, working for 10 years or more and the rest, have significant differences in employee engagement (a continuous variable), we will use the **independent-samples *t* test** (see Chapter 2).

To do an **independent-samples *t* test in SPSS**, open the file "*Ch3_HR_Data.sav.*" Go to *Analyze > Compare Means and Proportions > Independent-Samples t test.* Select T1_Engage_Mean as the *Test Variable(s).* Select Tenure as the *Grouping Variable.* Click *Define Groups.* In the "Define Groups" pop-up dialog box, enter "10" as the *Cut point.* Click *Continue.* Click *OK.* The result is in the output viewer. In the table "Group Statistics," the mean employee engagement for a tenure of10 years or more is 3.111, while for tenure which is less than 10 years is 3.952. In the table "Independent Samples Test," it shows that Levene's test for equality of variances is significant ($p < 0.001$), indicating that equal variances cannot be assumed. Therefore, we will read the significance of the second row (i.e., equal variances not assumed), and it is significant ($p < 0.001$). This means that the mean employee engagement of employees working for 10 years or more is lower than the rest at the level of 0.841 (i.e., 3.952 minus 3.111), and it is a significant difference. So, H_1 is accepted, and H_0 is rejected. The steps and the result are shown in Figure 3.16.

To do an **independent-samples *t* test in Excel**, open the file "*Ch3_HR_Data.xlsx.*" Go to worksheet "3. Ind-Samples T Test (Tenure)." Employee engagement of employees with tenure less than 10 years is in Column G,

File: *Ch3_HR_Data.sav*
Analyze > Compare Mean and Proportions > Independent-Samples T Test

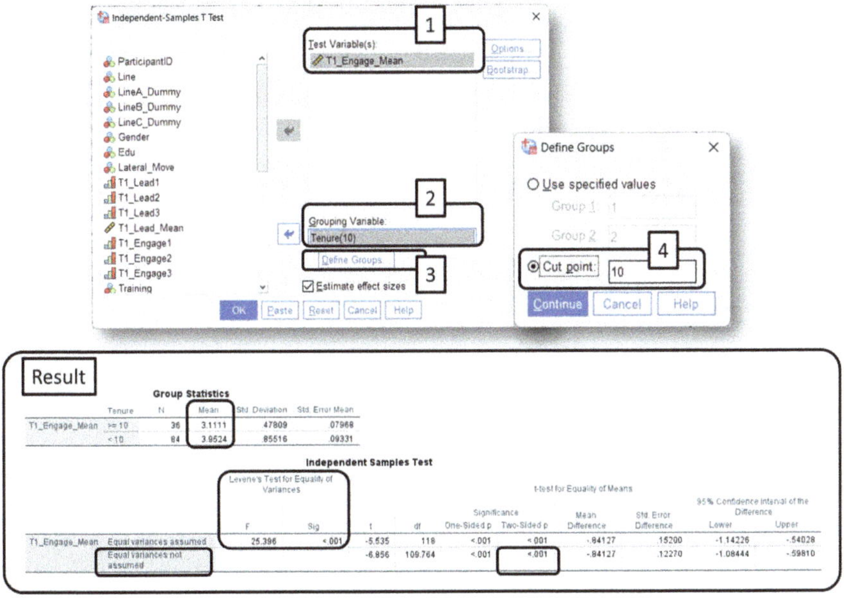

FIGURE 3.16
Independent-Samples *t* Test in SPSS

while those with a tenure of 10 years or more are in Column H. Go to *Add-ins > Real Statistics > Data Analysis Tools*. In the pop-up dialog box, click the tab page *Misc*, click *T Test and Non-parametric Equivalents,* and then click *OK*. In the "T Test and Non-parametric Equivalents" pop-up dialog box, select Column G as the *Input Range 1*. Select Column H as the *Input Range 2*. Choose *Two Independent Samples* as *Options*. Tick *T Test* as the *Test Type*. Enter the cell L1 as *Output Range*. Click *OK*. In the result area, in the table "SUMMARY," the mean employee engagement for tenure of 10 years or more is 3.111, while for tenure less than 10 years is 3.952. There is no Levene's test for equality of variances here. Therefore, we will read the *p*-value for both equal and unequal variances, and both are significant ($p < 0.001$). It means that the mean engagement level of employees working for 10 years or more is lower than the rest at the level of 0.841 (i.e., 3.952 minus 3.111), and it is a significant difference. So, H_1 is accepted, and H_0 is rejected. The steps and the result are shown in Figure 3.17.

Data analytics is not a one-off process. After finding evidence indicating employees working for 10 years or more have lower employee engagement, the HR team will continue to find its factors and figure out ways to improve the situation.

File: *Ch3_HR_Data.xlsx (Worksheet: 3. Ind-Samples T Test (Tenure))*
Add-ins > Real Statistics > Data Analysis Tools (Misc > T Test and Non-parametric Equivalents)

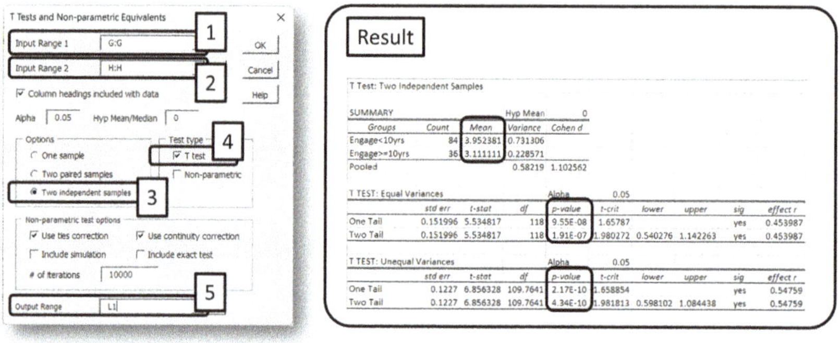

FIGURE 3.17
Independent-Samples *t* Test in Excel

Apart from Nielsen, there are also many other case studies about HR analytics. One of the classics is **Google**'s quest for better managers. Let us go through this case study.

3.8 CASE STUDY: GOOGLE'S PROJECT OXYGEN FOR BETTER MANAGERS

Google is a multinational technology company that specializes in internet-related services and products. It was founded by Larry Page and Sergey Brin in 1998. It is not surprising that a technology company makes engineering decisions based on data evidence. In Google, they bring this rigorous evidence-based decision-making practice to the next level in making people decisions (Garvin, 2013).

In the earlier days of Google, one software engineer questioned,

We are a company built by engineers for engineers; do we need managers?

The co-founders of Google considered it a valid question that challenged traditional assumptions, and their highly skilled, handpicked employees deserved to have an answer. In 2002, they experimented with a completely flat organization, eliminating the engineering managers in order to speed up the idea development to implementation from the engineers to the co-founders. However, this no-manager situation lasted only for a few months because there were too many daily operational issues, like expense reports and interpersonal conflicts, which made the company simply unable to function well. This experiment failed, which may be argued as a single incident, so Google continued to seek a solid proof.

To make evidence-based decisions, there are two crucial criteria: (1) the data and (2) the skills to analyze the data. Google understood this well and started this journey. In 2006, Laszlo Bock led People Operations to collect data via 360° performance reviews and employee surveys about career development and company culture. In the next year, Prasad Setty led the People Analytics group and built their analytics skill set by recruiting PhDs to perform hypothesis-driven analyses. With the data and the skills ready, Google started their **Project Oxygen** in 2009 to answer the question:

Do the managers matter?

Google hypothesized that managers do NOT matter, as the engineers suspected. Based on the collected data via performance reviews and employee surveys, they found that even the smallest increase in manager quality had powerful impacts on employees' performance and happiness. Google then had the solid proof to convince their employees that managers DO matter. They also analyzed the qualitative data to identify the top eight good manager behaviors, including being a good coach, having concerns for team members' success and well-being, and being a good communicator. These evidence-based results convinced the Googlers that managers mattered and gave their employees a set of shared vocabulary for discussing good manager behaviors. Google also implemented trainings and assessments around the findings. In 2012, the manager assessment scores had significantly increased compared with those data 2 years earlier.

In this case study, we can see that from the business question through the analytics process to the significant improvements made, it took Google 10 years. If companies are still skeptical about analytics, by the time they witness their competitors achieve success via analytics, it may have already been 10 years behind. It is no doubt that there is a lot of hard work in the journey of analytics. However, it is not a question of doing it or not, it is instead how soon the analytics journey should begin.

Let us get started now and try how we can replicate Google's analytics process in our Best Toy Company to find *how* managers' leadership behavior may influence employees' performance, *how* we can track the performance of interventions such as management training, and *how* to compare differences among different interventions.

3.9 LEADERSHIP BEHAVIOR AND EMPLOYEE PERFORMANCE – AN EXAMPLE OF MULTIPLE LINEAR REGRESSION

Best Toy Company treasures employees' effort, voice and contributions. The company believes that employees are in a unique position to understand customer needs because they directly contact customers, and their opinions reflect what customers value most. The company has a culture of participating employees in its decision-making process. In fact, this leadership style of having employees' participation when making decisions, known as **participative leadership**, has been well established in academic circles by scholars worldwide (Arnold et al., 2000; Huang, 2012; Lam et al., 2015; Tang & Lam, 2020). Research has shown that the participative leadership style improves **employee performance** and **helping behavior**. Although helping behavior among employees may not be assessed formally in performance reviews, these behaviors are crucial to organizational success (Ozer, 2011). Imagine if employees are not helping each other at all, organizations cannot function properly. Best Toy Company therefore also encourages their managers to promote helping behavior among the employees on top of improving performance. Now, the company starts an analytics process to find out the level of impact of participative leadership on their employees' performance.

Business Problem: The company would like to know the level of positive influence of managers' participative leadership behavior on employee performance in order to better convince its managers about the benefits of being participative.

Research Question: Is employee performance improvement one of the consequences of managers' participative leadership behavior?

Following that, they have built the **hypotheses** and the **model**:

H_1: Participative leadership improves employee performance.
H_0: Participative leadership does not improve employee performance.

In the hypothesized model, participative leadership is the independent variable, and employee performance is the dependent variable (Figure 3.18).

They hypothesize that participative leadership behavior demonstrated at Time 1 positively influences employee performance at Time 2, which is 1 year later.

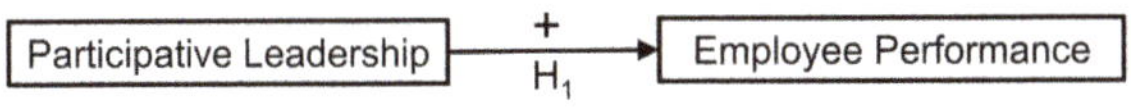

FIGURE 3.18
The Hypothesized Model for the Impact of Participative Leadership on Employee Performance

Participative leadership refers to the shared influence and joint decision-making between a leader and employees in an attempt to share power and information with employees and involve them to improve problem-solving and decision-making (Arnold et al., 2000; Huang, 2012; Lam et al., 2015; Tang & Lam, 2020). Behaviors such as encouraging employees to express suggestions and listening to and considering employees' opinions when making decisions reflect the adoption of participative leadership (Arnold et al., 2000). The HR team has adapted the survey items from Arnold et al.'s research and prepared the following three survey items, measured on a 7-point Likert scale (1 – Strongly disagree; 2 – Disagree; 3 – Slightly disagree; 4 – Neutral; 5 – Slightly agree; 6 – Agree; 7 – Strongly agree) in their annual employee survey rated by their direct subordinates:

1. My direct supervisor encourages me to express my thoughts at work.
2. My direct supervisor listens to my suggestions at work.
3. My direct supervisor considers my suggestions when making decisions.

The **employee performance variable** is the annual performance rating rated by the direct supervisors and retrieved from the HR database. It is measured by a 5-point Likert scale (1 – Very poor; 2 – Poor; 3 – Average; 4 – Good; 5 – Very good).

The survey items of participative leadership reflect its defined behaviors in the literature, and this construct passes **face validity**. The HR team confirms that the employee performance retrieved from the HR data is measuring what is intended, so it also passes **face validity**. There is only one item for employee performance, and hence no construct validity and reliability tests are required. There are three items for participative leadership, and this construct will go through the construct validity and reliability tests. Use the SPSS file "*Ch3_HR_Data.sav*" and the Excel file "*Ch3_HR_Data.xlsx.*" In the Excel file, go to the worksheet "Validity & Reliability."

Construct validity test for participative leadership at Time 1 shows that all the three factor loadings (0.964, 0.974 and 0.969, respectively) are greater than 0.6, indicating the measure is valid (Figures 3.19, 3.20).

File: *Ch3_HR_Data.sav*
Analyze > Dimension Reduction > Factor

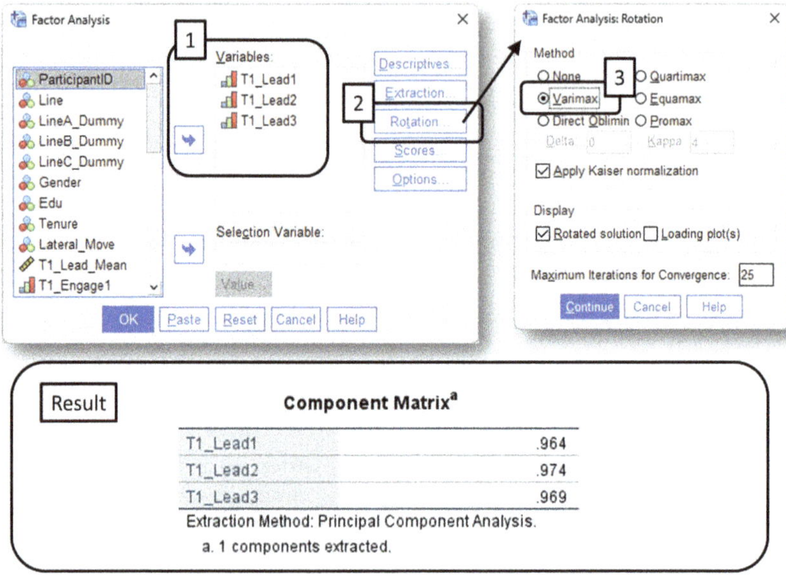

FIGURE 3.19
Factor Analysis for Participative Leadership in SPSS

File: *Ch3_HR_Data.xlsx (Worksheet: Validity & Reliability)*
Add-ins > Real Statistics > Data Analysis Tools (Multivar > Factor Analysis)

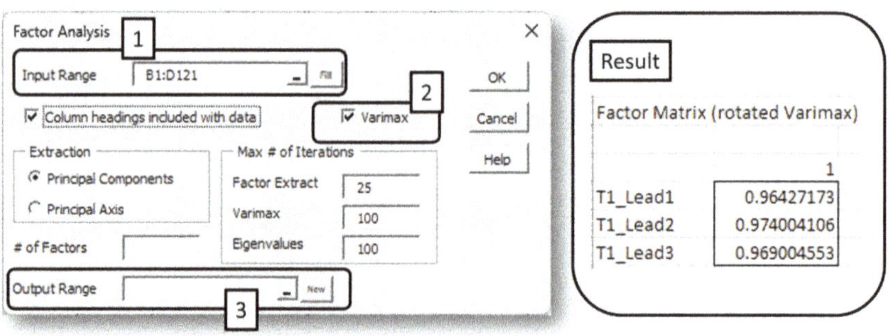

FIGURE 3.20
Factor Analysis for Participative Leadership in Excel

Reliability test for participative leadership at Time 1 shows that Cronbach's alpha equals 0.967, which is greater than 0.7, indicating that the measure is reliable (Figures 3.21 and 3.22).

We are now certain about the validity and reliability of the constructs. We can then test the hypothesis. To test the hypothesis whether employee

File: *Ch3_HR_Data.sav*
Analyze > Scale > Reliability Analysis

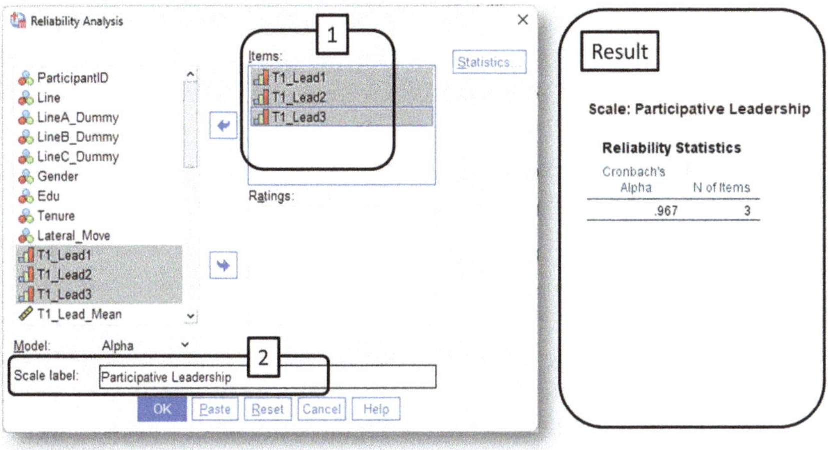

FIGURE 3.21
Reliability Test for Participative Leadership in SPSS

File: *Ch3_HR_Data.xlsx (Worksheet: Validity & Reliability)*
Add-ins > Real Statistics > Data Analysis Tools (Corr > Internal Consistency Reliability)

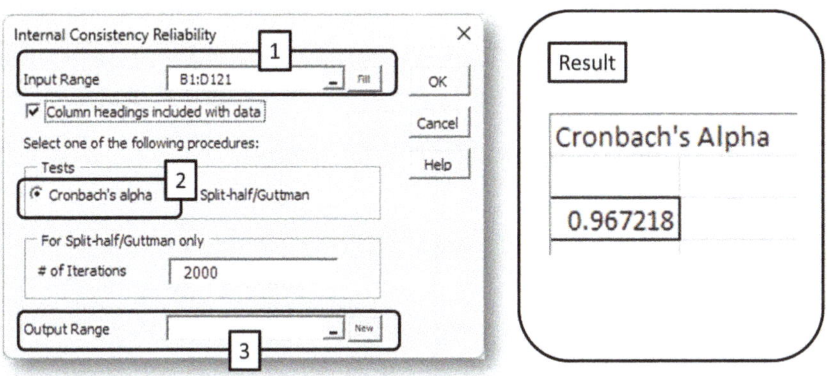

FIGURE 3.22
Reliability Test for Participative Leadership in Excel

performance (**a continuous variable**) is **a consequence** of participative leadership, we will use **multiple linear regression** (see Chapter 2). We will also include *Gender*, *Education*, *Tenure*, *LineB_Dummy* and *LineC_Dummy* as the control variables.

To do this **multiple linear regression in SPSS**, open the file "*Ch3_HR_Data.sav*." Go to *Analyze > Regression > Linear*. Select T2_Perform as *Dependent*. Select Gender, Edu, Tenure, LineB_Dummy, LineC_Dummy, and T1_Lead_Mean as *Independent(s)*. Click *OK*. The result is in the output viewer. The table "Model Summary" shows that R Square = 0.496, indicating that the control and independent variables account for 49.6% variance in employee performance. In the table "ANOVA," it shows that the model is significant ($p < 0.001$). In the "Coefficients" table, read columns Unstandardized B and Sig. Identify those significant variables (i.e., Sig. < 0.05). Gender (0 – Male; 1 – Female) is negatively and significantly related to performance ($B = -0.594$, $p < 0.001$), meaning that male employees perform better than their female counterparts. Participative leadership is positively and significantly related to employee performance ($B = 0.239$, $p < 0.001$), meaning that participative leadership improves employee performance. So, H_1 is accepted, and H_0 is rejected. The steps and the result are shown in Figure 3.23.

To do this **multiple linear regression in Excel**, open the file "*Ch3_HR_Data.xlsx*." Go to worksheet "4. MLR (Leadership)." Go to *Add-ins > Real Statistics > Data Analysis Tools*. In the pop-up dialog box, click the tab page *Reg*, click *Multiple Linear Regression* and *OK*. In the "Linear Regression"

File: *Ch3_HR_Data.sav*
Analyze > Regression > Linear

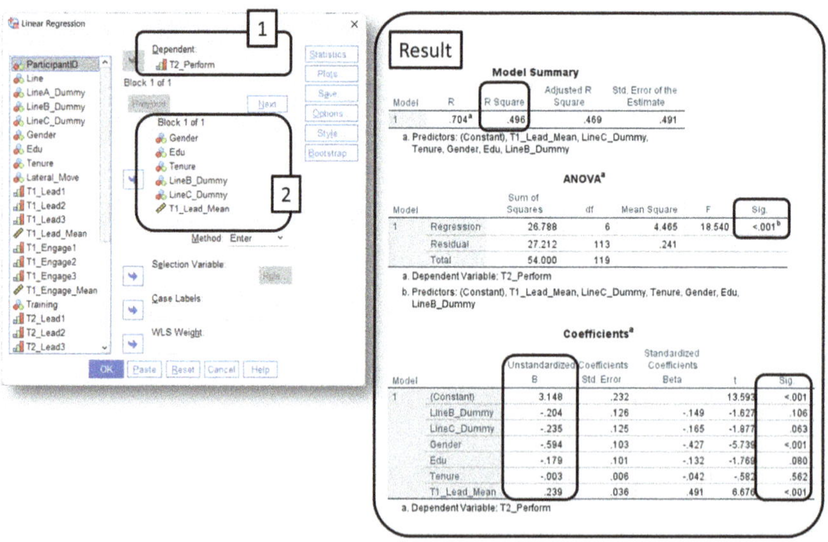

FIGURE 3.23
Multiple Linear Regression in SPSS

pop-up dialog box, select cells B1 to G121 (control variables and the independent variable) as the *Input Range X*. Select cells H1 to H121 (dependent variable) as the *Input Range Y*. Enter cell M1 as the *Output Range*. Click *OK*. In the result area, the table "OVERALL FIT" shows that R Square = 0.496, indicating that the control and independent variables account for 49.6% of the variance in employee performance. In the table "ANOVA," it shows that the model is significant ($p < 0.001$). In the coefficient table, identify those significant variables (i.e., p-value < 0.05). Gender (0 – Male; 1 – Female) is negatively and significantly related to performance ($B = -0.594, p < 0.001$), meaning that male employees perform better than their female counterparts. Participative leadership is positively and significantly related to employee performance ($B = 0.239, p < 0.001$), meaning that participative leadership improves employee performance. So, H_1 is accepted, and H_0 is rejected. The steps and the result are in Figure 3.24.

To predict an employee's performance, we can use the following equation formed from the result of multiple linear regression. Because the model is significant, all the control and independent variables will be included in Equation 3–8. By substituting the values of the control and independent

File: *Ch3_HR_Data.xlsx (Worksheet: 4. MLR (Leadership))*
Add-ins > Real Statistics > Data Analysis Tools (Reg > Multiple Linear Regression)

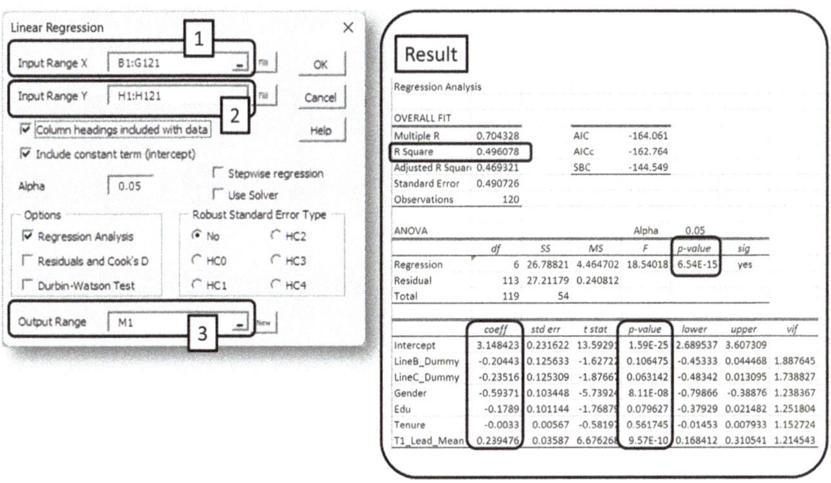

FIGURE 3.24
Multiple Linear Regression in Excel

variables (e.g., if that employee is male, substitute *Gender* with 0), the engagement level can be predicted.

$$\begin{aligned} Performance = {} & 3.148 \\ & -0.204 \times LineB\_Dummy \\ & -0.235 \times LineC\_Dummy \\ & -0.594 \times Gender \\ & -0.179 \times Edu \\ & -0.003 \times Tenure \\ & +0.239 \times T1\_Lead\_Mean \end{aligned} \quad (3\text{–}8)$$

Based on the statistical result, the HR team now has evidence to show that participative leadership will improve employee performance. At every 1-unit increase in the leader's participative leadership behavior on a 7-point Likert scale, their employees' performance will have significant improvements of 0.239-unit increase on a 5-point Likert scale. You can also interpret it like this. If the leader increases 4 units of participative behavior, the employee will increase almost 1 unit (0.239 × 4 = 0.956) in performance. By reading the descriptions of the two constructs' Likert scales, you may further interpret the result. If a leader demonstrates more participative behaviors (e.g., at a level from seldom to always being participative), an average employee could become a good performer.

The HR team now has evidence of the positive impact of participative leadership on employee performance to better convince their managers to practice participative behaviors. The HR department can prepare materials or training to better promote participative leadership practices.

3.10 LEADERSHIP BEHAVIOR AND HELPING BEHAVIOR – AN EXAMPLE OF MULTIPLE LINEAR REGRESSION

Apart from employee performance, Best Toy Company also acknowledges the importance of helping behavior among employees and would also like to find evidence to support whether participative leadership improves helping behavior. The HR team thus carries out another round of the analytics process.

Business Problem: The company would like to know the level of positive influence of managers' participative leadership on employee helping behavior to better convince its managers of the benefits of being participative.

Research Question: Is improvement in employee helping behavior one of the consequences of the managers' participative leadership?

Following that, they have built the **hypotheses** and the **model**:

H_1: Participative leadership improves employee helping behavior.
H_0: Participative leadership does not improve employee helping behavior.

In our hypothesized model, we have participative leadership as the independent variable and employee helping behavior as the dependent variable, as shown in Figure 3.25.

We hypothesize that participative leadership behaviors demonstrated at Time 1 positively influence employee performance at Time 2, which is 1 year later.

Helping behaviors among the employees are crucial to organizational effectiveness. In management literature, helping behavior is known as **organizational citizenship behavior toward other individuals (OCBI)**. OCBI refers to discretionary employee behavior that is usually not directly recognized by the formal reward system but improves the effective functioning of the organization (Lam et al., 2014; Lee & Allen, 2002; Organ, 1988; Podsakoff et al., 2009; Smith et al., 1983). The HR department of Best Toy Company has also measured the helping behaviors of the employees using the adapted survey items from the research of Lee and Allen (2002), rated by the employees' direct supervisor measured in a 7-point Likert scale (1 – Strongly disagree; 2 – Disagree; 3 – Slightly disagree; 4 – Neutral; 5 – Slightly agree; 6 – Agree; 7 – Strongly agree):

1. Help others who are in need at work.
2. Reschedule to accommodate others' requests for time off.
3. Welcome new employees.

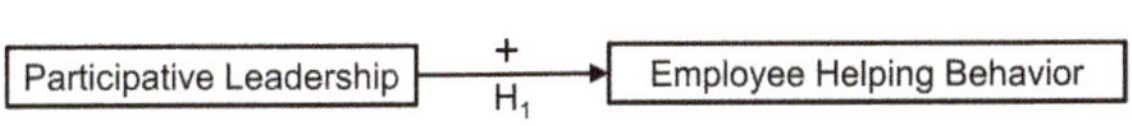

FIGURE 3.25
The Hypothesized Model for the Impact of Participative Leadership on Employee Helping Behavior

4. Show courtesy toward coworkers.

Participative leadership at Time 1 has been tested and passed the **face validity** test, the **construct validity** test in SPSS (Figure 3.19) and in Excel (Figure 3.20), and the **reliability** test in SPSS (Figure 3.21) and in Excel (Figure 3.22), as shown in the previous section.

For helping behavior at Time 2, its survey items' meanings reflect the definition from the literature; it is thus considered passing the **face validity**. Its **construct validity test** shows that all the four factor loadings (0.876, 0.901, 0.826 and 0.940, respectively) are greater than 0.6, indicating that the measure is valid (Figures 3.26 and 3.27). Its **reliability test** shows that Cronbach's alpha equals 0.906, which is greater than 0.7, indicating that the measure is reliable (Figures 3.28 and 3.29). To run these tests, use the SPSS file "*Ch3_HR_Data.sav*" and the Excel file "*Ch3_HR_Data.xlsx.*" In the Excel file, go to the worksheet "Validity & Reliability."

We are now certain about the validity and the reliability of the constructs. We can then test the hypothesis. To test the hypothesis of whether employee helping behavior (**a continuous variable**) is **a consequence** of participative

File: *Ch3_HR_Data.sav*
Analyze > Dimension Reduction > Factor

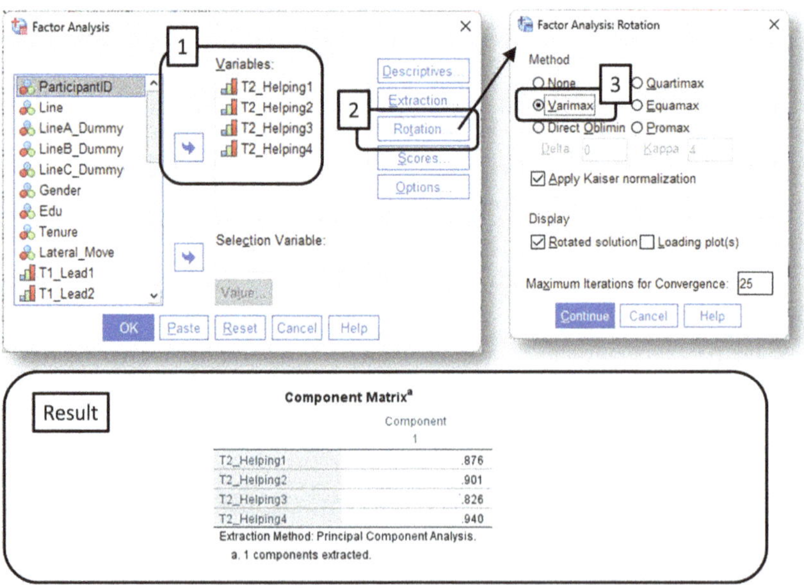

FIGURE 3.26
Factor Analysis for Helping Behavior in SPSS

File: *Ch3_HR_Data.xlsx (Worksheet: Validity & Reliability)*
Add-ins > Real Statistics > Data Analysis Tools (Multivar > Factor Analysis)

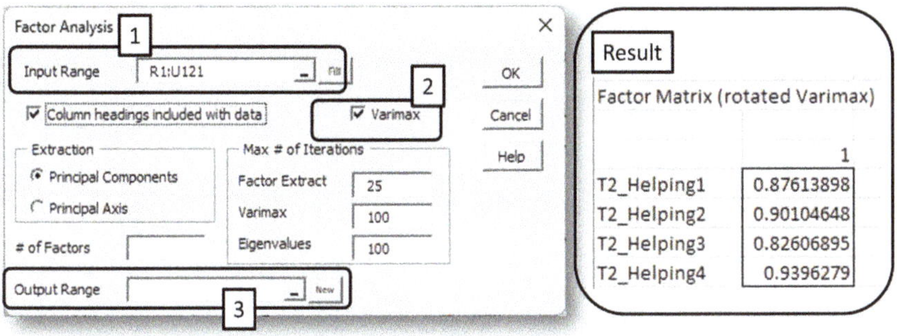

FIGURE 3.27
Factor Analysis for Helping Behavior in Excel

File: *Ch3_HR_Data.sav*
Analyze > Scale > Reliability Analysis

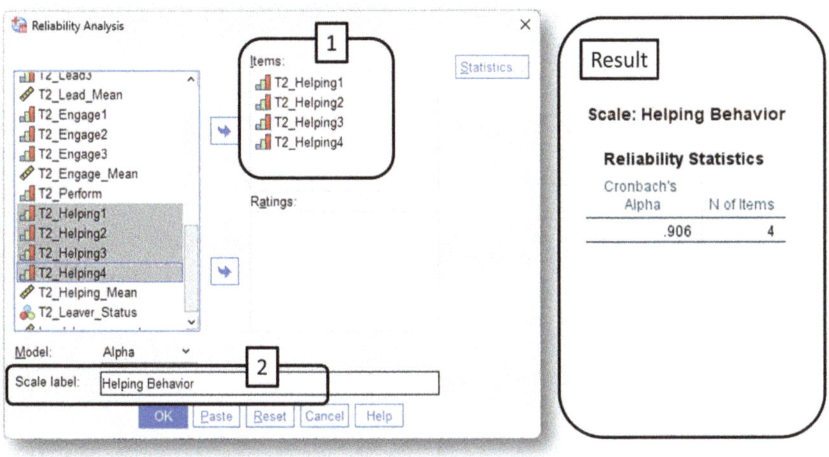

FIGURE 3.28
Reliability Test for Helping Behavior in SPSS

leadership, we will use **multiple linear regression** (see Chapter 2). We will also include *Gender*, *Education*, *Tenure*, *LineB_Dummy* and *LineC_Dummy* as the control variables. Use the file "*Ch3_HR_Data.sav*" to run this test in SPSS. Use worksheet "4. MLR (Leadership)" in the file "*Ch3_HR_Data.xlsx*" to run it in Excel. The steps for running multiple linear regression in SPSS and Excel were explained in the previous session. As a refresher, the steps are

File: *Ch3_HR_Data.xlsx (Worksheet: Validity & Reliability)*
Add-ins > Real Statistics > Data Analysis Tools (Corr > Internal Consistency Reliability)

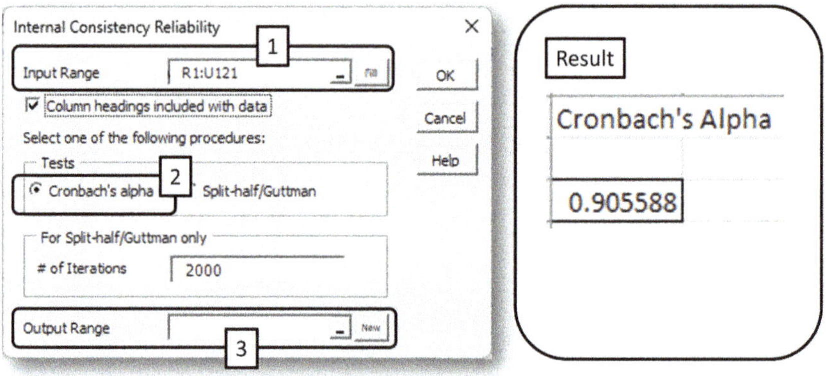

FIGURE 3.29
Reliability Test for Helping Behavior in Excel

File: *Ch3_HR_Data.sav*
Analyze > Regression > Linear

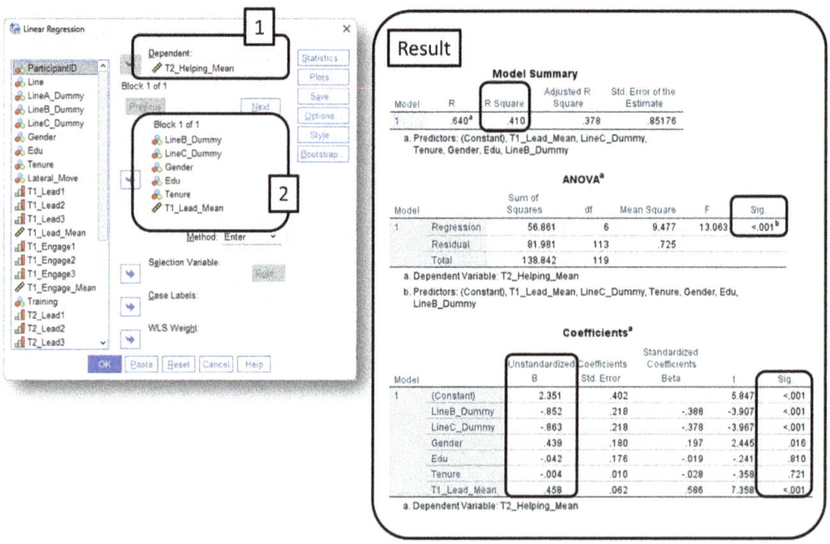

FIGURE 3.30
Multiple Linear Regression in SPSS

captured in Figure 3.30 for SPSS and Figure 3.31 for Excel. The results are also in these figures, and we will go through the results together.

In the result, R Square = 0.410 indicates that the control and independent variables account for 41.0% of the variance in employee helping behavior. In the table "ANOVA," it shows that the model is significant ($p < 0.001$). Line B, compared with Line A (i.e., the reference production line), is negatively and significantly related to helping behavior ($B = -0.852, p < 0.001$), meaning employees in Line B have demonstrated less helping behavior than their Line A counterparts. Employees in Line C have demonstrated less helping behavior than their Line A counterparts ($B = -0.863, p < 0.001$). Gender (0 – Male; 1 – Female) is positively and significantly related to helping behavior ($B = 0.439, p < 0.001$), meaning female employees have demonstrated more helping behavior. Participative leadership is positively and significantly related to employee helping behavior ($B = 0.458, p < 0.001$), meaning participative leadership improves employee helping behavior. So, H_1 is accepted, and H_0 is rejected.

Based on the statistical results, the HR team now has evidence to show that participative leadership will improve employee helping behavior: for every 1-unit increase in a leader's participative leadership behavior on a 7-point Likert scale, employees' helping behavior will have significant improvements of 0.458-unit

File: *Ch3_HR_Data.xlsx (Worksheet: 4. MLR (Leadership))*
Add-ins > Real Statistics > Data Analysis Tools (Reg > Multiple Linear Regression)

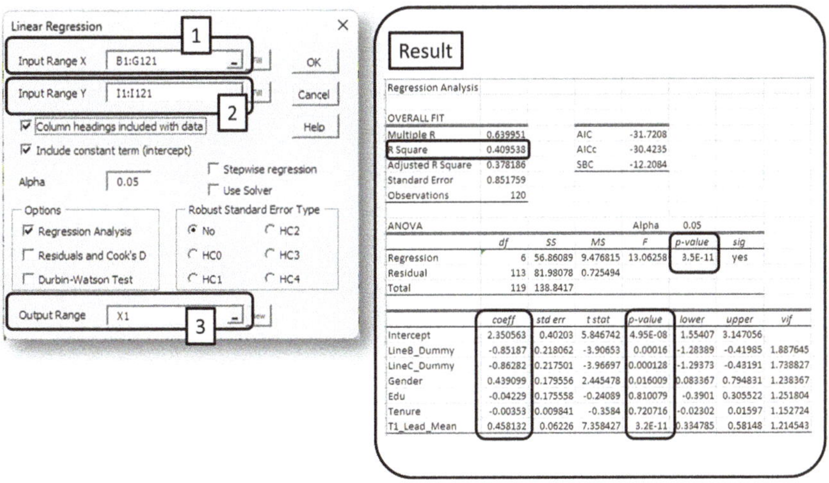

FIGURE 3.31
Multiple Linear Regression in Excel

increase on the same scale. You can also interpret it like this. If the leader increases 2 units of participative behavior, the employee will increase almost 1 unit (0.458 × 2 = 0.916) in helping behavior.

The HR team now has evidence to support their participative leadership training programs.

3.11 MEASURING THE RESULT OF AN INTERVENTION – AN EXAMPLE OF PAIRED-SAMPLES T TEST

Participative leadership is important for improving employee performance and their helping behavior. To equip the managers with participative leadership skills, the HR department organizes different managerial trainings every year, including preparing pamphlets, training courses and personal coaching. Each manager can choose to attend one of these trainings. Trainings are interventions. **Interventions** are actions which are implemented to *monitor* changes, *create* changes or *stop* changes in attitudes or behaviors. These interventions in our case here include improving leadership skills or maintaining improved skills from dropping.

As we mentioned at the beginning of this chapter, apart from showing the tasks completed, HR now needs to demonstrate their positive impacts and contributions to the company. Therefore, the HR team initiated an analytics process to measure the impact of these managerial trainings to the managers' participative leadership behavior.

Business Problem: The HR department would like to figure out whether the managerial trainings improve the managers' participative leadership behavior.

Research Question: Do the managers demonstrate more participative behaviors after the managerial training?

The HR team has built the **hypotheses** and the **model** (Figure 3.32):

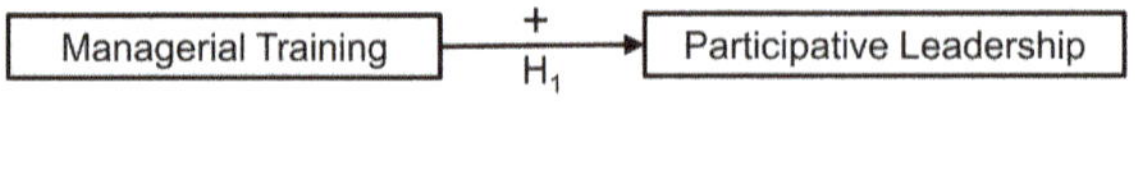

FIGURE 3.32
The Hypothesized Model for the Impact of the Managerial Training

H_1: Managers demonstrate more participative behaviors after the managerial training.

H_0: Managers do not demonstrate more participative behaviors after the managerial training.

Participative leadership for Time 1 has passed the **face validity** test, **construct validity** test in SPSS (Figure 3.19) and in Excel (Figure 3.20) and the **reliability** test in SPSS (Figure 3.21) and in Excel (Figure 3.22), shown in the previous section. Because we are comparing the differences in participative leadership within the same group of managers, we must use the same set of survey items for both Time 1 and Time 2. As it is the same set of survey items in Time 2, we do not need to check the face validity again. We will test validity test and reliability test for participative leadership in Time 2. Its **construct validity test** shows that all the three factor loadings (0.942, 0.970, and 0.954, respectively) are greater than 0.6, indicating that the measure is valid (Figures 3.33 and 3.34). Its **reliability test** for participative leadership at Time 2 shows that Cronbach's alpha equals 0. 951, which is greater than 0.7, indicating that the measure is reliable (Figures 3.35, 3.36). To run these tests, use the SPSS file "*Ch3_HR_Data.sav*" and the Excel file "*Ch3_HR_Data.xlsx.*" In the Excel file, go to the worksheet "Validity & Reliability."

File: *Ch3_HR_Data.sav*
Analyze > Dimension Reduction > Factor

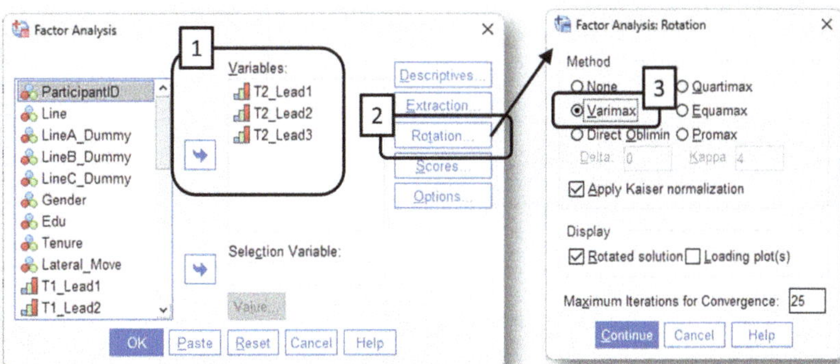

Result

Component Matrix[a]

	Component 1
T2_Lead1	.942
T2_Lead2	.970
T2_Lead3	.954

Extraction Method: Principal Component Analysis.
a. 1 components extracted.

FIGURE 3.33
Factor Analysis for Participative Leadership in SPSS

File: *Ch3_HR_Data.xlsx (Worksheet: Validity & Reliability)*
Add-ins > Real Statistics > Data Analysis Tools (Multivar > Factor Analysis)

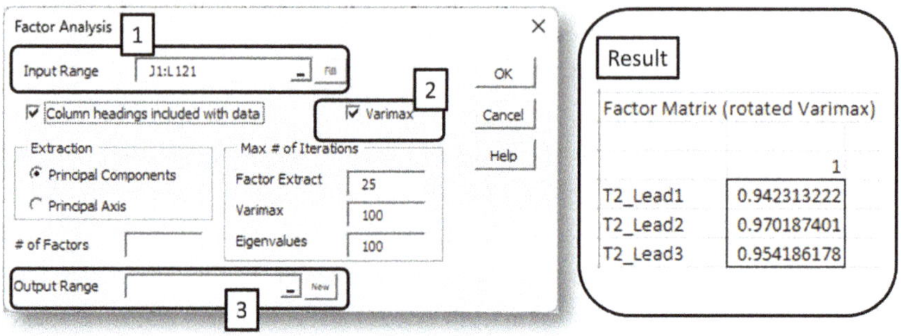

FIGURE 3.34
Factor Analysis for Participative Leadership in Excel

File: *Ch3_HR_Data.sav*
Analyze > Scale > Reliability Analysis

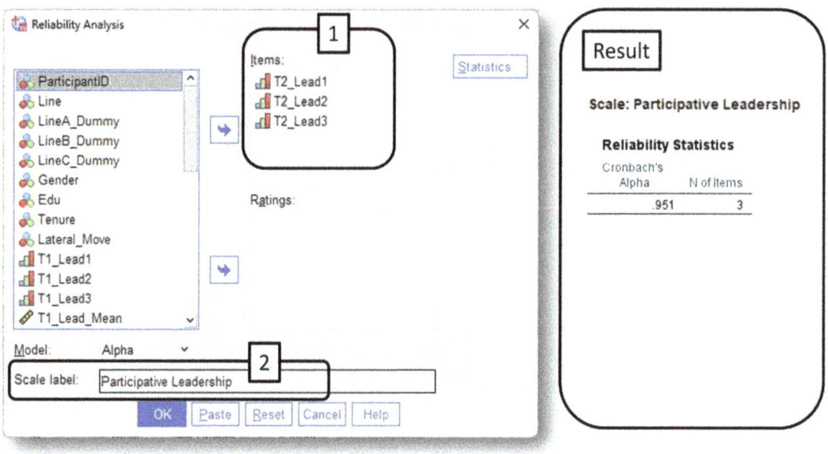

FIGURE 3.35
Reliability Test for Participative Leadership in SPSS

To test the hypothesis of finding whether the same group of managers has significant differences in participative leadership behavior (a continuous variable at two different times) after the training, we will use a **paired-samples *t* test** (see Chapter 2).

To do a **paired-samples *t* test in SPSS**, open the file "*Ch3_HR_Data.sav*." Go to *Analyze > Compare Means and Proportions > Paired-Samples t Test*. Select T2_Lead_Mean as *Variable1* and T1_Lead_Mean as *Variable2*. Click *OK*. The result is in the output viewer. In the table "Paired Samples

File: *Ch3_HR_Data.xlsx (Worksheet: Validity & Reliability)*
Add-ins > Real Statistics > Data Analysis Tools (Corr > Internal Consistency Reliability)

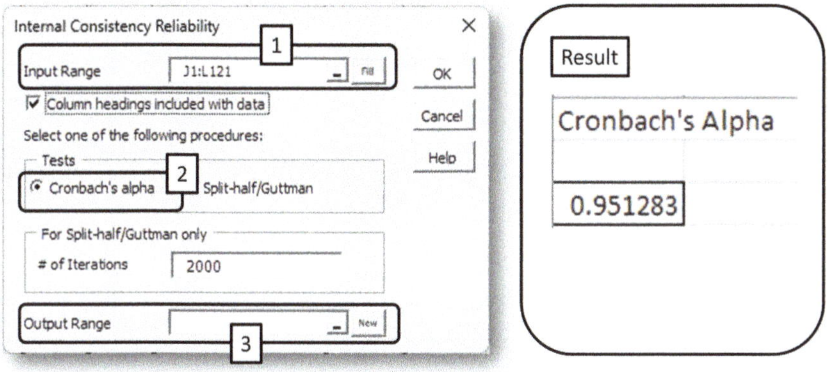

FIGURE 3.36
Reliability Test for Participative Leadership in Excel

Statistics," the mean participative leadership for Time 2 is 5.056, while for Time 1 it is 4.178. In the table "Paired Samples Test," it shows that the mean has a significant difference of 0.878 ($p < 0.001$). It means the leadership rating increases significantly after the training. So, H_1 is accepted, and H_0 is rejected. The steps and the result are shown in Figure 3.37.

To do a **paired-samples *t* test in Excel**, open the file "*Ch3_HR_Data.xlsx.*" Go to the worksheet "5. Paired-Samples T Test (Lead)." The participative leadership data after training are in Column C, while those before training are in Column B. Go to *Add-ins > Real Statistics > Data Analysis Tools.* In the pop-up dialog box, click the tab page *Misc,* then click *T Test and Non-parametric Equivalents* and click *OK.* In the "T Test and Non-parametric Equivalents" pop-up dialog box, select cells C1 to C121 as the *Input Range 1.* Select cells B1 to B121 as the *Input Range 2.* Choose *Two paired samples* as the *Options.* Tick *T Test* as the *Test Type.* Enter the cell G1 as *Output Range.* Click *OK.* In the result area, in the table "SUMMARY," the mean participative leadership for Time 2 is 5.056, while for Time 1 it is 4.178. The mean difference is 0.878. In the table "T Test," it shows that the mean difference is significant ($p < 0.001$). It means the participative leadership rating increases significantly after the training. So, H_1 is accepted, and H_0 is rejected. The steps and the result are shown in Figure 3.38.

Now the HR team is certain that the trainings significantly improve the managers' participative behavior at the level of 0.878 on a 7-point Likert scale. In the previous analytics processes, evidence has shown that for every 1-unit increase in the leader's participative leadership behavior, employees'

File: *Ch3_HR_Data.sav*
Analyze > Compare Means and Proportions > Paired-Samples T Test

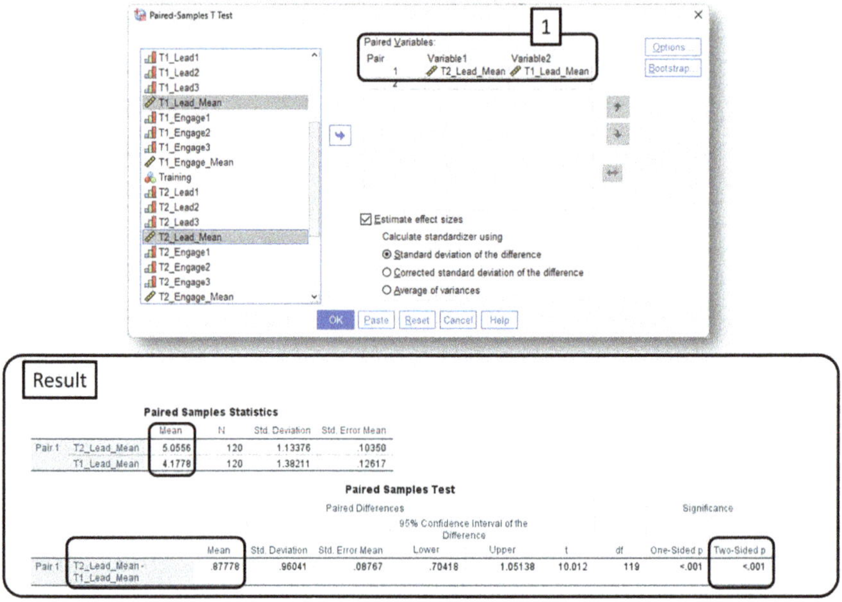

FIGURE 3.37
Paired-Samples *t* Test in SPSS

File: *Ch3_HR_Data.xlsx (Worksheet: 5. Paired-Samples T Test (Lead))*
Add-ins > Real Statistics > Data Analysis Tools (Misc > T Test and Non-parametric Equivalents)

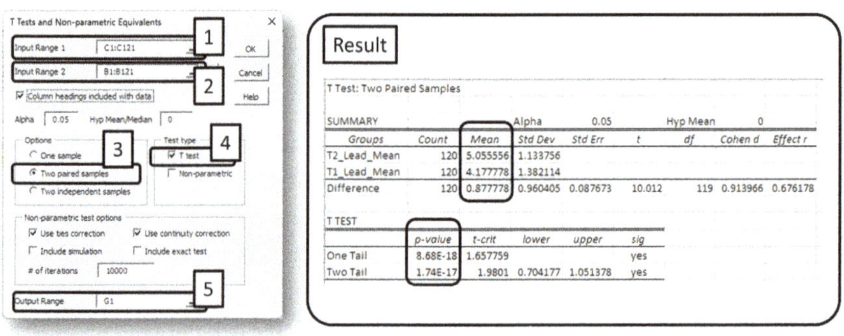

FIGURE 3.38
Paired-Samples *t* Test in Excel

performance will increase by 0.239 unit on a 5-point Likert scale and employees' helping behavior will increase by 0.458-unit on a 7-point Likert scale. This shows that these trainings improve the participative leadership behavior, which in turn improves the employee performance and helping behavior, which are crucial to the organization's performance.

Therefore, the HR team now has evidence to continue these training programs.

3.12 COMPARING THE RESULTS OF INTERVENTIONS – AN EXAMPLE OF ONE-WAY ANOVA

In Best Toy Company, as we have mentioned in the previous section, the HR department offers three different managerial trainings, including pamphlets, training courses and personal coaching. Each manager can choose to attend one of them. You can imagine different trainings may improve participative leadership skills at different levels and incur different costs. The HR team would like to start an analytics process to find out at what level each training improves the managers' leadership skills. If there are differences, the HR team would like to know if these differences are significant so they can find out the most suitable and the most cost-effective training for different managers.

Business Problem: The HR department would like to know if different trainings impose different levels of influence in participative leadership behavior.

Research Question: Do different trainings influence participative leadership behavior at different levels significantly?

The HR team has built the **hypotheses** and the **model** (Figure 3.39):

H_1: Different trainings influence participative leadership behavior differently.

H_0: There is no significant difference in influencing participative leadership behavior through different trainings.

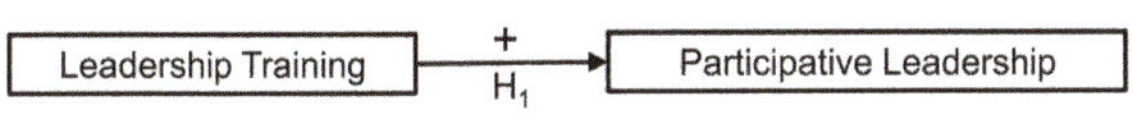

FIGURE 3.39
The Hypothesized Model for the Impact of Managerial Training on Participative Leadership

The variable *Lead_Improvement* is the difference in leadership score after training, calculated by deducting the participative leadership score at Time 1 from the participative leadership score at Time 2. If it is a positive number, it is an improvement. If it is a negative number, it is a weakening in the participative leadership behavior. The variable *Training* is the type of training attended (1 – Pamphlet; 2 – Training course; 3 – Personal coach). The statistical test one-way ANOVA will compare the mean values of the leadership improvements for each of these three types of training and tell whether the differences are significant.

To do **one-way ANOVA in SPSS**, open the file "*Ch3_HR_Data.sav.*" Go to *Analyze > Compare Means and Proportions > One-Way ANOVA*. Select Lead_Improvement as *Dependent List* and Training as the *Factor*. Click *Post Hoc*. In the pop-up dialog box "One-Way ANOVA: Post Hoc Multiple Comparisons," tick *Tukey* for *Equal Variances Assumed* and tick *Games-Howell* for *Equal Variances Not Assumed*. Click *Continue*. Back in the "One-Way ANOVA" pop-up dialog box, click *Options*. In the pop-up dialog box "One-Way ANOVA: Options," tick *Descriptives* and *Homogeneity of variance test*. Click *Continue*. Then click *OK*. The result is in the output viewer. In the table "Descriptives," the mean values of leadership score improvement by different training are shown: 0.222 for reading a pamphlet, 0.939 for attending a training course, and 1.400 for having a personal coach. The "ANOVA" table shows that the differences are significant. So, H_1 is accepted, and H_0 is rejected. In the table "Tests of Homogeneity of Variances," Levene's test shows a significant result, meaning that equal variances cannot be assumed. As we have chosen to show Games-Howell when equal variances cannot be assumed, we will read the result of Games-Howell instead of Tukey in the table "Post Hoc Tests." It shows that the difference in leadership score between a training course and a pamphlet (0.717) is significant. The difference in the leadership score between a personal coach and a pamphlet (1.178) is significant, while the difference between a training course and a personal coach is not significant. The steps and the result are shown in Figure 3.40.

To do **one-way ANOVA in Excel**, open the file "*Ch3_HR_Data.xlsx.*" Go to the worksheet "6. One-Way ANOVA (L Training)." Columns I to K contain the variable *Lead_Improvement* for the three trainings. They are required to be in a specific format. Column I includes the difference in the mean leadership score for those who attended Training 1 (i.e., reading a pamphlet). There are 36 managers who attended Training 1; including the header row, the next empty row is row 38. So, column J starts from row 38 onward, placing the difference of the mean leadership score for those who attended Training 2 (i.e., attending a training course). Similarly, do the same

File: *Ch3_HR_Data.sav*
Analyze > Compare Means and Proportions > One-Way ANOVA

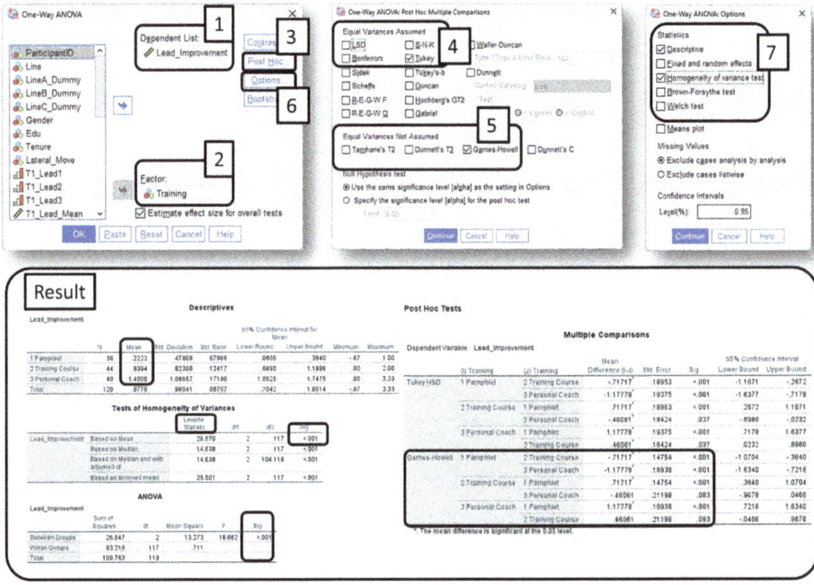

FIGURE 3.40
One-Way ANOVA in SPSS

for column K for those who attended Training 3 (i.e., having a personal coach). Go to *Add-ins > Real Statistics > Data Analysis Tools.* In the pop-up dialog box, click the tab page *Anova*, then click *One Factor Anova* and *OK.* In the "ANOVA: Single Factor" pop-up dialog box, select columns I to K as the *Input Range.* Click the radio-button *Excel format.* Tick *ANOVA*, *Levene's Test*, *Tukey HSD,* and *Games-Howell.* Input O1 as the *Output Range.* Click *OK.* In the table "DESCRIPTION," the mean values of the leadership score improvements for the three trainings are shown: 0.222 for reading a pamphlet, 0.939 for attending a training course, and 1.400 for having a personal coach. The table "ANOVA" shows that the differences are significant. So, H_1 is accepted, and H_0 is rejected. In the table "Levene's Tests," it shows a significant result, meaning that equal variances cannot be assumed. So, we will read the result of Games-Howell instead of Tukey. In the table "Q TEST" under "GAMES HOWELL," it shows that the difference in leadership score between a training course and a pamphlet (0.717) is significant. The difference in the leadership score between a personal coach and a pamphlet (1.178) is also significant, while the difference between a training course and a personal coach is not significant.

File: *Ch3_HR_Data.xlsx (Worksheet: 6. One-Way ANOVA (L Training))*
Add-ins > Real Statistics > Data Analysis Tools (Anova > One Factor Anova)

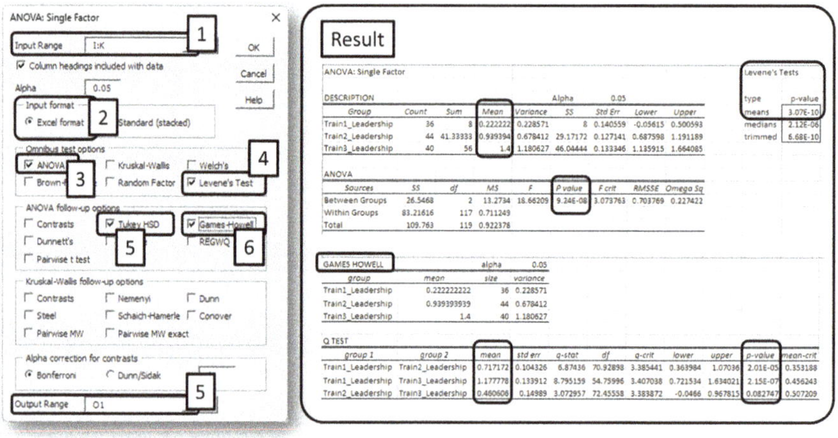

FIGURE 3.41
One-Way ANOVA in Excel

The HR team now knows that having a personal coach makes the most improvements in leadership score (1.400), the next is attending a training course (0.939) and the last is reading a pamphlet (0.222). Attending a training course or having a personal coach makes significant improvements in leadership score compared to reading a pamphlet, while the difference between attending a training course and having a personal coach is not significant. Although having a personal coach improves leadership score more than attending a training course, the statistical test shows that this difference is not significant. Therefore, depending on the difference between the costs of a training course and personal coaching, if the difference is small, the company may choose personal coaching; otherwise a training course may be more cost-effective.

3.13 A GRAPHICAL COMPARISON OF INTERVENTIONS

After doing all the hard work of statistical analysis, we would propose our actionable recommendations based on data and evidence. In the proposal, one major task is to help the audience visualize the statistical results and make evidence-based decisions.

In our comparison of interventions in the last section, there are three trainings, and each of them improves the leadership score at different

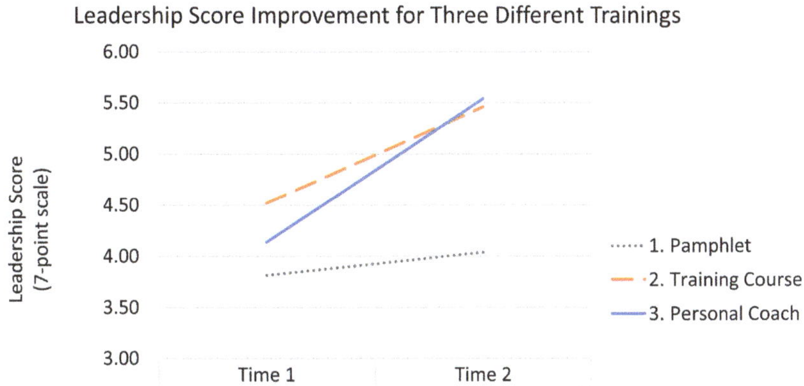

	Time 1	Time 2
1. Pamphlet	3.81	4.04
2. Training Course	4.52	5.45
3. Personal Coach	4.13	5.53

Time 2 is one year after the Training at Time 1

FIGURE 3.42
A Graphical Comparison of Interventions in Excel

levels. How can we show this result graphically? We can use a single line chart showing the changes in leadership improvement for the three trainings using three lines, as shown in Figure 3.42. The dotted line represents a pamphlet, which shows the smallest increase in leadership score. The dashed line represents a training course, and the solid line represents personal coaching. These two lines show a similar increase in the leadership score. By showing this, it will help the decision-maker visualize the impact of the difference training courses.

Now let us try to prepare this **graphical comparison chart of interventions in Excel**. Open the file "*Ch3_HR_Data.xlsx.*" Go to the worksheet "6. Intervention Chart." This worksheet contains columns A to C: *Training_Attended*, *T1_Lead_Mean*, and *T2_Lead_Mean*. First, we will prepare a PivotTable. Follow the numbers in Figure 3.43, which highlight the steps in the following text. Go to *Insert* > *PivotTable.* In the pop-up dialog box "PivotTable from table or range," select cells A1 to C121 as the *Table/Range.* Enter G1 as the *Location* in the *Existing Worksheet* to tell Excel to show the pivot table starting from cell G1. Click *OK.* Click on the pivot table. In the "PivotTable Fields" area, drag *Training_Attended* to *Columns.* Drag *T1_Lead_Mean* to *Values.* Click the inverted triangle next to it to have the dialog box "Value Field Settings" pop up. Rename it "Time 1" in the field *Custom Name.* Choose "Average" as *Summarize value field by.* Click *OK.* Back to the "PivotTable Fields" area, drag *T2_Lead_Mean* to *Values.* Click the inverted triangle next to it to have the dialog box "Value Field Settings" popped up. Rename

File: *Ch3_HR_Data.xlsx (Worksheet: 6. Intervention Chart)*
Insert > PivotTable

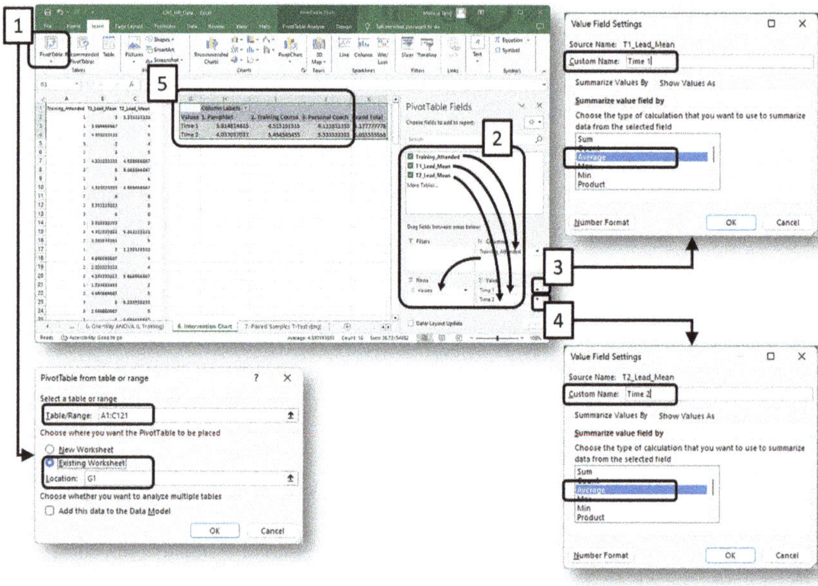

FIGURE 3.43
A Graphical Comparison of Interventions in Excel: Add a PivotTable

it "Time 2" in the field *Custom Name.* Choose "Average" as *Summarize value field by.* Click *OK.* Back in the "PivotTable Fields" area, drag *Values* from *Columns* to *Rows.* You will have the pivot table from cell G1 to K4 showing the mean leadership ratings for the three trainings for both Time 1 and Time 2.

We will now make use the PivotTable to prepare the comparison chart. Follow the numbers in Figure 3.44, which highlight the steps in the following text. Select the area from Cells G2 to J4, which are the data required for the chart. Go to *Insert > Recommended Charts.* In the pop-up dialog box "Insert Chart," choose "Line." Click *OK.* The chart will appear. Click the chart, and then click the *Chart Element* button (i.e., the green "+" button in the top right-hand corner of the chart). Tick the checkbox for *Axes, Axis Title, Chart Title, Data Table, Gridlines* and *Legend.* Update the title accordingly, and you will have the chart ready.

A good diagram saves a thousand words. Presenting a chart showing your statistical results graphically helps your audience understand and memorize the impact instantly. Practicing and rehearsing your presentation is also important. Together with good narratives, you can help to highlight the key points to your audience (Knaflic, 2015).

File: *Ch3_HR_Data.xlsx (Worksheet: 6. Intervention Chart)*
Insert > Recommended Charts > Line

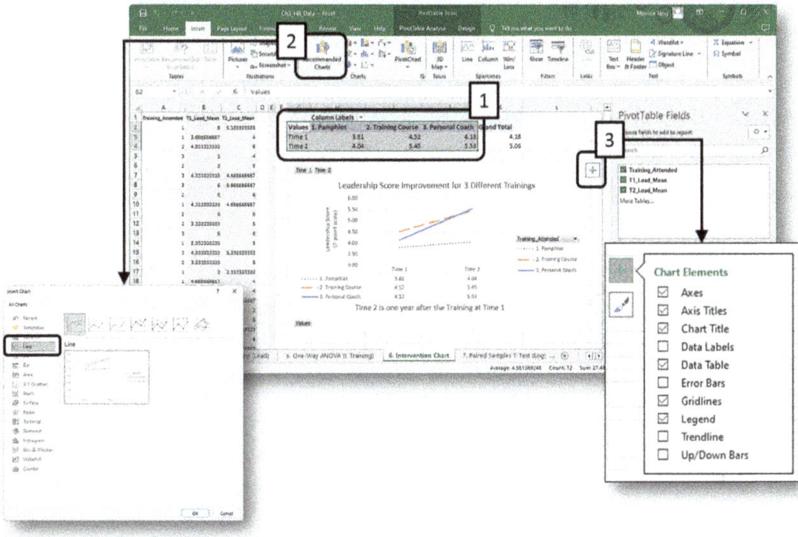

FIGURE 3.44
A Graphical Comparison of Interventions in Excel: Add a PivotChart

We have so far read the case studies of Nielsen and Google and had hands-on statistical exercises to replicate their analytics processes. These are cases which show us how to identify key factors, find solutions, monitor, and compare the results of the solution. In fact, data analytics can also help organizations prevent biases. Let us go through the case study from **Amazon**, and I will show you how to identify if biases exist in an organization via data analytics.

3.14 CASE STUDY: AMAZON'S MACHINE LEARNED FROM GENDER-BIASED DATA

Amazon is an American international e-commerce company. It is not surprising that the company makes use of automation in its business and processes. Since 2014, the team had been building computer programs to review the job applicants' resumes to identify, for example, the top five talents. One year later, in 2015, the company realized that the system preferred males to females for technical positions. Amazon tried to edit the program, but there was no guarantee of avoiding gender discrimination, as the program could deduce the gender with the information provided in the resumes, with identifiers like "women's" or "all-women's colleges." Ultimately, the company dismissed the project, and Amazon's recruiters claimed that they did not solely rely on this program for hiring (Dastin, 2018).

Applying artificial intelligence (AI) and machine learning (ML) to improve business efficiency is an inevitable trend. Apart from rule-based business programs (i.e., programs that rely on if-then-else logic to provide results), AI programs now learn from data (i.e., the programs identify patterns in the data provided to predict results). If the data provided to the machines are biased, the machines will magnify it and provide biased results. Therefore, it is important that we are able to identify whether the data are biased before providing them for machine learning. How can we do this? Let us use the recruitment data in our Best Toy Company to demonstrate how to identify if the data may have gender bias.

3.15 DETECTING GENDER BIAS IN RECRUITMENT DATA: AN EXAMPLE OF CHI-SQUARE TEST

Before we do a statistical test to check if there may be significant gender bias in the recruitment process, we will first observe whether there seems to be gender bias, for example, by using a chart to visualize the *proportions* of jobs offered to the number of applicants of the two genders largely differed. Using the recruitment data in Best Toy Company, the following chart is prepared in Excel (Figure 3.45). You can see that out of 22 male applicants, 8 of them are offered a job. There are 38 female applicants, and only five of them are offered a job. So, 36.4% (i.e., 8 ÷ 22 × 100% = 36.4%) of male applicants are offered a job, while 13.2% (i.e., 5 ÷ 38 × 100% = 13.2%) for the female counterparts. We can easily visualize that there seems to be a large difference in the proportions of jobs offered between the two genders.

Now let us try to prepare this **Graphical Comparison of Job Offered by Gender in Excel**. Open the file "*Ch3_Job_Applicant_Data.xlsx*" Go to the worksheet "Data." This worksheet contains columns A to C: *ApplicantID*, *Gender* (0 – Male; 1 – Female) and *Job_Offered* (0 – No; 1 – Yes). We will prepare a PivotChart. Follow the numbers in Figure 3.46, which highlight the steps in the following text. Go to *Insert* > *PivotChart*. In the pop-up

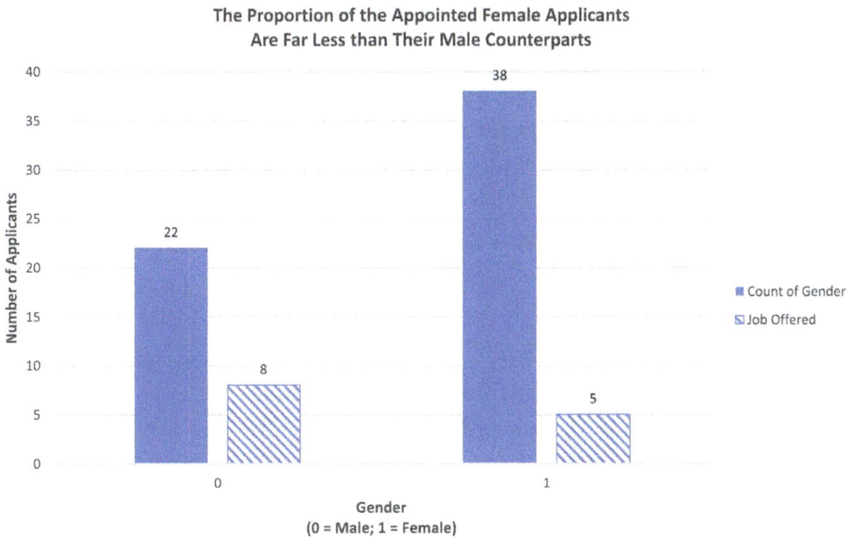

FIGURE 3.45
A Graphical Comparison of Job Offered by Gender

File: *Ch3_Job_Applicant_Data.xlsx (Worksheet: Data)*
Insert > PivotChart

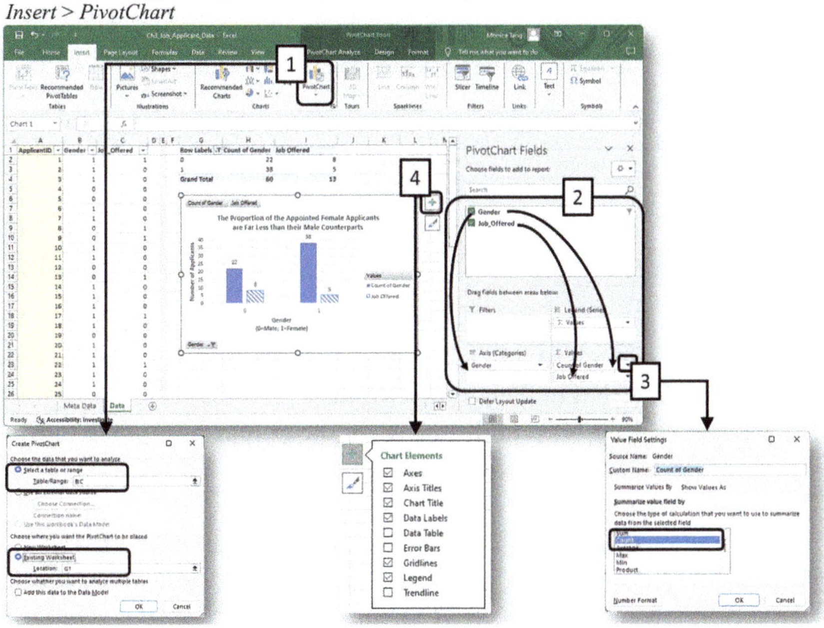

FIGURE 3.46
A Graphical Comparison of Job Offered by Gender Proportion: Add a PivotChart in Excel

dialog box "Create PivotChart," select columns B to C as *Table/Range*. Enter G1 as *Location* in the *Existing Worksheet* to tell Excel to show the pivot table starting from cell G1. Click *OK*. In the "PivotTable Fields" area, drag *Gender* to *Axis (Categories)*. Drag *Gender* to *Values*. Click the inverted triangle next to it to have the dialog box "Value Field Settings" pop up. Choose "Count" as *Summarize value field by*. Click *OK*. Back in the "PivotTable Fields" area, drag *Job_Offered* to *Values*. You will now have the pivot table and the pivot chart shown. Click the chart, and click the button *Chart Element* (i.e., the green "+" button at the top right-hand corner of the chart). Tick the checkbox for *Axes, Axis Title, Chart Title, Data Labels, Gridlines* and *Legend*. Update the title accordingly, and you will have the chart ready.

There is an observation of a difference in the proportions of jobs offered between the two genders. Subsequently, we need to test whether this difference is statistically significant. So, the HR team starts another round of the analytics process.

Business Problem: The HR department would like to know if gender bias exists in the recruitment process.

Research Question: Is the proportion of jobs offered significantly different between the male and female applicants?

The HR team has built the **hypotheses** and the **model** (Figure 3.47):

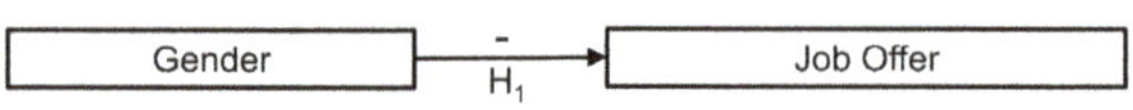

FIGURE 3.47
The Hypothesized Model for the Impact of Gender on Job Offer

H_1: The proportion of jobs offered to male applicants is significantly higher than that to female applicants.

H_0: There is no significant difference in the proportions of jobs offered between male and female applicants.

To test the hypothesis whether gender (**a categorial variable**) influences job offered (**a categorial variable**), we will use the **chi-square test** (see Chapter 2).

To do this **chi-square test in SPSS**, open the file "*Ch3_Job_Applicant_Data.sav*." Go to *Analyze* > *Descriptive Statistics* > *Crosstabs*. Drag Gender to *Row(s)*. Drag Job_Offered to *Column(s)*. Click *Statistics*. In the "Crosstabs:

File: *Ch3_Job_Applicant_Data.sav*
Analyze > Descriptive Statistics > Crosstabs

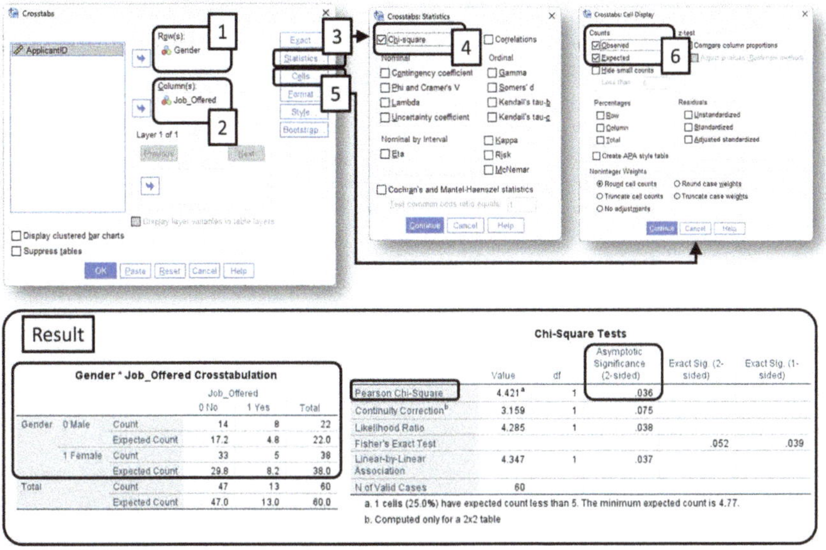

FIGURE 3.48
Chi-Square Test in SPSS

Statistics" pop-up dialog box, tick "Chi-square." Click *Continue*. Back in the "Crosstabs" dialog box, click *Cells*. In the "Crosstabs: Cell Display" dialog box, tick "Observed" and "Expected" for Counts. Click *Continue*. Click *OK*. The result is in the output viewer. The table "Gender * Job_Offered Crosstabulation" shows the actual counts (also called the observed counts) and the expected counts (i.e., the expected number of jobs offered if there is no bias and the proportions of jobs offered to males and females are the same). It shows differences in the actual counts and the expected counts. The table "Chi-Square Tests" shows that Pearson chi-square is significant ($p < 0.05$), indicating that the difference is significant. So, H_1 is accepted, and H_0 is rejected. The steps and the result are shown in Figure 3.48.

To do a **chi-square test in Excel**, open the file "*Ch3_Job_Applicant_Data.xlsx*." Go to the worksheet "Data." Columns A to C contain the variables *ApplicantID*, *Gender* (0 – Male; 1 – Female), and *Job_Offered* (0 – No; 1 – Yes). Go to *Add-ins > Real Statistics > Data Analysis Tools*. In the pop-up dialog box, click the tab page *Misc*, click *Chi-Square Test for Independence,* and then click *OK*. Select cells B1 to C121 as the *Input Range*. Click the radio button *Standard format*. Leave the *Output Range* blank to have the result shown on a new worksheet. In the table "Chi-square summary data,"

File: *Ch3_Job_Applicant_Data.xlsx (Worksheet: Data)*
Add-ins > Real Statistics > Data Analysis Tools (Misc > Chi-square Test for Independence)

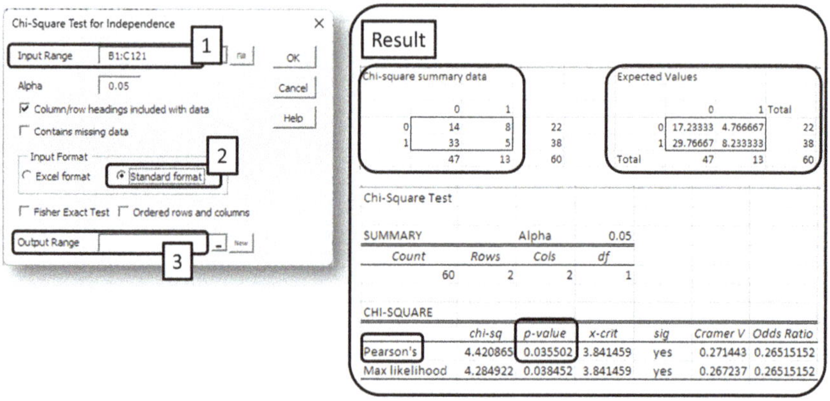

FIGURE 3.49
Chi-Square Test in Excel

it shows the actual number (i.e., the observed counts) of jobs offered to male and female applicants. In the table "Expected Values," it shows the expected numbers of jobs offered to the male and female applicants if they are in the completely same proportion. The table "CHI-SQUARE" shows that the difference is significant ($p < 0.05$). So, H_1 is accepted, and H_0 is rejected. The steps and the result are shown in Figure 3.49.

So, now you know how to identify whether there are significant biases in the data.

The HR department of Best Toy Company then runs some equality programs to improve the company's equality and diversity awareness. They will also regularly measure whether there are improvements in the gender equality in their recruitment process using the process mentioned earlier.

3.16 ORGANIZATIONAL NETWORK ANALYSIS

We have covered different metrics and commonly used statistical tests in HR. Before the end of this chapter, one new trend in HR analytics worth mentioning is **organizational network analysis (ONA)**.

ONA is a process to understand the communication structures in an organization (Krackhardt & Hansons, 1993). ONA usually presents as a diagram, with nodes to represent each employee and the edges to represent their communication and relationship paths. These paths together form a network of communications within the organization. This network of organizational communication is usually different from the formal hierarchy of the organization. The formal hierarchy is set up to handle routine, well-defined and anticipated problems. When unexpected problems arise, the informal communication network (which is highly adaptive and moves diagonally and elliptically) kicks in to have the problems solved. That is the reason why organizations start to analyze this informal communication network such that the most suitable team can be identified to solve these problems.

There are three types of organizational networks which solve different problems. First, the **advice network** shows the network which others depend on to solve problems and provide technical information. This network helps achieve strategic objectives. Second, the **trust network** identifies the network in which employees share delicate political information and support one another in a crisis. This network helps implement a major change or overcome a crisis. Third, the **communication network** shows that the network employees communicate work-related matters on a day-to-day basis. This network helps improve productivity.

To identify these networks in an organization, data can be collected via surveys by asking each employee with whom they exchange information for these three types of networks. You can imagine three large networks will be formed with these data collected. These data can be managed by software like UCINET or Pajek.

The afore-mentioned covers a brief discussion of ONA. ONA is a special type of social network analysis (SNA). Interested readers may refer to books (e.g., Galety, 2022; Nooy et al., 2011) on SNA to learn more about the technical calculations and applications.

This chapter covered different data analytics applications in HR, ranging from identifying recruitment gender bias to finding factors of performance and measuring intervention improvements by different statistical techniques. These applications were also illustrated by real-world case studies. The future trend of data analytics was also discussed. With practice, these analytical skills can be applied to solving different HR problems in different situations.

REFERENCES

Arnold, J. A., Arad, S., Rhoades, J. A., & Drasgow, F. (2000). The empowering leadership questionnaire: the construction and validation of a new scale for measuring leader behaviors. *Journal of Organizational Behavior, 21*(3), 249–269.

Boudreau, J. W., Cascio, W. F., & Fink, A. A. (2019). *Investing in People: Financial Impact of Human Resource Initiatives.* Society For Human Resource Management.

Dastin, J. (2018, October 11). *Amazon scraps secret AI recruiting tool that showed bias against women.* Reuters. https://www.reuters.com/article/us-amazon-com-jobs-automation-insight-idUSKCN1MK08G

Edwards, M. R., Edwards, K., & Jang, D. (2024). *Predictive HR Analytics: Mastering the HR Metric* (3rd ed.). Kogan Page Limited.

Galety, M. G. (2022). *Social Network Analysis: Theory and Applications.* John Wiley & Sons, Inc.

Garvin, D. A. (2013). How Google sold its engineers on management. *Harvard Business Review, 91*(12), 74–82.

HireVue. (2020). *Cathay Pacific improves hiring time over 90% with video interviewing.* https://www.hirevue.com/case-studies/cathay-pacific-ondemand-case-study

Huang, X. (2012). Helplessness of empowerment: the joint effect of participative leadership and controllability attributional style on empowerment and performance. *Human Relations, 65*(3), 313–334.

Knaflic, C. N. (2015). *Storytelling with Data: A Data Visualization Guide for Business Professionals.* Wiley.

Krackhardt, D., & Hansons, J. R. (1993). Information networks: the company behind the chart. *Harvard Business Review, 71*(4), 104–111.

Lam, C. K., Huang, X., & Chan, S. C. H. (2015). The threshold effect of participative leadership and the role of leader information sharing. *Academy of Management Journal, 58*(3), 836–855.

Lam, C. K., Walter, F., & Ouyang, K. (2014). Display rule perceptions and job performance in a Chinese retail firm: the moderating role of employees' affect at work. *Asia Pacific Journal of Management, 31*(2), 575–597.

Lee, K., & Allen, N. J. (2002). Organizational citizenship behavior and workplace deviance: the role of affect and cognitions. *Journal of Applied Psychology, 87*(1), 131–142.

Nooy, W. D., Mrvar, A., & Batagelj, V. (2011). *Exploratory Social Network Analysis with Pajek* (2nd ed.). Cambridge University Press.

Organ, D. W. (1988). *Organizational Citizenship Behavior: The Good Soldier Syndrome.* Lexington, MA: Lexington Books.

Ozer, M. (2011). A moderated mediation model of the relationship between organizational citizenship behaviors and job performance. *Journal of Applied Psychology, 96*(6), 1328–1336.

Podsakoff, N. P., Whiting, S. W., Podsakoff, P. M., & Blume, B. D. (2009). Individual- and organizational-level consequences of organizational citizenship behaviors: a meta-analysis. *Journal of Applied Psychology, 94*(1), 122–141.

Schaufeli, W. B., Bakker, A. B., & Salanova, M. (2006). The measurement of work engagement with a short questionnaire: a cross-national study. *Educational and Psychological Measurement, 66*(4), 701–716.

Smith, C. A., Organ, D. W., & Near, J. P. (1983). Organizational citizenship behavior: its nature and antecedents. *Journal of Applied Psychology, 68*(4), 653–663.

Steiner, K. (2017, March 9). *People analytics isn't as hard as you think – Nielsen proves why.* LinkedIn. https://www.linkedin.com/business/talent/blog/talent-engagement/how-nielsen-used-people-analytics-to-increase-retention

Tang, M. W. M., & Lam, C. K. (2020, April 23–25). Skip-level participation and helping behavior: the role of leader-leader exchange [Poster session]. *35th Annual Conference of the Society for Industrial and Organizational Psychology (SIOP 2020)*, Austin, TX, United States.

4

Data Analytics in Marketing

4.1 AN INTRODUCTION TO DATA ANALYTICS IN MARKETING

Marketing is a practice in which marketers identify the right target customers and sell them the right products or services. By raising the customers' brand awareness and providing values to the customers, the company gains better brand impressions, improves customer loyalty, drives sales and, as a result, boosts the market share.

In this marketing process, marketers get to understand the customer persona and identify the customer segments for different products. The marketers aim to drive the customers through the **AIDA model** (also considered the sales funnel) from knowing the product to buying it. AIDA is an acronym for **attention** to the product (a cognitive response), **interest** in the product (an affective response), **desire** to have the product (an affective response), and **action** to buy the product (a behavioral response) (Ullal & Hawaldar, 2018). This process can be taken through different channels, both the traditional and the new ones, like direct mails, TV advertisements, emails, social media and livestream e-commerce. More and more livestream e-commerce events are emerging on different online platforms, including Facebook, Amazon, YouTube, Instagram, Twitter, Twitch, Taobao, or TikTok. In 2023, sales from these livestream e-commerce events reached nearly 5 trillion yuan in China (Ou, 2024) and 50 billion U.S. dollars in the United States (Chevalier, 2024). As technology advances, more and more new marketing channels will likely arise. There is no one-size-fits-all best channel, but rather a proper mixture of traditional and new channels for the whole marketing campaign can bring success. For example, the livestream e-commerce events may be advertised using traditional media to draw more audience to the events.

DOI: 10.1201/9781032642307-4

Data analytics for marketing is about using data and measurements to help marketers make better business decisions. Some measurements are common to both traditional and new marketing channels, while some are specific to a certain channel; for example, click-through rate (CTR) is unique to online platforms.

This chapter will cover the most popular measurements and scenarios of different marketing channels. By using the hypothetical data in our Best Toy Company and real-world case studies, we will know how data analytics can be applied in helping marketers make better decisions. This chapter will start by introducing some common marketing metrics, which give a quick overview of business situation. Some key metrics will be displayed in a dashboard to help visualize the data. Different statistical tools will also be applied to help marketers make better decisions in customer segmentation, comparing marketing choices and even real-time monitoring during peak-season sales. The future trend of data analytics in marketing will also be discussed.

4.2 METRICS

Metrics are indicators that give marketers a quick overview of the marketing situations in an organization (Farris et al., 2006). Some popular marketing metrics are **retention rate**, **churn rate**, **customer lifetime value** (**CLV**), **return on marketing investment** (**ROMI**), and **Net Promoter Score** (**NPS**). Some are more specific to digital marketing, including **number of impressions**, **cost per thousand impressions** (**CPM**), **click-through rate** (**CTR**), **abandonment rate** and **conversion rate**. Let us go through them one by one.

Retention rate is the percentage of retained customers at the end of the period divided by the total number of the customers at the beginning of the period, as shown in Equation 4–1. Make sure the number of retained customers does not include the newly acquired customers.

$$Retention\ Rate = \frac{\begin{array}{c}Number\ of\ Customers\ Stay\\ from\ the\ First\ Day\ to\ the\ Last\ Day\\ of\ the\ period\end{array}}{\begin{array}{c}Number\ of\ Customers\\ on\ the\ First\ Day\ of\ the\ Period\end{array}} \times 100\% \qquad (4–1)$$

Retention rate ranges from 0% (all customers moved on) to 100% (all customers stay). A higher percentage means more customers are retained. The complement of retention rate is **churn rate,** which means the percentage of moved-on customers. If the retention rate is 80%, the churn rate is 20%.

Customer lifetime value (CLV) is the projected cash flow generated from the customer over the whole period of the commercial relationship with your customer. CLV can be predicted based on the RFM model (i.e., recency, frequency, and monetary of the customer's buying behavior) and the customer's likelihood of buying, which requires historical data and regression analysis. In fact, there are different ways to project CLV. Here is one common and more straightforward CLV calculation: multiplying the average profit of the sales transaction, the number of transactions in the measured period (e.g., 1 year) and the customer retention period (e.g., the number of years the customers do business with the company before they move on), as shown in Equation 4–2.

$$\begin{aligned} CLV = {} & \textit{Average Profit of a Sales Transaction} \\ & \times \textit{Number of Transactions} \\ & \times \textit{Customer Retention Period} \end{aligned} \qquad (4\text{–}2)$$

When we consider the sales of the customers may not stay the same year after year, we also take inflation (i.e., the discount rate in the equation) into account, as shown in Equation 4–3.

$$\textit{Traditional CLV} = \textit{Gross Margin per Customer} \times \frac{\textit{Retention Rate}}{1 + \textit{Discount Rate} - \textit{Retention Rate}} \qquad (4\text{-}3)$$

CLV helps marketers to have an idea of the maximum costs to acquire and retain a customer because that is the maximum profit a customer would likely generate in the whole business relationship.

Return on marketing investment (ROMI) is a measure of how the rate of investment (some may consider it spending) on marketing contributes to the profits. You may be familiar with return on investment (ROI), which means the rate of the net profit over the investment required to generate that profit. ROMI is a similar concept but only considering the part of revenue attributable to the marketing activities, excluding the marketing spending, over marketing spending, as shown in Equation 4–4.

$$ROMI = \frac{\textit{Revenue Attributable to Marketing Activities} - \textit{Marketing Spending}}{\textit{Marketing Spending}} \times 100\% \qquad (4\text{–}4)$$

Net Promoter Score (NPS) is a metric measuring the act of customers' loyalty (Baehre et al., 2021; Reichheld, 2003). NPS is measured by a single-question survey asking the customers whether they will recommend a product to a friend, using a Likert scale from 0 to 10, where 0 is the most unlikely and 10 is the most likely. Customers who responded 0 to 6 are **detractors,** unhappy customers who may even discourage others from buying your product. Customer who responded 7 to 8 are **passives,** satisfied customers but not enthusiastic enough to promote your product to others. Customers who responded 9 or 10 are **promoters,** loyal customers who will spread positive word of mouth for your product. The calculation of NPS is performed by subtracting the percentage of detractors from the percentage of promotors, hence the name "net promoter," as shown in Equation 4–5.

$$NPS = Percentage\ of\ Promoters - Percentage\ of\ Detractors \tag{4-5}$$

The NPS score ranges from −100% (all customers are detractors) to 100% (all customers are promoters). Therefore, a higher score means a larger proportion of net promoters in your customer pool. NPS is also commonly used to understand customers' experience after a digital online service.

The advancement of technology empowers businesses to measure figures that were previously only able to be roughly estimated. Digital marketing via different online platforms, like The Trade Desk, Google Ads, Facebook Ads, and Twitter Ads, provides detailed figures to help marketers understand data-driven insights into the performance of marketing campaigns in different stages of the AIDA model.

In the AIDA model, the first stage is to let the potential customers be aware of the product. The **number of impressions** is the number of times an advertisement is viewed (Equation 4–6). This number indicates the level of potential customers' awareness of the product. **Cost per thousand impressions** (**CPM**) measures the cost-effectiveness to increase awareness of the product by calculating the cost of advertising divided by the number of thousands of impressions generated (Equation 4–7). The next stages in the AIDA module include having the customers' interest and desire of the product. The potential customers clicking on the online advertisement is a good indicator of their interest in knowing more about the product. **Click-through rate** (**CTR**) is the percentage of the number of click-throughs over the number of impressions (Equation 4–8). This measures the effectiveness of whether the online advertisement is sufficiently intrigued to raise customers' interest in, or even the desire for, the product. **Abandonment rate** (also called **bounce rate**) is measuring the percentage of the number of uncompleted purchases over the number of purchases started (Equation 4–9). A high abandonment rate may be a warning of a weak design or even an error on the online shopping site. The last stage of the AIDA model is taking action to purchase. **Conversion rate** measures the percentage of the number of purchases over the number of visitors to an online shopping site (Equation 4–10). The text earlier gives the general meanings of the metrics. The specific details (e.g., which online action indicates starting a purchase) depend on the design of individual shopping sites and the digital marketing platforms. Readers are advised to well define the specific actions of the customers as a measure for these metrics.

$$Number\ of\ Impressions = Number\ of\ Times\ an\ Advertisement\ is\ Viewed \tag{4–6}$$

$$CPM = \frac{Cost\ of\ Adverstising}{The\ Number\ of\ Thousands\ of\ Impressions\ Generated} \times 100\% \tag{4–7}$$

$$CTR = \frac{Number\ of\ Click\ throughs}{Number\ of\ Impressions} \times 100\% \tag{4–8}$$

$$Abandonment\ Rate = \frac{Number\ of\ Uncompleted\ Purchases}{Number\ of\ Purchases\ Started} \times 100\% \tag{4–9}$$

$$Conversion\ Rate = \frac{Number\ of\ Purchases}{Number\ of\ Visitors\ of\ the\ Online\ Shoppoing\ Site} \times 100\% \tag{4–10}$$

Marketing is a practice racing against time. Some data patterns may be seasonal; for example, sales volume is likely to be peak during holiday seasons. On the other hand, some data patterns require real-time monitoring; for example, a sudden drop in the conversion rate may reflect some errors in the online shopping platform which needs a quick fix in order not to lose sales in a peak season. In the coming section, I will use the data from our hypothetical Best Toy Company to show a marketing dashboard in Excel with both seasonal and real-time marketing metrics. Moving average, a smoothing technique, will also be introduced for an overall trend of seasonal data patterns. More Excel dashboard functions have been discussed in Chapter 3, and I am not going to repeat them here. Interested readers may refer to the dashboard section in the previous chapter.

4.3 DASHBOARD

Now, let us use the data from our hypothetical Best Toy Company to demonstrate a marketing dashboard. The company is going to launch a new series of jigsaw puzzles in the coming holiday season and would like to analyze this product category in detail. This marketing dashboard shows the real-time online shopping metrics, sales, and marketing spending information for the past 5 years, with a moving average line of sales to observe the trend, as shown in Figure 4.1.

The left-hand side of the dashboard shows the hypothetical data for the real-time online shopping platform metrics, including the number of impressions, CTR, abandonment rate and conversion rate. These figures can usually be found on online marketing platforms like Google Ads or Facebook Ads. Our focus here is to build the line chart on the right-hand side of this **dashboard in Excel**. Open the file "*Ch4_Marketing_Dashboard.xlsx.*" Go to worksheet "Data." This worksheet contains four columns: product category, period, sales ($K) and marketing spending ($K). We are going to use these data to prepare this dashboard with data lines in (1) **sales** (the dotted line) and **marketing**

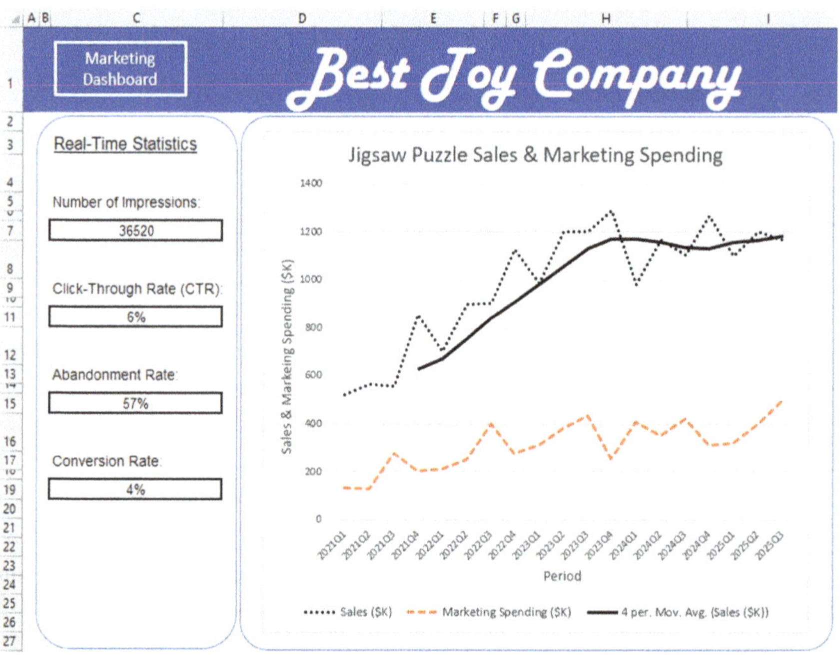

FIGURE 4.1
A Marketing Dashboard about Trends of Sales and Marketing Spending

spending (the dashed line) to observe if there seems to be a relationship between sales and marketing spending and (2) **a moving average line to show the sales trend** (the solid line). Go to worksheet "Dashboard". The dashboard is already prepared. You may observe that the volume of marketing spending in the previous quarter will affect the sales in the next quarter. For example, the increase in marketing spending in Q3 of 2023 reflects an increase in sales in Q4 of 2023. Let us look at the moving average sales line. It shows that the sales went up from 2021 to 2023 but have plateaued from 2024. If you want to try building this line chart, follow the steps in the next paragraph.

We will prepare a **line chart** of jigsaw puzzle sales and marketing spending for the past 5 years. A **line with moving average of sales** will be added to better show the sales trend across years. After preparing the sales line of jigsaw puzzle in the chart, you will see that there is a wavelike pattern, and it is difficult to tell the general trend across years. In Best Toy Company, the sales volume of jigsaw puzzle is seasonal, following a four-quarter cycle. The peak season is in quarter 4 (Q4), which is the holiday season. The sales will then usually drop in Q1, go up a bit in Q2 because of the school holiday, and drop again in Q3. Therefore, we will use a four-period moving average to see the overall trend in sales. Follow the numbers in Figure 4.2, which highlight the steps in the following text. Go to worksheet "Data." Select the table with cells from B1 to D20. To prepare the line chart, go to *Insert* > *Recommended Charts*. In the "Insert Chart" pop-up dialog box, click the "All Charts" tab. Click "Line" and *OK*. Update the chart title and axis titles accordingly. To add a moving-average trendline for sales, right-click on the Sales line and click *Add Trendline*. In the "Format Trendline" dialog box, choose "Moving Average" and enter "4" as Period. Click *OK*. You can then copy the chart to the worksheet "Dashboard."

Now, we can see the overall sales trend by the moving average line without being distracted by the wave-like patterns in the sales line. Here, I am going to explain the logic of a moving average trendline. **Moving average** is a smoothing technique to analyze the overall trend of the data points by a series of averages of subsets of the data. In our example, the seasonal data are in four-period subsets (e.g., Q1–Q4 every year). As the name "moving average" suggests, we move through the periods and continuously calculate the average of the four-period subsets (as it is a four-period cycle in this example). As shown in Figure 4.3, we calculate the average of the first four consecutive periods as a data point. Then, we move one period forward and calculate the average of the next four consecutive periods as another data point. Usually, this calculated data point is placed in the middle of the periods. In Excel, this calculated data

File: *Ch4_Marketing_Dashboard.xlsx*

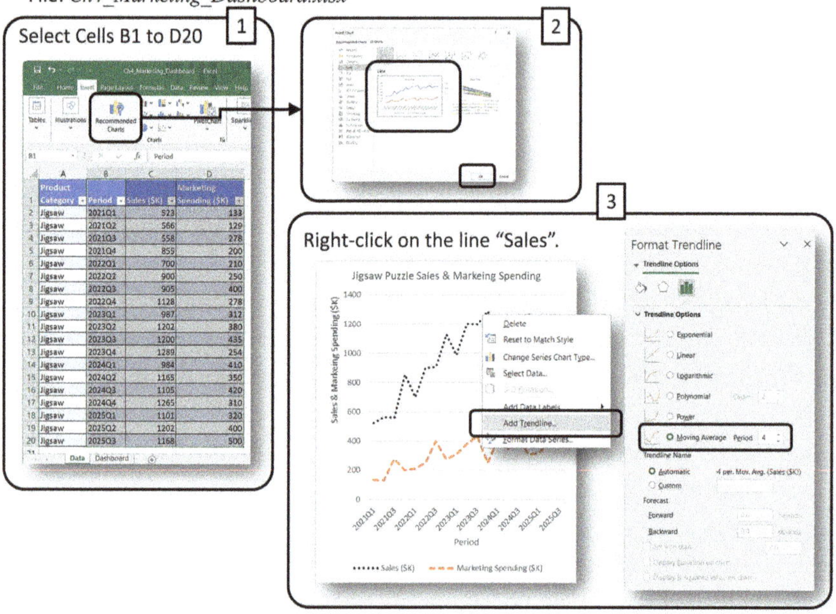

FIGURE 4.2
Marketing Dashboard: Moving Average Line

File: *Ch4_Marketing_Dashboard.xlsx*

	A	B	C	D	E
1	Product Category	Period	Sales ($K)	Moving Average	Formulas of Moving Average (for 4-period)
2	Jigsaw	2021Q1	523		
3	Jigsaw	2021Q2	566		
4	Jigsaw	2021Q3	558		
5	Jigsaw	2021Q4	855	625.5	=SUM(C2:C5)/4
6	Jigsaw	2022Q1	700	669.75	=SUM(C3:C6)/4
7	Jigsaw	2022Q2	900	753.25	=SUM(C4:C7)/4
8	Jigsaw	2022Q3	905	840	=SUM(C5:C8)/4
9	Jigsaw	2022Q4	1128	908.25	=SUM(C6:C9)/4
10	Jigsaw	2023Q1	987	980	=SUM(C7:C10)/4
11	Jigsaw	2023Q2	1202	1055.5	=SUM(C8:C11)/4
12	Jigsaw	2023Q3	1200	1129.25	=SUM(C9:C12)/4
13	Jigsaw	2023Q4	1289	1169.5	=SUM(C10:C13)/4
14	Jigsaw	2024Q1	984	1168.75	=SUM(C11:C14)/4
15	Jigsaw	2024Q2	1165	1159.5	=SUM(C12:C15)/4
16	Jigsaw	2024Q3	1105	1135.75	=SUM(C13:C16)/4
17	Jigsaw	2024Q4	1265	1129.75	=SUM(C14:C17)/4
18	Jigsaw	2025Q1	1101	1159	=SUM(C15:C18)/4
19	Jigsaw	2025Q2	1202	1168.25	=SUM(C16:C19)/4
20	Jigsaw	2025Q3	1168	1184	=SUM(C17:C20)/4
21					

Data | Dashboard | Moving Average

2021Q4

$$\frac{523 + 566 + 558 + 855}{4} = 625.5$$

2022Q1

$$\frac{566 + 558 + 855 + 700}{4} = 669.75$$

.
.
.

2025Q3

$$\frac{1265 + 1101 + 1202 + 1168}{4} = 1184$$

FIGURE 4.3
Marketing Dashboard: Moving Average Line

point is placed in the last period. This difference makes the resulting line shift to the right in Excel. Apart from this, the trendline pattern is the same as that with the data point placed in the middle of the periods.

From the moving average sales trendline, we can see that the sales volume of jigsaw puzzle has plateaued, as indicated in the marketing dashboard of Best Toy Company (Figure 4.1). A new glowing jigsaw puzzle series is going to launch in the coming holiday peak season to improve sales. The marketing team is going to take actions to drive customers through the AIDA model. Like many other companies, they start by analyzing the customer segments. **Nike**, an international sportswear company, applied marketing analytics to optimally define the customer segments. Let us go through this case study in the next section.

4.4 CASE STUDY: NIKE'S SUCCESS BY MARKET SEGMENTATION

Nike, Inc. is an American athletic sportswear corporation. The company successfully identifies different market segments by understanding each segment's specific needs well (Ng, 2018).

Nike started its business (as "Blue Ribbon Sports" in 1964) with the tailored running shoes designed to be more durable, increase runners' speed and provide better protection from injuries to specifically suit runners' needs. This identified niche segment brought Nike a competitive advantage. The brand soon became one of the best-in-class products in athletic footwear. In the 1980s, Nike expanded its market coverage and successfully identified the basketball segment which leveraged air-cushion technology to optimize athletes' performance.

You may wonder whether Nike had continued to target different sports, like cycling and yoga, as a specific segment. To answer this question, one needs to consider the resources invested in and the return generated from that segment. Each segment requires different resources to support the products and services offered to the customers. Over-segmentation will lead to an ineffective use of resources and an unclear brand message.

Nike knew the objective of segmentation well. When they came to start the line of business for sportswomen, they dug deep to understand sportswomen's persona and found that women are more willing to pay a premium than men for stylish sportswear. Therefore, they decided to target women as a single segment. The result shows it was a good decision, and this new segment led to a significant revenue growth for Nike.

4.5 MARKET SEGMENTATION – AN EXAMPLE OF K-MEANS CLUSTERING AND ELBOW METHOD

Market segmentation is a process of grouping customers with similar characteristics so that the company can tailor the right message to the right group of customers for more effective customer connection (Kotler & Keller, 2016). As you have seen in the case of market segmentation in Nike, they segmented the markets by demographic segmentation (e.g., gender) and behavioral segmentation (e.g., different types of sports require different footwear support). Other ways include geographical segmentation (e.g., different weather conditions require different footwear materials) and psychographic segmentation (e.g., achievers versus self-expressers). This method of segmentation is done via an analysis of different customers' **personas** (i.e., a description of the customer characteristics).

Apart from descriptive insights, we can use statistical analyses, such as k-means clustering and elbow method, to show how customer clusters can be segmented (Venkatesan et al., 2015). **K-means clustering** algorithm requires you to provide the number of clusters you want to segment in the group of data (i.e., the number *k*). The algorithm will first generate *k* random number of centroids and assign the data points to the nearest centroid to form groups of membership. According to each membership group, the new centroid (i.e., the arithmetic mean of the data points) will be generated, and the membership of the data points will be reassigned until the memberships do not change over several such iterations. According to the membership group of the result of k-means clustering, a bar chart can be produced to visualize the clusters. You may ask how we can know the number *k* is an appropriate number of clusters. **Elbow method** may shed light on determining the number *k*. To do this analysis, we will repeat the process of k-means clustering for a range of *k* (Syakur et al., 2018). For each k-means clustering result, calculate the square of the distance between each data point and its within-cluster centroid, and then sum them up. We call this number **within-cluster sum of square (WCSS)**. Do an elbow plot, which shows the WCSS against the number of clusters *k*. The marginal gain from an additional cluster will drop. Thus, we can identify the optimal *k*, which has no significant gain by adding additional number of clusters. Using the elbow method to determine *k* is not without criticism (Schubert, 2023). Yet, at the point of time the author writes this text, the elbow method remains a common way to determine *k*.

Let us use the data in our Best Toy Company to demonstrate how to do k-means clustering and the elbow method. The company uses the data from customers who bought jigsaw puzzles from the company last year (for demonstration purposes, we use 120 customers' data). The marketing team conducted a qualitative survey with the salespersons and got a sense that customers living farther away from the City Central and who are parents with young kids living in the suburbs contribute to higher sales volume. The second high-sales-volume group of customers is the jigsaw lovers. The customers in the third group only sometimes buy jigsaw puzzles, which contributes to a smaller volume of the total sales. The data gathered contain the customer's home distance from City Central (in kilometers), the number of kids (younger than 12 years old) the customer has and the sales generated from their jigsaw puzzle purchases last year.

You can imagine that the range of these three variables varies largely. For example, the number of kids ranges from zero to a single-digit value, while the sales of jigsaw puzzle purchases are in the thousands. As mentioned previously, a bar chart will be produced to visualize the clusters. If the value ranges of the variables differ largely, the clusters will be difficult to be visualized. For better data comparison and visualization purpose, standardized values will be used. Standardized values (also called z-score or mean-centered values) will adjust the normally distributed data such that the mean of the data becomes 0 and the standard deviation becomes 1. I will later demonstrate the difference between a chart using standardized values and one using unstandardized values when we prepare the cluster chart. Now, before we do k-means clustering in SPSS, we will first prepare the standardized values.

In **SPSS**, open the file "*Ch4_Segmentation_Data.sav.*" In this file, the variable *Home_Distance* represents the customer's home distance from City Central (in kilometers). The variable *Kids_Number* means the number of kids (younger than 12 years old) the customer has. The variable *Jigsaw_Sales* represents the sales generated from their jigsaw puzzle purchases last year.

First, we will prepare the **standardized values** of the three data columns: ZHome_Distance, ZKids_Number and ZJigsaw_Sales. To standardize the data: Go to *Analyze > Descriptive Statistics > Descriptives.* Select Home_Distance, Kids_Number and Jigsaw_Sales as *Variable(s).* Tick "*Save standardized values as variables.*" Click *OK.* The three new variables of standardized values are created: ZHome_Distance, ZKids_Number and ZJigsaw_Sales The steps and the result are in Figure 4.4.

Second, we will do **k-means cluster analysis in SPSS** to calculate and assign the memberships of the three clusters. We assume there are three clusters, as the marketing team gathered qualitative data from the salespersons suggesting that there are likely three groups of customer personas. In SPSS, go to *Analyze > Classify > K-Means Cluster.* Select Home_Distance,

File: *Ch4_Segmentation_Data.sav*
Analyze > Descriptive Statistics > Descriptives

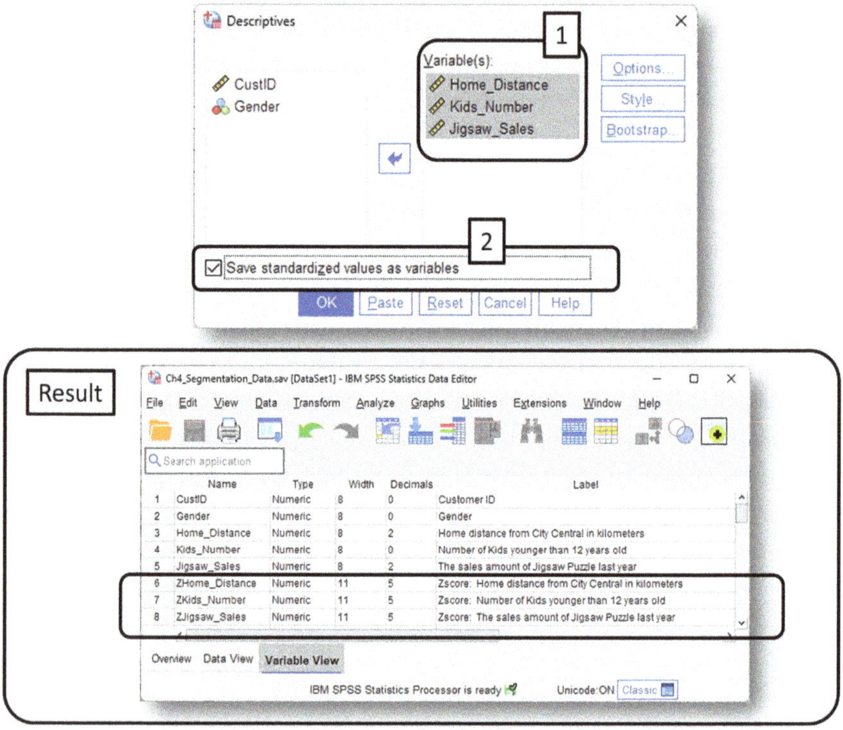

FIGURE 4.4
Standardized Values in SPSS

Kids_Number, and Jigsaw_Sales as *Variable(s).* Enter "3" as *Number of Clusters.* Click the *Save* button. In the "K-Means Cluster: Save New Variable" pop-up dialog box, tick *Cluster membership.* Click *Continue.* Click the *Options* button. In the "K-Means Cluster Analysis: Options" pop-up dialog box, tick *ANAOVA table.* Click *Continue.* Click *OK.* You can then see a newly added variable, QCL_1, which is the cluster membership assigned by the program. In the output viewer, the table "ANOVA" shows that all three variables are significant (i.e., Sig. < 0.05). The table "Number of Cases in Each Cluster" shows the count of cases assigned to each cluster. As you may recall that the centroids are at first assigned randomly, so, this algorithm may in fact have multiple valid solutions. Therefore, if you rerun this analysis, you may find the memberships assigned differently. The table "Final Cluster Centers" shows the values of the final centroids. Double-click this table, select the nine values, right-click and choose *Create Graph* and then *Bar.* You can see a bar chart showing the patterns of the three clusters. The steps and the result

File: *Ch4_Segmentation_Data.sav*
Analyze > Classify > K-Means Cluster

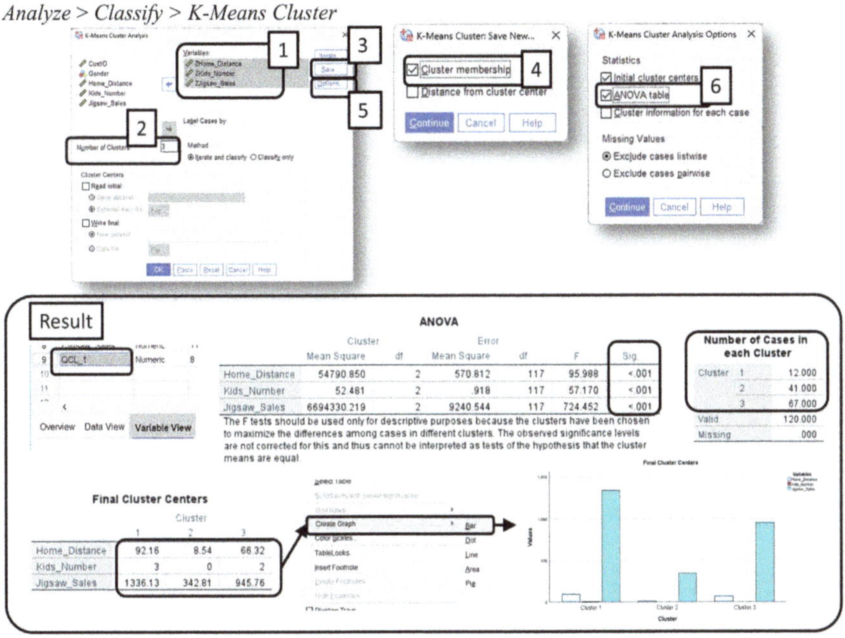

FIGURE 4.5
K-Means Cluster Analysis in SPSS

are in Figure 4.5. You may notice that the ranges of the three variables vary greatly; for example, the number of kids ranges from 0 to 4, while the jigsaw sales volume ranges from 130 to around 1,500. This makes the patterns of the three clusters difficult to be visualized in the bar chart. We will rerun the k-means cluster analysis using the standardized values, which will make the values more comparable and thus easier to visualize the patterns.

To do **k-means cluster analysis using standardized values in SPSS**, go to *Analyze > Classify > K-Means Cluster*. This time, select ZHome_Distance, ZKids_Number, and ZJigsaw_Sales as *Variable(s)*. Enter "3" as *Number of Clusters*. I will skip the analyses of other tables in the results, as they have been covered in the previous paragraph. We will focus on the bar chart with standardized values. Double-click the table "Final Cluster Centers." Select its nine values. Right-click and choose *Create Graph* and then *Bar*. You can see a bar chart showing the patterns of the three clusters. The steps and the result are in Figure 4.6. You can see that the patterns in the bar chart are more readily visible this time. Cluster 1 shows that this group of customers lives far away from City Central, has more kids, and spends the most on jigsaw puzzles. Customers in Cluster 2 live far from City Central (but not as far

File: *Ch4_Segmentation_Data.sav*
Analyze > Classify > K-Means Cluster

FIGURE 4.6
K-Means Cluster Analysis Using Standardized Values in SPSS

as those in Cluster 1), have relatively fewer kids, and spend some money on jigsaw puzzles. Customers in Cluster 3 live around City Central, have even fewer kids, and spend the least on jigsaw puzzles.

The marketing team profiles the three clusters of customers and names Cluster 1 as "Parent with Young Kids Living in Suburbs," Cluster 2 as "Jigsaw Lover" and Cluster 3 as "Casual Jigsaw Player".

To do this **k-means cluster analysis in Excel**, open the file "*Ch4_Segmentation_Data.xlsx.*" Go to the worksheet "Data." Go to *Add-ins > Real Statistics > Data Analysis Tools.* In the pop-up dialog box, click the tab page *Multivar,* click *K-Means Cluster Analysis,* and click *OK.* In the "K-Means Cluster Analysis" pop-up dialog box, select cells C9 to E129 (i.e., the three variables Homd_Distance, Kids_Number and Jigsaw_Sales) as the *Input Range.* Enter "3" as the *Number of Clusters.* Leave the *Output Range* blank. Click *OK.* The result is prepared in the worksheet "b. 3-Cluster." (As you may recall, the centroids are at first assigned randomly, so, this algorithm may have multiple valid solutions. Therefore, if you run this analysis, your memberships assigned may differ from mine.) In worksheet "b. 3-Cluster," column B shows the cluster membership assigned for each row. The centroids

File: *Ch4_Segmentation_Data.xlsx (Worksheet: Data)*
Add-ins > Real Statistics > Data Analysis Tools (Multivar > K-Means Cluster Analysis)

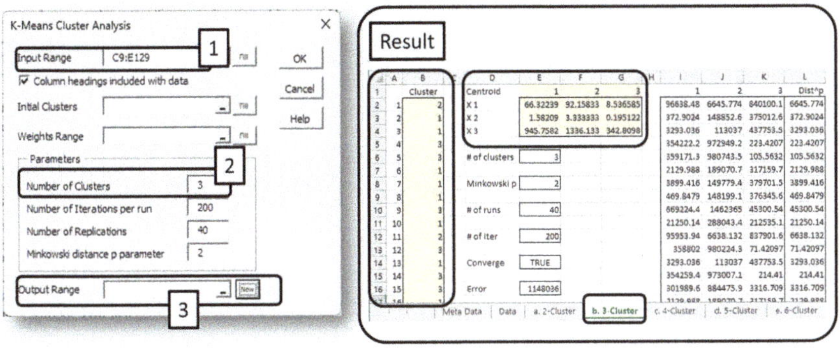

FIGURE 4.7
K-Means Cluster Analysis in Excel

for each variable in each cluster are also shown. For example, the centroid of the variable "Home_Distance" (i.e., X1) for Cluster 2 is 92.1583. The steps and the result are in Figure 4.7. Interested readers can prepare the standardized values for the set of data by the function "=standardize(*variable value, mean of the variable, standard deviation of the variable*)" in Excel and prepare the bar chart similar to what we did in SPSS. I am not going to repeat the steps here. Instead, I will do the elbow method in Excel.

To do the **elbow method in Excel** to determine the optimal number of clusters, again, open the file "*Ch4_Segmentation_Data.xlsx.*" Repeat the steps for doing k-means cluster analysis in Excel in the last paragraph for two clusters, four clusters, up to six clusters. These results have been prepared in the worksheets "a. 2-Cluster," "c. 4-Cluster," "d. 5-Cluster," and "e. 6-Cluster." As explained in the last paragraph, the centroids are calculated and shown in these worksheets. The **elbow plot** is a line chart of within-cluster sum of square (WCSS) against the number of clusters. WCSS is the sum of all the squares of the distances between the data point and the within-cluster centroid. The results of WCSS are calculated and highlighted in row 131 for each number of clusters in the worksheet "Data." The elbow plot is shown in the worksheet "Elow Plot" (Figure 4.8). You can see that there is a significant drop in the within-cluster sum of squares of the distances between the data points and the centroid from two clusters to three clusters. That means, the data points with three clusters are much closer to each other than those with two clusters. Moving from three clusters onward, the gain is much less significant. Therefore, we identify that the optimal grouping for this dataset is with three clusters.

File: *Ch4_Segmentation_Data.xlsx (Worksheet: Elbow Plot)*

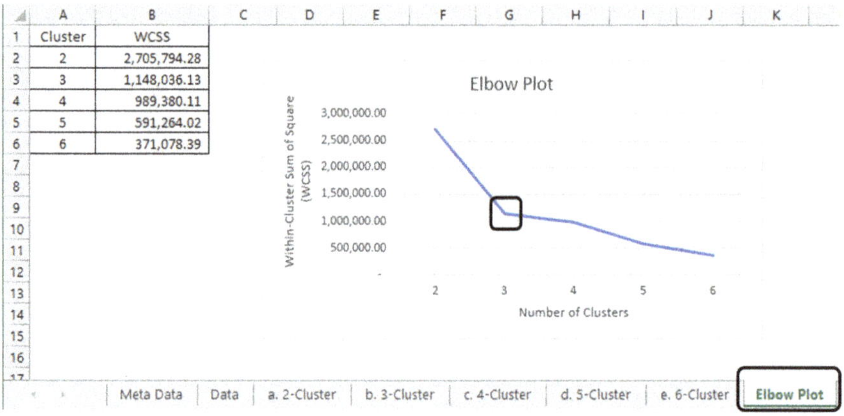

FIGURE 4.8
Elbow Plot in Excel

As mentioned earlier, the marketing team profiles the three clusters of customers. The company is going to launch a new glowing jigsaw series in the coming holiday season in Q4. It is now Q3, and the company has designed a new set of online promotional materials tailored for each customer segment. Will this new design improve sales, have no impact on sales, or even reduce sales? Let us look at a case study about **Microsoft Bing,** which may bring some insights on how to answer this question.

4.6 CASE STUDY: AN EXPERIMENT IN MICROSOFT BING BROUGHT HIGH REVENUE

Microsoft Bing is one of the most popular online search engines in the world. You can imagine that the revenue generated from advertisements on Bing is enormous. Many employees work to propose improvements to this search engine in different ways. The program managers always receive hundreds of proposed ideas. One of these ideas was a slight change in displaying the advertisement headlines. The program managers considered it a low-priority proposal, and it remained pending for months without a decision. One engineer thought it was a relatively low-cost technical change and launched a simple online experiment to test users' responses. The response was astonishingly good and generated unexpectedly high revenue within hours. If this experiment was not carried out, this very best revenue-generated idea in Bing's history may never be uncovered. This case study also reflects that reality can sometimes largely differ from our intuition or experience. One may never think that a slight change may generate huge revenue (Kohavi & Thomke, 2017).

Many companies nowadays adopt this experimental approach with robust A/B tests to guide their evidence-based decisions. In an A/B test, two groups of customers are randomly assigned to two different treatments. For example, group A customers receive a promotional email with the existing design, and group B customers receive a newly designed promotional email. The result is then compared between these two groups of customers to see if there are statistically significant differences in measurements such as CTR or sales revenue (Gallo, 2017). Similar comparisons can be applied in different marketing events, for example, comparing the customers' engagement levels (e.g., customers engaging in polls, expressing opinions and emotions through emojis) of livestream e-commerce events between two influencers or key opinion leaders (KOLs). Another example may be to compare the likelihood of buying the products with different packaging between two groups of customers.

Therefore, to collect evidence to make better decisions, sometimes experiments are required, and an A/B test is a straightforward way to test the result's significance. An independent-samples *t* test is one way to carry out an A/B test.

4.7 AN EXPERIMENT ON PROMOTION DESIGN – AN EXAMPLE OF INDEPENDENT-SAMPLES T TEST

Let us get back to our Best Toy Company. The holiday season is approaching. This is the peak period that generates a lot of revenue for the company. The marketing team has designed a set of new promotional email materials tailored for each group of the customer segments. The team targets to find evidence to see whether the newly designed promotional emails will generate higher revenue before a full-scale launch of the marketing campaign to all customers in the holiday season. To find evidence to better predict whether the new promotion design will improve sales, the marketing team starts the **five-step data analytics process** (see Chapter 2). We will demonstrate this process using data in the customer segment "Parents with Young Kids Living in Suburbs."

Business Problem: The marketing team randomly picks a sample of 60 customers in the segment "Parents with Young Kids Living in Suburbs" for preorder sales, with half of them receiving a promotional email with the existing design (let us call them group A), while the other half receiving a promotional email with the new design (group B). They aim to compare if the two sample groups will generate significant different preorder sales in two weeks' time.

Research Question: In the segment "Parents with Young Kids Living in Suburbs," do group B customers receiving the new promotional email generate more preorder sales than group A customers who receive the existing promotional email?

The marketing team has then built the **hypotheses** and the **model** (Figure 4.9):

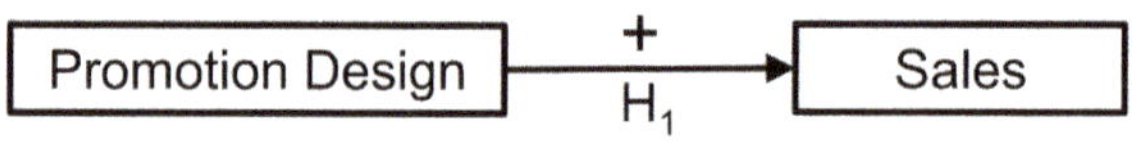

FIGURE 4.9
The Hypothesized Model for the Impact of Promotion Design on Sales

H_1: In the segment "Parents with Young Kids Living in Suburbs," group B customers receiving the new promotional email generate more preorder sales than group A customers who receive the existing promotional email.

H_0: In the segment "Parents with Young Kids Living in Suburbs," group B customers receiving the new promotional email do not generate significantly different preorder sales compared to group A customers who receive the existing promotional email.

Look at the data in the SPSS file "*Ch4_Marketing_Data.sav*" and the Excel file "*Ch4_Marketing_Data.xlsx.*" In these files, the variable *Membership* represents the customer segment that a customer is in: segment 1 as "Parent with Young Kids Living in Suburbs," segment 2 as "Jigsaw Lover" and segment 3 as "Casual Jigsaw Player." The variable *PreOrderSales_in_2weeks* is the sales amount of jigsaw Puzzle in the 2 weeks after a customer receives the promotional email.

The marketing team has checked that the sales amount represents the correct amount generated within 2 weeks after the promotional emails were sent. So, it passes **face validity**. As it only contains one question, construct validity and reliability tests are not required.

To test the hypothesis of finding whether the two groups of customers, receiving the existing or new promotional email, have significant differences in generating the preorder sales amount (a continuous variable), we will use the **independent-samples *t* test** (see Chapter 2).

Let us read the file "*Ch4_Marketing_Data.sav.*" This dataset contains data for all three segments. In this test, we will compare the difference for segment 1 (i.e., "Parents with Young Kids Living in Suburbs"). So, we first select the data for the variable Membership that equals 1. To do this in SPSS, go to *Data* > *Select Cases*. Choose *If condition is satisfied.* Click the *If* button. In the "Select Cases: If" pop-up dialog box, enter "Membership = 1" as the condition. Click *Continue*. Click *OK*. The result is shown in the "Data View." You can see that those rows where membership does not equal 1 are crossed out. There is also an additional variable, *filter_$,* where the value 1 means that row is selected, while 0 means that row is not selected. The steps and the result are in Figure 4.10. Please note that the crossed-out rows are not deleted. They only indicate that the following analysis will not include those

File: *Ch4_Marketing_Data.sav*
Data > Select Cases

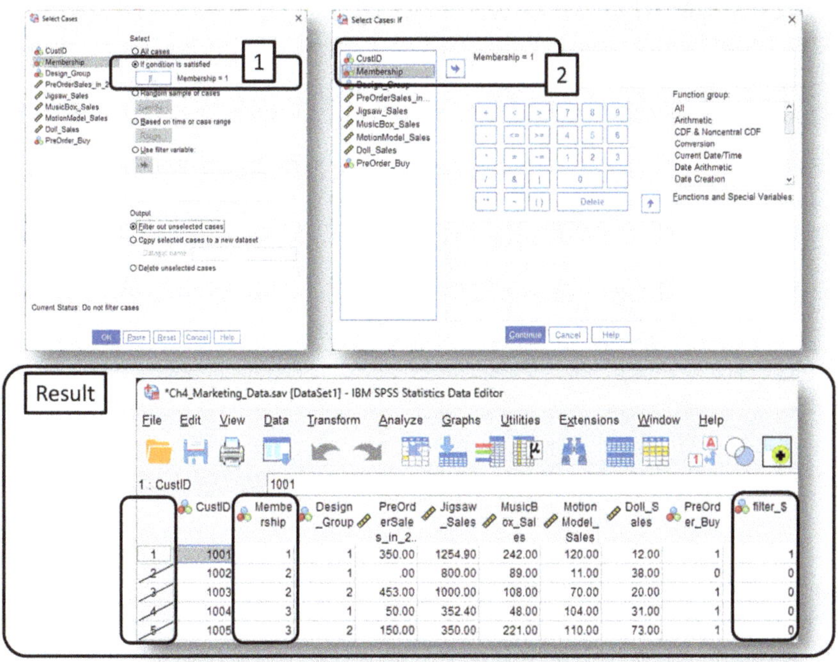

FIGURE 4.10
Select Cases in SPSS

crossed-out rows. I will later show you how to remove the filter after finishing the independent-samples *t* test.

To do an **independent-samples *t* test in SPSS**, go to *Analyze > Compare Means and Proportions > Independent-Samples t Test.* Select PreOrderSales_in_2weeks as *Test Variable(s).* Select Design_Group as the *Grouping Variable.* Click *Define Groups.* In the "Define Groups" pop-up dialog box, enter "1" as *Group 1* and "2" as *Group 2.* Click *Continue.* Click *OK.* The result is in the output viewer. In the table "Group Statistics," the mean value of preorder sales for Group A (those receiving the existing promotional email) is 144.333 while Group B (those receiving the new promotional email) is 426.533. In the table "Independent Samples Test," Levene's test for equality of variances is significant (p = 0.006), indicating that equal variances cannot be assumed. Therefore, we will read the significance of the second row (i.e., equal variances not assumed), and it is significant ($p < 0.05$). It means that the mean value of preorder sales for Group B is higher than Group A by 282.2 (i.e., 426.533 minus 144.333), and it is a significant difference. So, H_1 is accepted, and H_0 is rejected. The steps and the result are in Figure 4.11.

File: *Ch4_Marketing_Data.sav*
Analyze > Compare Mean and Proportions > Independent-Samples T Test

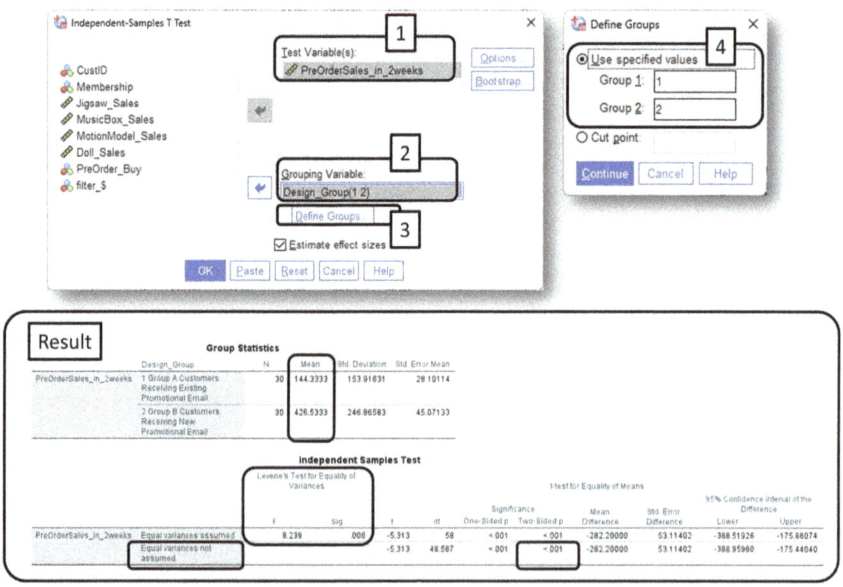

FIGURE 4.11
Independent-Samples *t* Test in SPSS

Remember that we have filtered the data for the previous test. To remove the filter in SPSS, go to *Data > Select Cases.* Choose *All cases.* Click *OK.* In the "Data View," you can see that no rows are now crossed out. You may note that variable *filter_$* remains. You can simply select that variable and press the Delete key on the keyboard to delete it. The steps and results are shown in Figure 4.12.

Now, it is the turn for Excel. Open the Excel file "*Ch4_Marketing_Data.xlsx.*" In the worksheet "Data," it contains the data the same as those in the SPSS file which have already been explained earlier. So, I am not going to describe the data here again. To filter in Excel, simply go to *Data > Filter.* Click the drop-down button in the column header and select the required values. In the Excel file, the selected data are already prepared for you.

To do an **independent-samples *t* test in Excel**, open the file "*Ch4_Marketing_Data.xlsx.*" Go to the worksheet "1. Ind-Samples T Test." Preorder sales data of Group A customers (those who receive the existing promotional email) are in Column A, while those for Group B customers (those who receive the new

File: *Ch4_Marketing_Data.sav*
Data > Select Cases

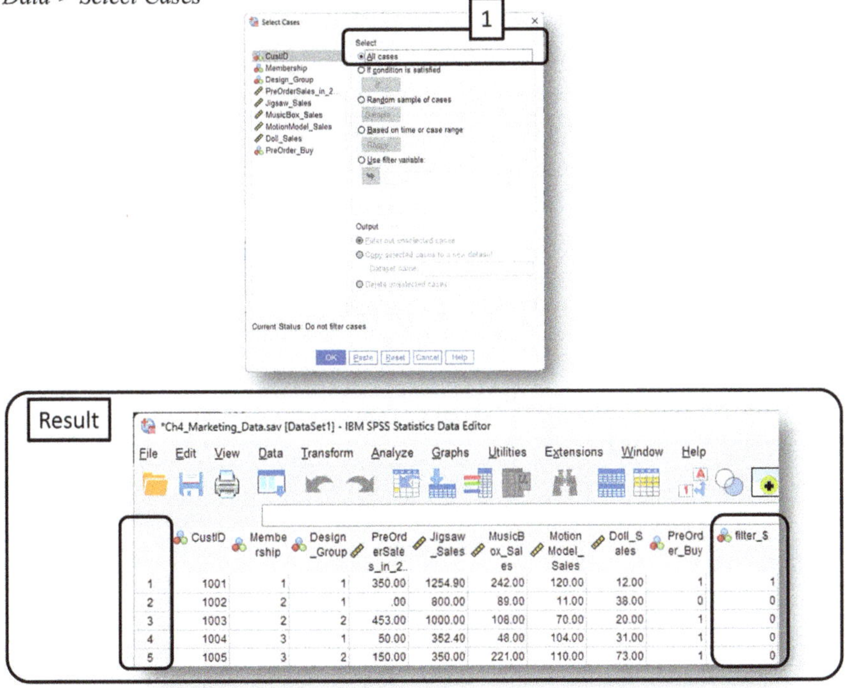

FIGURE 4.12
Select All Cases in SPSS

promotional email) are in Column B. Go to *Add-ins > Real Statistics > Data Analysis Tools*. In the pop-up dialog box, click the tab page *Misc*, click *T Test and Non-parametric Equivalents,* and *OK*. In the "T Test and Non-parametric Equivalents" pop-up dialog box, select Column A as *Input Range 1*. Select Column B as *Input Range 2*. Choose *Two independent samples* as *Options*. Select *T Test* as *Test Type*. Enter the cell F1 as *Output Range*. Click *OK*. In the result area, in the table "SUMMARY," the mean value of preorder sales for Group A (those receiving the existing promotional email) is 144.333, while for Group B (those receiving the new promotional email) is 426.533. There is no Levene's test for equality of variances here. Therefore, we will read the *p*-value of both equal and unequal variances, and both are significant ($p < 0.05$). It means that the mean value of preorder sales for Group B is higher than Group A by 282.2 (i.e., 426.533 minus 144.333), and it is a significant difference. So, H_1 is accepted, and H_0 is rejected. The steps and the result are in Figure 4.13.

The earlier text has demonstrated how independent-samples *t* test can be applied to compare the difference in the impact on sales of the two different promotional emails for the segment "Parent with Young Kids Living in Suburbs." The result shows that the new promotional email significantly increases sales. Can you try the same test for the two other segments, "Jigsaw Lover" and "Casual Jigsaw Player"?

After you have done the tests for all the three segments, you will find that the statistical results support that the new promotional emails improve the sales for all three segments significantly. Therefore, the marketing team has data-driven support to decide to launch the new set of promotional emails on a full scale in the coming holiday season.

File: *Ch4_Marketing_Data.xlsx (Worksheet: 1. Ind-Samples T Test)*
Add-ins > Real Statistics > Data Analysis Tools (Misc > T Test and Non-parametric Equivalents)

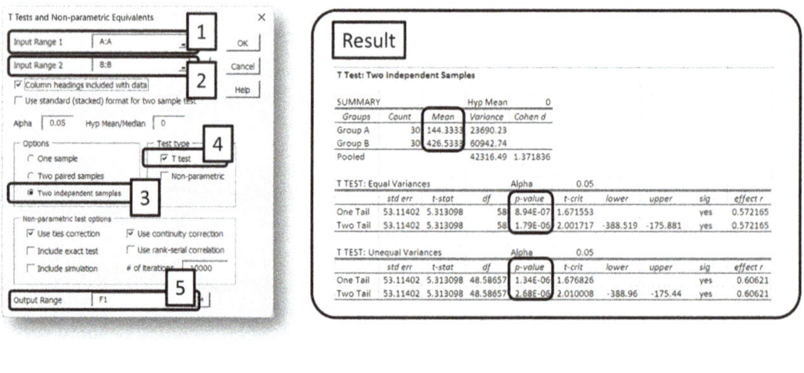

FIGURE 4.13
Independent-Samples *t* Test in Excel

4.8 CROSS-SELLING AND UP-SELLING

To further improve sales of this new series of glowing jigsaw puzzles, the marketing team plans to do this through cross-selling and up-selling. **Cross-selling** is a marketing technique that leverages the current customer relationship by selling additional products to the same customer in order to increase sales. **Up-selling,** on the other hand, increases sales by selling an upgrade of the product to the current customer (Kamakura, 2008). These common techniques are not without drawbacks if not done right. When customers are offered irrelevant additional products or upgrades, they may feel overwhelmed or even a detracted shopping experience. In our Best Toy Company, if every customer who buys in the shop is asked whether they want to buy the new series of glowing jigsaw puzzles, some customers who find this an irrelevant product may feel annoyed, or worse, the relationship with this customer will be negatively affected. If so, can marketing analytics help to identify those customers who will most likely buy this product such that the salesperson only cross-sells or up-sells to these customers? Yes, we can use logistic regression to predict which customers are more likely to buy this product.

4.9 PREDICTING WHICH CUSTOMERS WILL BUY – AN EXAMPLE OF LOGISTIC REGRESSION

The marketing team of Best Toy Company interviewed the frontline salespersons, who are in a privileged position to interact with and understand the customers, to identify the potential buyers for this new series of glowing jigsaw puzzles. The salespersons have commented that the customers who have bought music boxes, motion models (e.g., car models) or dolls may be interested in this new series of glowing jigsaw puzzles, while customers who have bought jigsaw puzzles may want a new challenge with this new series. In other words, the customers who have bought music boxes, motion models or dolls may be target customers to cross-sell, while those who have bought jigsaw puzzles may be target customers to up-sell.

The marketing team targets to have data-driven support before making this cross-selling and up-selling decision. The team gathered the data from their experiment to test the new promotional email, along with the data from the marketing database, including the sales of music boxes, motion models, dolls, and jigsaw puzzles to these customers in the last year. Let us open the SPSS file "*Ch4_Marketing_Data.sav*" and the Excel file "*Ch4_Marketing_Data.xlsx*" to read the data. The variables Jigsaw_Sales, MusicBox_Sales, MotionModel_Sales and Doll_Sales represent the sales amounts of jigsaw puzzles, music boxes, motion models and dolls of that customer, respectively, last year. The variable PreOrder_Buy is a categorical variable with the values 1 or 0, where 1 indicates that the customer has ordered the glowing jigsaw puzzle in their preorder sales experiment, while 0 indicates that the customer has not. The marketing team will use the data for those customers who received the new promotional email in this analysis because the marketing team has decided to use this new promotional email on a full scale in the holiday season.

The marketing team now has the data ready. They have also followed the **five-step data analytics process** (see Chapter 2) and have formulated the business problem and research question as follows:

Business Problem: The marketing team wants to identify the potential cross-sell or up-sell customers who may be interested in the glowing jigsaw puzzle series.

Research Question: Are the customers who have bought jigsaw puzzles, music boxes, motion models and dolls more likely to buy the glowing jigsaw puzzle?

Following that, they have built the **hypotheses** and the **model**:

H_1: Sales amount of jigsaw puzzles last year positively predicts the purchase of glowing jigsaw puzzles.

H_2: Sales amount of music boxes last year positively predicts the purchase of glowing jigsaw puzzles.

H_3: Sales amount of motion models last year positively predicts the purchase of glowing jigsaw puzzles.

H_4: Sales amount of dolls last year positively predicts the purchase of glowing jigsaw puzzles.

In our hypothesized model, we have sales amounts of jigsaw puzzles, music boxes, motion models, and dolls last year as the independent variables (IVs), and preorder sales buying status as the dependent variable (DV), as shown in Figure 4.14.

The marketing team has checked that the corresponding sales amounts represent the correct amounts for individual products of that customer last

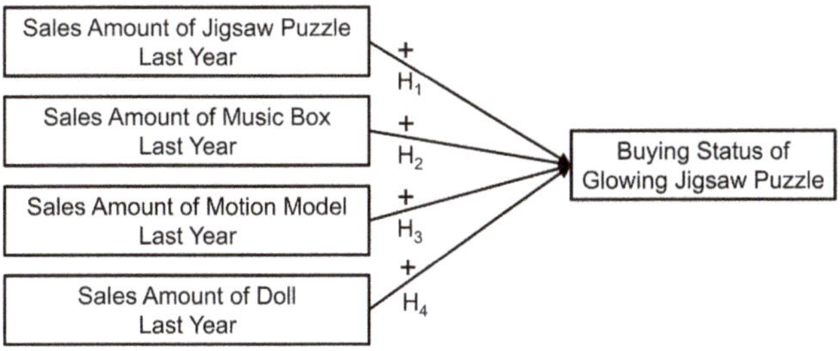

FIGURE 4.14
The Hypothesized Model for the Factors Predicting Which Customers Will Buy

year. The preorder sales status also correctly indicates whether that customer has bought the glowing jigsaw puzzles in the preorder sales. So, they pass **face validity**. As all these variables contain only one question, construct validity and reliability tests are not required.

In this hypothesized model, we are **finding factors predicting the buying status**, a categorical variable. It is categorical because it contains only the values 0 (i.e., not buy) and 1 (i.e., buy). So, we will use **logistic regression** (see Chapter 2).

Let us read the SPSS file "*Ch4_Marketing_Data.sav.*" This dataset contains data for Group A customers (who received the existing promotional email) and Group B customers (who received the new promotional email). In this test, we will use data for Group B customers, as the full-scale promotion will use the new promotional email. So, we first select the data where the variable Design_Group equals 2 (i.e., Group B). To do this in SPSS, go to *Data > Select Cases*. Choose *If condition is satisfied*. Click the *If* button. In the "Select Cases: If" pop-up dialog box, enter "Design_Group = 2" as the condition. Click *Continue*. Click *OK*. The result is shown in the "Data View." You can see that rows where Design_Group does not equal 2 are crossed out. There is also an additional variable named *filter_$*, where the value 1 means that row is selected, while 0 means that row is not selected. The steps and the result are in Figure 4.15.

To do this **logistic regression in SPSS** in the file "*Ch4_Marketing_Data.sav,*" go to *Analyze > Regression > Binary Logistic*. Select PreOrder_Buy (i.e., DV) as *Dependent*. Select Jigsaw_Sales, MusicBox_Sales, MotionModel_Sales and Doll_Sales (i.e., IVs) as *Covariates*. Click *OK*. The steps and the result are shown in Figure 4.16.

The result is in the output viewer. In the table "Omnibus Tests of Model Coefficients," it shows that the model is significant ($p < 0.05$). In the table "Model Summary," the Nagelkerke R Square = 0.652, indicating that the

File: *Ch4_Marketing_Data.sav*
Data > Select Cases

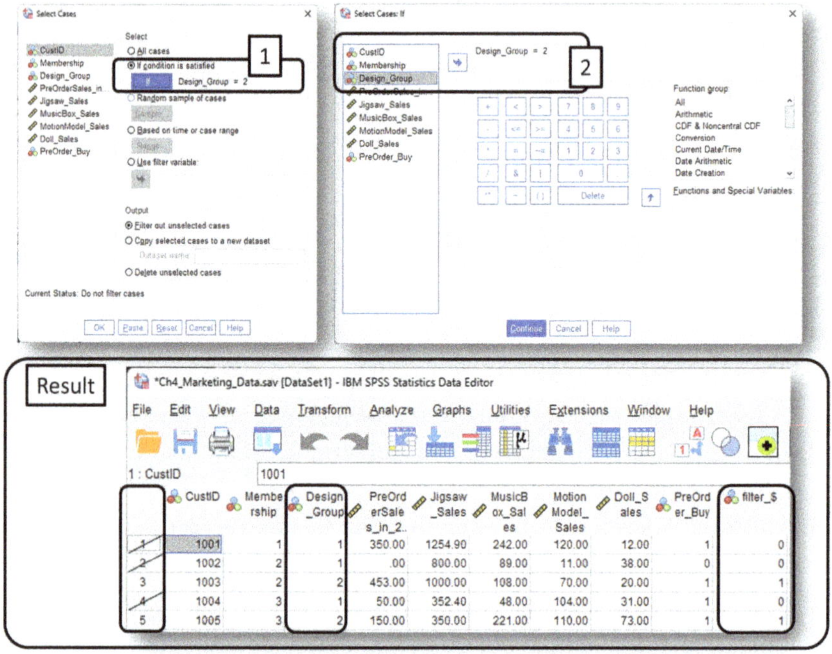

FIGURE 4.15
Select Cases in SPSS

independent variables account for 61.8% of the variance in the preorder buying status. In the table "Variables in the Equation," read columns Exp(B) and Sig. Identify those significant variables (i.e., Sig. < 0.05). We call Exp(B) the **odds ratio,** which represents the likelihood of an event occurring. Follow Equation 4–11 to interpret the meaning of the odds ratio:

$$Exp(B) = \frac{Probability\ of\ DV = 1}{Probability\ of\ DV = 0}\ when\ IV\ is\ 1\ unit\ higher \qquad (4\text{–}11)$$

The IV *Jigsaw_Sales* is significant ($p < 0.001$) and has an odds ratio of 1.003. Follow Equation 4–11 to interpret its meaning. The probability of buying (i.e., DV = 1) relative to the probability of not buying (i.e., DV = 0), when last year's jigsaw sales of that customer (i.e., IV) are 1 dollar higher instead of 1 dollar lower, is 1.003. A more interpretable way of saying this is that customers who spent 1 dollar more than those who spent 1 dollar less on jigsaw puzzles last year are 1.003 times more likely to buy the glowing jigsaw puzzle. So, H_1 is accepted.

File: *Ch4_Marketing_Data.sav*
Analyze > Regression > Binary Logistic

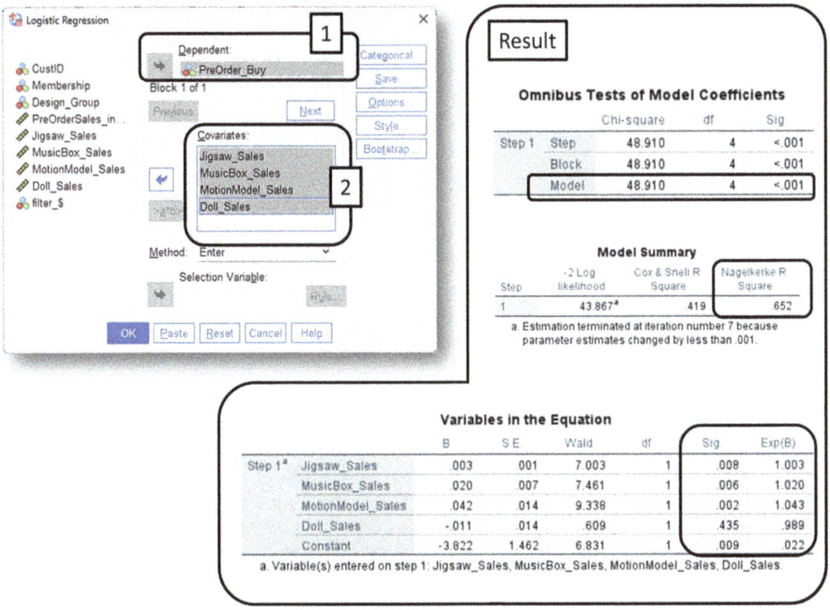

Omnibus Tests of Model Coefficients

		Chi-square	df	Sig
Step 1	Step	48.910	4	<.001
	Block	48.910	4	<.001
	Model	48.910	4	<.001

Model Summary

Step	-2 Log likelihood	Cox & Snell R Square	Nagelkerke R Square
1	43.867[a]	.419	.652

a. Estimation terminated at iteration number 7 because parameter estimates changed by less than .001.

Variables in the Equation

		B	S.E.	Wald	df	Sig.	Exp(B)
Step 1[a]	Jigsaw_Sales	.003	.001	7.003	1	.008	1.003
	MusicBox_Sales	.020	.007	7.461	1	.006	1.020
	MotionModel_Sales	.042	.014	9.338	1	.002	1.043
	Doll_Sales	-.011	.014	.609	1	.435	.989
	Constant	-3.822	1.462	6.831	1	.009	.022

a. Variable(s) entered on step 1: Jigsaw_Sales, MusicBox_Sales, MotionModel_Sales, Doll_Sales.

FIGURE 4.16
Logistic Regression in SPSS

The IV *MusicBox_Sales* is significant ($p < 0.001$) and has an odds ratio of 1.020. The IV *MotionModel_Sales* is significant ($p < 0.001$) and has an odds ratio of 1.043. So, H_2 and H_3 are accepted.

The IV *Doll_Sales* is insignificant ($p = 0.435$) and has an odds ratio of 0.022. So, H_4 is rejected. It indicates that customers who bought dolls last year are not predictor of buying the glowing jigsaw puzzle.

To do this **logistic regression in Excel**, open the file "*Ch4_Marketing_Data.xlsx.*" Go to the worksheet "2. Logistic Regression." Go to *Add-ins > Real Statistics > Data Analysis Tools.* In the pop-up dialog box, click the tab page *Reg,* click *Multinomial Logistic Regression,* and click *OK.* In the "Multinomial Logistic Regression" pop-up dialog box, select cells C1 to G91 (the values of the independent variables and the dependent variable, which must be in the last column) as the *Input Range.* Enter "4" in the field *# of Independent Variables.* Enter cell K1 as the *Output Range.* Click *OK.* In the result area, the table "R-square" shows that R-sq (N) = 0.652, meaning Nagelkerke R Square = 0.652, indicating that the independent variables account for 65.2% of the variance in the preorder buying status. In the table "Significance Test," p-value < 0.05, meaning the model is significant. (In Excel, when you see a number such

File: *Ch4_Marketing_Data.xlsx (Worksheet: 2. Logistic Regression)*
Add-ins > Real Statistics > Data Analysis Tools (Reg > Multinomial Logistic Regression)

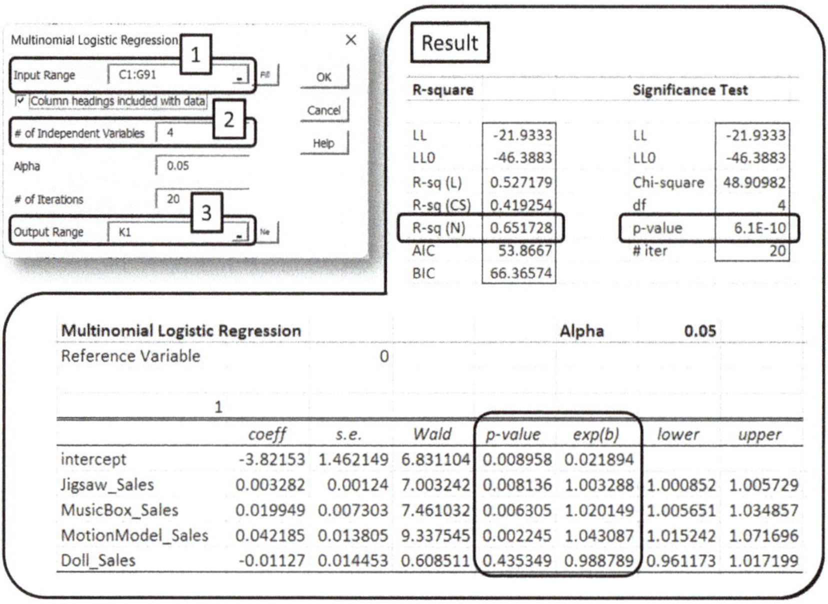

R-square	
LL	-21.9333
LL0	-46.3883
R-sq (L)	0.527179
R-sq (CS)	0.419254
R-sq (N)	0.651728
AIC	53.8667
BIC	66.36574

Significance Test	
LL	-21.9333
LL0	-46.3883
Chi-square	48.90982
df	4
p-value	6.1E-10
# iter	20

Multinomial Logistic Regression — Alpha 0.05
Reference Variable 0

1

	coeff	s.e.	Wald	p-value	exp(b)	lower	upper
intercept	-3.82153	1.462149	6.831104	0.008958	0.021894		
Jigsaw_Sales	0.003282	0.00124	7.003242	0.008136	1.003288	1.000852	1.005729
MusicBox_Sales	0.019949	0.007303	7.461032	0.006305	1.020149	1.005651	1.034857
MotionModel_Sales	0.042185	0.013805	9.337545	0.002245	1.043087	1.015242	1.071696
Doll_Sales	-0.01127	0.014453	0.608511	0.435349	0.988789	0.961173	1.017199

FIGURE 4.17
Logistic Regression in Excel

as 6.1E-010, it means 0.00000000061, which is smaller than 0.05.) Follow Equation 4–11 to interpret the results in the table "Reference Variable." The IV *Jigsaw_Sales* is significant ($p < 0.05$) and has an odds ratio of 1.003. The IV *MusicBox_Sales* is significant ($p < 0.05$) and has an odds ratio of 1.020. The IV *MotionModel_Sales* is significant ($p < 0.05$) and has an odds ratio of 1.043. So, H_1, H_2 and H_3 are accepted. The IV *Doll_Sales* is insignificant ($p = 0.435$) and has an odds ratio of 0.022. So, H_4 is rejected. The steps and the result are in Figure 4.17. The result details have already been discussed in the earlier paragraphs explaining the result using SPSS so I am not going to repeat them here.

The last step of an analytics process is to give actionable recommendations based on the statistical results. The marketing team makes use of these statistical insights to improve sales in both the physical and online shops. In the physical shops, information will be shown on the salespersons' screen indicating that a customer may be a potential buyer for the new glowing jigsaw puzzle if that customer bought jigsaw puzzles, motion models or music boxes last year. Thus, the salesperson can cross-sell or up-sell the glowing jigsaw puzzle. In the online shops, the glowing jigsaw puzzle will be suggested to customers on the first launching page if they bought jigsaw puzzles, motion models or music boxes last year. This is how data insights help provide a more personalized experience to the customers.

When it comes to the peak season in Q4 and full-scale promotional emails are sent to customers, the marketing team monitors the data in real time. These data can include real-time metrics on our dashboard, such as the conversion rate or the sales volume from the point-of-sale (POS) system. For example, unexpectedly low sales volume may indicate issues in the physical shop, such as stock not being displayed or technical issues in the online shop. If these issues are not solved in real-time, the sales during this period will be lost, perhaps to competitors.

The continuous advancement in technology helps companies provide more personalized service and hence a better shopping experience to the customers. Let us look at a real-world case study from **Tata AIA** on how they make use of technologies to improve their service.

4.10 CASE STUDY: TATA AIA IMPROVING CUSTOMER EXPERIENCE THROUGH TECHNOLOGIES

Tata AIA Life Insurance Company Limited (Tata AIA) is a joint venture between India-based Tata Sons Pvt. Ltd. and Hong Kong-based AIA Group Ltd., established in 2001. They initiated the digital customer-centric initiative in 2013, aiming to improve and automate most processes online in India. After this improvement, the customers do not need to submit physical documents anymore, and the customers can access information like policies via online platforms including the web portal, chatbots and interactive voice response system (IVRS). This strategic move has sustained the company's business as usual during the COVID-19 lockdown. The company has also applied predictive data analytics to identify which customers are more likely to pay their premium late and send reminders only to these customers without annoying punctual customers. They also applied analytics for customer profiling. The sales agents can make use of this profiling information via their mobile devices to sell customers the right products. These customer-focused and personalized services have largely improved the customer experience. They also make use of the Net Promoter Score (NPS) to understand the level of customer satisfaction. The company aims to continue driving more adoption of digital technologies in the way ahead (Siriguppi & Nair, 2021).

4.11 THE FUTURE OF MARKETING ANALYTICS

Marketers will need to make more use of marketing analytics to better personalize the way they promote services and products to customers. The advancement in data analytics and artificial intelligence (AI) will provide more applications of human-mimicking technologies and machines (Kotler et al., 2021). Imagine, in the future, machines with cameras and facial recognition functionalities can identify customers who walk into the shop, profile the customers via data analytics, suggest products for the customers via natural language processing (NLP) and generative AI capabilities, and get the physical products to the customers through their robotics functions. Machines will be a close coworker with marketers. These machine coworkers are built on big data with the logic from data analytics. Therefore, understanding data analytics will definitely be an essential skill for present and future marketers.

REFERENCES

Baehre, S., O'Dwyer, M., O'Malley, L., & Lee, N. (2021). The use of Net Promoter Score (NPS) to predict sales growth: insights from an empirical investigation. *Journal of the Academy of Marketing Science, 50*(1), 67–84.

Chevalier, S. (2024, March 28). *Live commerce sales in the U.S. 2022–2026.* Statista. https://www.statista.com/statistics/1276120/livestream-e-commerce-sales-united-states/

Farris, P. W., Bendle, N. T., Pfeifer, P. E., & Reibstein, D. J. (2006). *Marketing Metrics: 50+ Metrics Every Executive Should Master.* Wharton School Pub.

Gallo, A. (2017, June 28). *A refresher on A/B testing.* Harvard Business Review. https://hbr.org/2017/06/a-refresher-on-ab-testing

Kamakura, W. A. (2008). Cross-selling. *Journal of Relationship Marketing, 6*(3–4), 41–58.

Kohavi, R., & Thomke, S. (2017). The surprising power of online experiments. *Harvard Business Review, 95*(5), 74–82.

Kotler, P., Kartajaya, H., & Setiawan, I. (2021). *Marketing 5.0.* John Wiley & Sons.

Kotler, P., & Keller, K. L. (2016). *Marketing Management* (15th ed.). Pearson.

Ng, C. (2018, November 14). *Market segmentation – Nike case study.* LinkedIn. https://www.linkedin.com/pulse/market-segmentation-nike-case-study-chris-ng

Ou, X. (2024, April 5). *Market value of live commerce in China 2019–2026.* Statista. https://www.statista.com/statistics/1127635/china-market-size-of-live-commerce/

Reichheld, F. F. (2003). The one number you need to grow. *Harvard Business Review, 81*(12), 46–124.

Schubert, E. (2023). Stop using the elbow criterion for k-means and how to choose the number of clusters instead. *ACM SIGKDD Explorations Newsletter, 25*(1), 36–42.

Siriguppi, D., & Nair, J. (2021). TATA AIA Life leverages digital technologies to create a superior customer experience. *ICFAI Journal of Marketing Management, 20*(4), 400–411.

Syakur, M. A., Khotimah, B. K., Rochman, E. M. S., & Satoto, B. D. (2018). Integration k-means clustering method and elbow method for identification of the best customer profile cluster. *IOP Conference Series: Materials Science and Engineering, 336.*

Ullal, M. S., & Hawaldar, I. T. (2018). Influence of advertisement on customers based on AIDA model. *Problems and Prospective in Management, 16*(4), 285–298.

Venkatesan, R., Farris, P. W., & Wilcox, R. T. (2015). *Cutting-edge Marketing Analytics: Real World Cases and Data Sets for Hands on Learning.* Pearson Education.

5

Data Analytics in Supply Chain

5.1 AN INTRODUCTION TO DATA ANALYTICS IN SUPPLY CHAIN

Supply chain covers the planning and management of activities in the supply and demand cycles within and across companies. These activities include the management of the **flow of products, money and information**. If the process is done right, it can improve customer satisfaction, increase company profit and thus sustain the business growth.

In this supply chain process, supply chain professionals manage the flow of products, money and information through the **Supply Chain Operations Reference (SCOR) model** (Association for Supply Chain Management, 2022; Nguyen, 2024). The SCOR model is one of the most popular supply chain frameworks which supply chain professionals follow to manage the process of **planning** the supply chain processes, **sourcing** the suitable suppliers, **transforming** resources into products and services, ensuring smooth **ordering** by customers, **fulfilling** orders, and facilitating **returning** of products if needed. This model is pictured as two infinity loops illustrating the **orchestration** of business strategies, technologies, and human resources. To help this process to be done right, most companies capture the data in this process in Enterprise Resource Planning (ERP) systems. With the right data, data analytics can provide insights for better decision-making (Bowers et al., 2017). Companies like Coca-Cola Refreshment USA Inc. and Hanesbrands Inc. (an American multinational clothing company) apply analytics models to predict sales demands, prescribe available alternatives to address demands, as well as to mitigate the costs. These definitely bring business advantages to grasp better opportunities than their counterparts who make decisions just by intuitions.

This chapter will cover the most popular metrics, hands-on data analytics and case studies in supply chain management. By using the hypothetical data in our Best Toy Company, along with real-world case studies, we will

DOI: 10.1201/9781032642307-5

go through some practical scenarios on how data analytics can be applied in forecasting demands, minimizing costs, predicting delays and prescribing solutions. The future trends will also be discussed.

5.2 METRICS

Metrics are indicators which give the supply chain professionals a quick overview of the supply chain performance in an organization. Some popular supply chain metrics are **perfect order rate**, **order fulfillment cycle time**, **cash-to-cash (C2C) cycle time**, **upside supply chain flexibility,** and **cost per order (CPO)**. Let us go through them one by one.

Perfect order rate measures the percentage of orders that are delivered on time, complete, and without any damage, as shown in Equation 5–1. Different organizations may define their perfect orders differently. In general, the elements in defining a perfect order include order accuracy and efficiency, first-attempt completion, and customer satisfaction. Organizations with a high perfect order rate consistently perform better and have higher profit margins (Stock & Manrodt, 2020).

$$Perfect\ Order\ Rate = \frac{Number\ of\ Perfect\ Orders}{Total\ Number\ of\ Orders} \times 100\% \qquad (5\text{–}1)$$

When companies want to analyze how to improve its perfect order rate, they may first look into the customer feedback and satisfaction rate after the order delivery. They may also analyze the order accuracy and the order fulfillment cycle time.

Order fulfillment cycle time refers to the time taken from the receipt of an order to its delivery, as shown in Equation 5–2 (Hult et al., 2002). It reflects the efficiency of the flow of the product in the order delivery process. Obviously, the order fulfillment processes in different business services may differ. For example, an order from an online shop may involve arranging the products from a warehouse with packaging, via freight movement, and then delivery to the customers. On the other hand, an order from a courier service may involve picking up the package, sorting it, and transporting it to the destination. By further analyzing the detailed steps in the process by **supply chain mapping** (which I will introduce later in this chapter), organizations can identify bottlenecks in their order fulfillment process. These bottlenecks may be due to the delays in the flow of products, information or money.

$$\textit{Order Fulfillment Cycle Time} = \textit{Delivery Date} - \textit{Order Received Date} \quad (5\text{–}2)$$

Cash-to-cash (C2C) cycle time measures the efficiency of the supply chain in managing working capital and cash flow (Randall & Farris, 2009). This metric is associated with three variables, namely days of inventory (DOI), days of receivables (DOR) and days of payables (DOP). **Days of inventory (DOI)** is the average number of days the inventory is held before it is sold. **Days of receivables (DOR)** is the average number of days the payment is collected after a sale. **Days of payables (DOP)** is the average number of days to pay the suppliers. C2C cycle time is calculated by adding DOI and DOR, with DOP subtracted, as shown in Equation 5–3. The shorter the C2C cycle time indicates the more efficient the company is converting its investment into cash. From the equation, you can see that the shorter the time the inventory is in the warehouse, the faster the customers pay, and the longer the time to pay the supplier, the more the C2C cycle time will be reduced.

$$\textit{C2C Cycle Time} = \textit{DOI} + \textit{DOR} - \textit{DOP} \quad (5\text{–}3)$$

Upside supply chain flexibility measures how quickly the supply chain can adapt to an unplanned 20% increase in demand while maintaining service levels, as shown in Equation 5–4 (Association for Supply Chain Management, 2022). To calculate the number of days for the supply chain to adapt to a sudden increase in demand, it depends on a number of constraints, including manufacturing capacity (whether the machines are operating at their full potential), material availability (i.e., calculating the total lead time to build and deliver the components in the bills of materials (BOM)), and direct labor availability.

$$\textit{Upside Supply Chain Flexibility} = \textit{Time to Achieve 20\% Increase Unplanned Orders} \quad (5\text{–}4)$$

Cost per order (CPO) calculates the total cost involved in fulfilling an order, as shown in Equation 5–5. The types of costs included differ from industry to industry. In general, they cover direct and indirect costs, like raw material costs, labor costs, research and development costs, marketing costs, packaging costs, transportation costs, utility costs, insurance costs and management overhead costs (Stock & Manrodt, 2020).

$$CPO = \frac{Total\ Costs\ Incurred}{Total\ Number\ of\ Orders} \tag{5–5}$$

Supply chain management is a practice about accuracy and efficiency, not only within the company but also across companies of the suppliers. Different metrics help to identify opportunities (e.g., a reduction in cost per order) or risks (e.g., a decrease in perfect order rate), which may alert the company to act at the right time for getting business advantages or avoiding losses. **Deere & Company** has demonstrated a typical example of using metrics to optimize their supply chain, extending to improving suppliers' efficiency. Let us go through this case study together.

5.3 CASE STUDY: DEERE & COMPANY'S INSIGHTS FROM METRICS

Deere & Company, founded in 1837, is an American corporation that manufactures agricultural machinery. It also provides financial services and other related activities. Deere remains one of the top companies in the Fortune 500 list of the largest United States corporations, after operating for almost two centuries. Continuous improvements in its supply chain management definitely contribute to its success (Nelson, 2002). In 1996, Deere's leaders recognized that the costs from their suppliers made up to 70% of the total costs. By the good use of metrics, Deere was able to reduce $400 million in their purchase costs during 1996 and 2001. Let us see how they did it by improving the flow of products, costs and information.

After Deere had streamlined their internal costs, they found that 70% of its costs came from the suppliers. This big percentage implies that a big portion of their supply chain process was, in fact, extended to their suppliers' factory floor. If the suppliers are not as efficient as they could be, the cost and inefficiency simply transfer to Deere. Therefore, they started a project to understand their suppliers' supply chain efficiency.

One case was about a tillage equipment supplier with $6 million in sales per year to Deere (which was half of Deere's revenue) having difficulty with on-time delivery. Their problem transferred to Deere. Deere missed to fulfill three dealer's orders. In 1997, Deere spent 2 days in **supply chain mapping** (which is a useful tool to visualize a supply chain process) with this supplier and discovered the problem in its non-value-added job processes and the lack of parts tracking. With improvements in these areas, the supplier improved their on-time delivery up to 96.5% and tracked its most profitable year in the past decade at that time. Deere has performed these improvement processes with its different suppliers. Deere invested $7 million in such supplier development in the **flow of products** and, in return, saved $22 million.

Deere monitors the cost of the products starting from the design phase, not only within the company but also with its suppliers. Deere requires the suppliers to provide a detailed cost analysis for every part they quote. By monitoring the **flow of costs**, Deere aims to delight customers at the lowest cost starting from its design.

Deere has also made improvements in removing process redundancies between companies by supplier integration. They have employed the SAP business-to-business applications and provided suppliers with web-based access for immediate corrective attention in post-sales customer support. This improvement in the **flow of information** provides feedback from customers not only to Deere but also to its suppliers for better products.

Deere's case study demonstrates how a supply chain can be managed across companies. It requires cooperation and trust. You may imagine that if Deere's leaders did not have the metric of cost distribution in the first place, all these improvements may not have been possible.

Metrics can provide insights into the upstream of the supply chain, like suppliers' raw material as shown in Deere's case study. Metrics can also offer predictive information in the downstream of the supply chain like the appropriate number of units of products to be distributed to retail stores. In the coming section, I will use the data from our hypothetical company, Best Toy Company, to show a supply chain dashboard in Excel, with a line chart using data from a pivot table to show the trend of product units sold in different retail stores across years. For those Excel dashboard functions discussed in Chapters 3 and 4, I am not going to repeat them here. Interested readers may refer to the dashboard section in the previous chapters.

5.4 DASHBOARD

Now, let us use the data from our hypothetical Best Toy Company to demonstrate a supply chain dashboard. The company is going to promote a new series of jigsaw puzzle in the coming holiday season. The marketing team

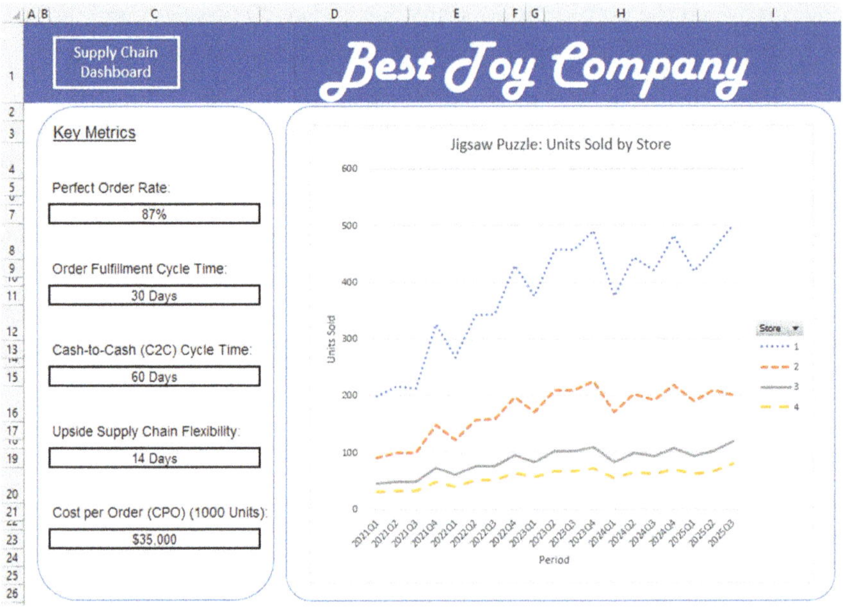

FIGURE 5.1
A Supply Chain Dashboard about Trends of Units of Jigsaw Puzzle Sold by Store

has predicted that the number of units sold in that period will be 1,000. The supply chain team looks at the supply chain dashboard to decide the number of units to be distributed to each of their four retail stores. This dashboard shows the key metrics and the trends of units of jigsaw puzzle sold by each store over the past 5 years, as shown in Figure 5.1.

The left-hand side of the dashboard shows the hypothetical data for the key supply chain metrics, including the perfect order rate, order fulfillment cycle time, cash-to-cash (C2C) cycle time, upside supply chain flexibility and cost per order (1,000 units). These figures are usually kept in the supply chain management system. Our focus here is to build the line chart on the right-hand side of this **dashboard in Excel**. Open the file "*Ch5_Supply_Chain_Dashboard.xlsx*." Go to worksheet "Data." This worksheet contains four columns: product category, period, store and units sold. We are going to use these data to prepare the dashboard with four data lines, each representing the trend of a store's units of jigsaw puzzle sold in the past 5 years. Go to the worksheet "Dashboard." The dashboard is already prepared. For demonstration purposes, only one product category, jigsaw, is included in the dataset. As indicated in the legend, the dotted line represents Store 1, the dashed line represents Store 2, the solid line represents Store 3 and the long-dash line represents Store 4. You may observe that the number of units

File: *Ch5_Supply_Chain_Dashboard.xlsx (Worksheet: Data)*
Insert > PivotChart

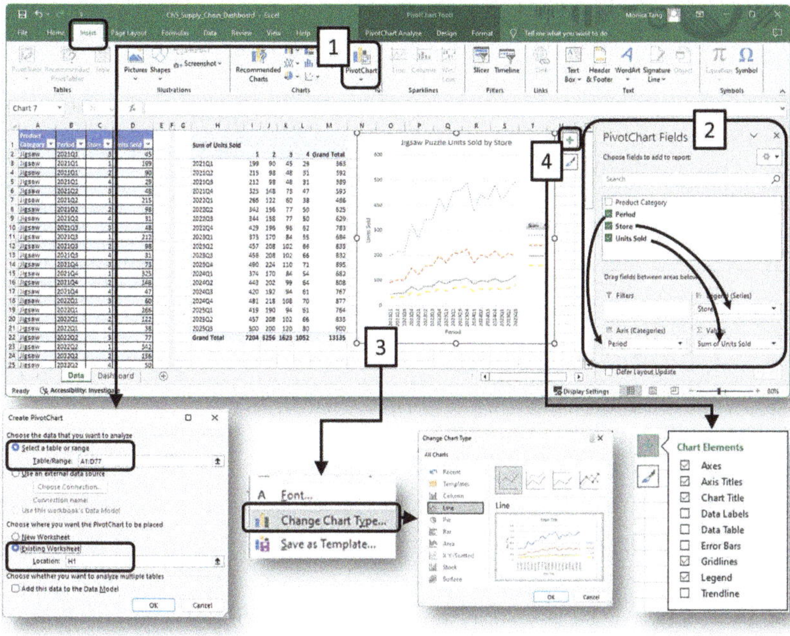

FIGURE 5.2
A Supply Chain Dashboard: Add a PivotChart in Excel

sold in Store 1 is almost double that in Store 2 consistently. While Store 2 usually sold almost double what Store 3 sold, and Store 3 sold slightly more than Store 4. If you want to try building this line chart, please follow the steps in the next paragraph.

To prepare this **line chart of trends of units of jigsaw puzzle sold by store in Excel**, open the file "*Ch5_Supply_Chain_Dashboard.xlsx.*" Go to worksheet "Data." This worksheet contains columns A to D: *Product Category*, *Period*, *Store* and *Units Sold*. Follow the numbers in Figure 5.2, which highlight the steps in the following text. Go to *Insert > PivotChart*. In the pop-up dialog box "Create PivotChart," select cells A1 to D77 as *Table/Range*. Enter H1 as *Location* in the *Existing Worksheet* to tell Excel to show the pivot table starting from cell H1. Click *OK*. In the "PivotTable Fields" area, drag *Period* to *Axis (Categories)*, *Store* to *Legend (Series)*, and *Units Sold* to *Values*. You will have the pivot table and the pivot chart shown. Right-click on the chart. Click *Change Chart Type*. In the "Change Chart Type" dialog box, click *Line* and then *OK*. Click the chart and click the button *Chart Element* (i.e., the green "+" button on the top right-hand corner of the chart). Tick the

TABLE 5.1

Transportation Cost per Unit of the Products

	Transportation Cost per Unit	
Store	**DC 1**	**DC 2**
Store 1	$6	$9
Store 2	$7	$12
Store 3	$6	$8
Store 4	$9	$10

checkbox for *Axes, Axis Title, Chart Title, Gridlines* and *Legend.* Update the titles accordingly, and you will have the chart ready.

Visualizing the trends of units of jigsaw puzzle sold being consistent in similar proportions for the four stores over the past 5 years, the supply chain team decides to allocate the 1,000 units of jigsaw puzzle to the stores according to the previous year's proportions (which was found to be the appropriate quantity in the past years): 55% to Store 1, 22% to Store 2, 13% to Store 3, and 10% Store 4.

The products will be transported from two distribution centers (DCs) to these four stores. DC 1 can store 550 units of jigsaw puzzle, while DC 2 can store 500 units. The costs of transporting each unit of the products from the distribution centers to the stores are different, as shown in Table 5.1.

The supply chain team wants to minimize the transportation costs, like many other companies do. Do you know how to do this? Let us gain insight from a case study of **DHL** to see how they plan their transportation network, minimizing the costs while satisfying other constraints.

5.5 CASE STUDY: DHL (HONG KONG)'S TRANSPORTATION NETWORK PLANNING

DHL, founded in the United States in 1969, is an international logistics company providing courier, package delivery and express mail services. Its major markets are in Europe and the Asia-Pacific (AP) region. Hong Kong (HK) is one of their largest service subregions (Cheung et al., 2001).

In 1998, the Hong Kong International Airport was relocated from the center of the city to Chek Lap Kok on Lantau Island, which is much farther from the city. The increase in size of the new airport brought opportunities to DHL (HK), but its remote location also brought challenges. Air-express market operates under highly competitive industry standards: overnight service within the AP region, next-day service to Europe and North America, money-back guarantees in case of delivery failure and, of course, at a competitive price. A more remote airport shortens the window of processing time after the package pickup cutoff time at 5:15 p.m. After this cutoff time, the packages are picked up from these "demand zones," which are mostly in the city where most offices are located. These packages are then transported to "depots" for consolidation and delivery to the corresponding service centers. "Service centers" handle all major processing, including labeling, X-ray screening, reweighting, sorting, document and formality follow-up and transferring to the appropriate aircraft at the airport. The airport relocation requires this process from pickup to delivery at the airport more effectively in this a-few-hour processing window. The transportation network was restudied to fulfill these requirements.

A later pickup cutoff time and wider demand zones (i.e., service coverage) will definitely be an advantage for better business. Yet it risks missing some successful deliveries (i.e., reliability). To find out the possible best network solutions that balance service coverage and reliability, a framework with **objectives** and **constraints** was defined. The key objective was minimizing the fixed costs and variable costs. There were 820 constraints collected such that the processing time must be within the time window. **Linear programming** was applied with model simulation. The senior management of DHL (HK) found the analysis both scientific and practical. Before this, they could only make decisions based on intuition. With this information, they can decide on a solution that balances the relationships among service coverage, reliability, and costs.

Although this case study does not disclose the detailed results to protect the information at DHL (HK), the method employed is enlightening and can be applied to different supply chain problems, including the minimizing transportation cost problem in our Best Toy Company.

5.6 MINIMIZING TRANSPORTATION COST – AN EXAMPLE OF LINEAR PROGRAMMING

In our example in Best Toy Company, the supply chain team wants to minimize transportation costs to deliver the 1,000 units of products from the two DCs to the four retail stores according to the units required. DC 1 has 550 units of jigsaw puzzles, while DC 2 has 500 units. Store 1 requires 550 units,

Store 2 requires 220, Store 3 requires 130 and Store 4 requires 100. The costs of transporting each unit of the products from the distribution centers to the stores are different, as shown in Table 5.1.

We can apply **linear programming** with **Excel Solver** to find the solution (Robertson, 2021). First, we list our objective and constraints.

Objective: Minimize total transportation cost
Constraints: (1) The defined number of units is delivered to the stores.
(2) The DCs have enough inventory for delivery.

Second, we input the information we have in Excel. Open the file "*Ch5_Supply_Chain_Data.xlsx.*" Go to worksheet "Linear Programming." This worksheet contains four parts of information: transport cost per unit, units needed per store, warehouse inventory, and total transportation cost. The information is placed in Excel, as shown in Figure 5.3. The following text describes the detail.

The part "Transportation Cost per Unit" shows the cost of transporting each unit from a DC to a store (i.e., the data in Table 5.1).

File: *Ch5_Supply_Chain_Data.xlsx (Worksheet: Linear Programming)*
Data > Solver

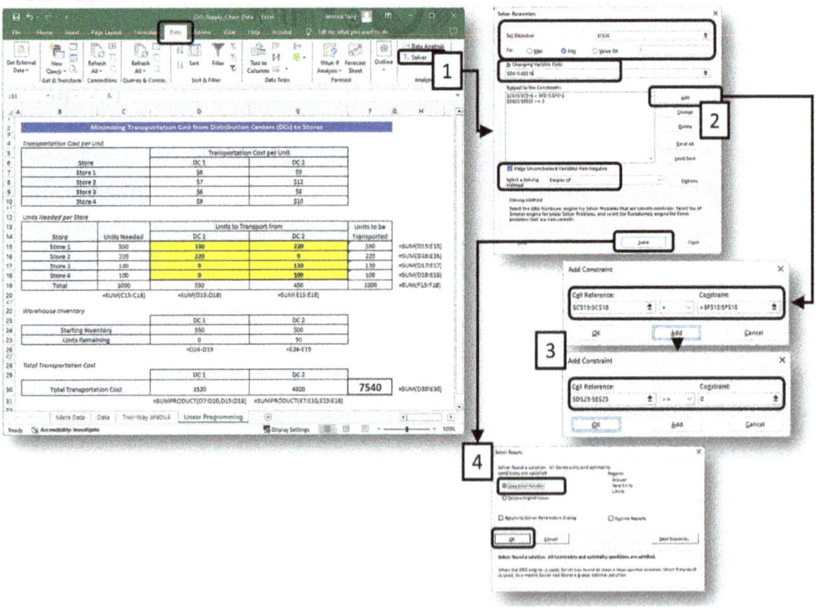

FIGURE 5.3
Minimizing Transportation Cost by Solver in Excel

The part "Units Needed per Store" shows the units to be delivered to each store. The highlighted cells with numbers (i.e., cells D15 to E18) are to be calculated by Solver. Solver will need to know the total units transported from each DC, and the total transported units from all DCs should be 1,000. Therefore, we put the summation formulas in cells F15 to F18 for the units transported to each store, with cell F19 showing the grand total. We also put the summation formulas in cells C19 to E19 for the total units needed for all the stores and the total units transported from each DC. The summation formulas are shown in Figure 5.3, next to or below the corresponding cells.

The part "Warehouse Inventory" shows the starting inventory for each DC. The units transported should not be more than the inventory that each DC has. Later, we will add this constraint to Solver. We calculate the units remaining after delivery in cells D25 and D26. The formulas are shown in Figure 5.3, below the corresponding cells.

The part "Total Transportation Cost" shows the total transportation costs for each DC (cells D30 and E30) and their total cost (F30). The Excel formulas are shown in Figure 5.3, next to or below the corresponding cells.

Having the data and formulas prepared, we are ready to use Solver to calculate the units to be transported from each DC to each store (i.e., cells D15 to E18, the highlighted cells with numbers).

To run Solver, go to *Data* > *Solver*. Follow the numbers in Figure 5.3. In the pop-up dialog box "Solver Parameters," select cell F30 (i.e., the total transportation cost) as the *Set Objective*. Choose *Min* because we aim to find the minimum total transportation cost. Enter D15:E18 (i.e., the units to be transported from each DC to each store) as the *By Changing Variable Cells*. Tick the checkbox *Make Unconstrained Variables Non-Negative*. Choose "Simplex LP" in *Select a Solving Method*. Enter the first constraint that the total units transported to the stores should be the same as the units needed by each store. Click *Add*. In the pop-up dialog box "Add Constraint," select cells C15:C18 as *Cell Reference*, choose the "=" sign, and select cells F15:F18 as *Constraint*. Enter the second constraint. After transporting the units, the number of remaining units in the DCs must be bigger than 0. Click *Add*. In the pop-up dialog box "Add Constraint," select cells D25:E25 as *Cell Reference*, choose the ">=" sign, and enter "0" as *Constraint*. Click *OK*. Click *Solve*. In the pop-up dialog box "Solver Results," choose *Keep Solver Solution* and click *OK*. You will find the number of units to be transported in cells D15 to E18, as highlighted in Table 5.2. Solver finds the minimum total transportation cost, which is $7,540.

TABLE 5.2

Solver Result of Units Transported for Each DC to Each Store for Minimizing the Total Transportation Cost

Store	Units Needed	Units to Transport from		Units to be Transported
		DC 1	DC 2	
Store 1	550	**330**	**220**	550
Store 2	220	**220**	**0**	220
Store 3	130	**0**	**130**	130
Store 4	100	**0**	**100**	100
Total	1,000	550	450	1,000

Apart from determining the appropriate number of units to be transported and lowering costs, on-time delivery is another key factor for success in the supply chain. Let us read the case study of **Kamaths Ourtimes Ice Creams Pvt. Ltd (KOI)** about their considerations regarding delivery delays.

5.7 CASE STUDY: KAMATHS OURTIMES ICE CREAMS' DELAY ISSUES

Natural Ice Cream is an Indian ice cream brand owned by Kamaths Ourtimes Icecreams Pvt. Ltd. (KOI). It was founded by R.S. Kamath in 1984, with the first store in Mumbai. KOI distinguishes itself by using natural fruit flavors (without artificial ones) in its products, which are welcomed by the customers (Dhaigude et al., 2018).

KOI runs its business in over 100 stores, with a mix of about 5% company-owned stores and the rest franchised. It has one manufacturing unit located in Mumbai, transporting ice cream via rail to retailers outside Mumbai and via trucks to retailers in the city.

In 2017, the company was at a point where the management saw an opportunity but also a risk. The demand grew steadily, indicating that the company should expand its production capacity. On the other hand, various delays in order fulfillment were observed. Girish Pai, Director of Operations at that time, had to decide whether to expand or fix the delay issues first. His gut feeling was that delays required immediate attention, or they would adversely affect the expansion and fail to support the increased capacity. However, if the delays were only isolated incidents and happened by chance, fixing the delay issues now would miss the expansion opportunity.

If you were Pai, how would you decide?

Making decisions without data-driven evidence is hard. In fact, we can use data analytics to find statistical support to determine whether the timing of delays on some routes is significantly higher than on others.

Now, let us use data from our Best Toy Company to demonstrate how to identify if some routes have significantly longer delays.

5.8 FINDING ROUTES WITH SIGNIFICANTLY LONGER DELAYS – AN EXAMPLE OF TWO-WAY ANOVA

In Best Toy Company, as we have mentioned in the previous section, products are transported from the two distribution centers (DCs) to the four retail stores. The company records the product-sending DC, the receiving store, the expected delivery time and the actual delivery time in minutes for every order. Such that, they can calculate the delay time in minutes. By collecting these data, the company can identify if significant delays occur in a specific DC, a specific store or a combination of both (i.e., a specific route) using the **five-step data analytics process** (see Chapter 2).

Business Problem: The supply chain team would like to identify if significant longer delays occur in a specific DC, a specific store or a combination of both (i.e., a specific route).

Research Question: Does a specific DC, a specific store or a combination of both (i.e., a specific route) have significant delays compared to others?

The supply chain team has built the **hypotheses** and the **model** (Figure 5.4):

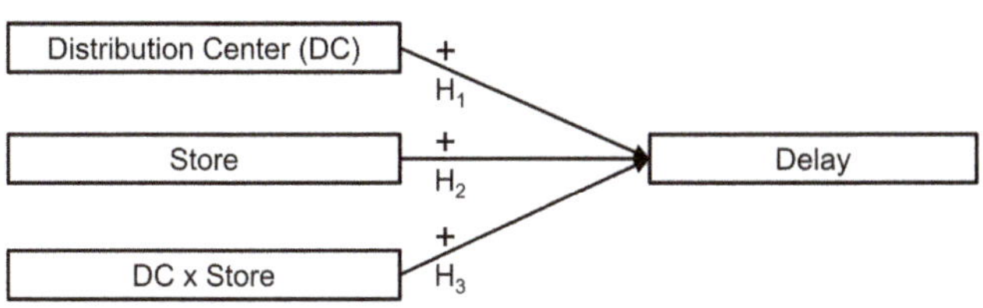

FIGURE 5.4
The Hypothesized Model for the Two Factors (DCs and Stores) Influencing Delays

H_1: Different DCs significantly influence delays differently.
H_2: Different stores significantly influence delays differently.
H_3: Different combinations of DCs and stores significantly influence delays differently.
H_0: There is no significant difference in delays in DCs, or stores, or a combination of both.

Look at the data in the SPSS file "*Ch5_Supply_Chain_Data.sav*" and the Excel file "*Ch5_Supply_Chain_Data.*" The variable *DC* is the DC number, including 1 and 2, while the variable *Store* is the store number, ranging from 1 to 4. The variable *TimeDelayed* is the time delayed in minutes. If the actual delivery time is shorter than the expected delivery time, this value is 0.

The supply chain team has checked that the variables represent the correct meanings. So, it passes the **face validity**. As it contains only one question for all the variables, construct validity and reliability tests are not required.

In our hypotheses, there are two factors, DCs and stores, that potentially influence the delay time. Therefore, the statistical test two-way ANOVA will compare whether the differences in the mean values of the delays among the DCs, stores and their combinations are significant (see Chapter 2).

To do **two-way ANOVA in SPSS**, open the file "*Ch5_Supply_Chain_Data.sav.*" The following steps are also shown in Figure 5.5. Go to *Analyze > General Linear Model > Univariate.* In the "Univariate" pop-up dialog box, select TimeDelayed as *Dependent Variable* and DC and Store as the *Fixed Factor(s).* Click *Plots.* In the "Univariate: Profile Plots" pop-up dialog box, drag DC to the *Horizontal Axis* and click *Add* to add the DC plot. Drag Store to *Horizontal Axis,* click *Add* to add the Store plot. Drag DC to *Horizontal Axis,* drag Store to *Separate lines,* click *Add* to add the DC*Store plot. Click *Continue.* Back in the "Univariable" pop-up dialog box, click *Post Hoc.* In the pop-up dialog box "Univariate: Post Hoc Multiple Comparisons for Observed Means," drag Store to *Post Hoc Test for* (DC is not required here because there are only two DCs). Tick *R-E-G-W-Q* for *Equal Variances Assumed.* Click *Continue.* Back in the "Univariable" pop-up dialog box, click *EM Means.* Drag (OVERALL), DC, Store and DC*Store to *Display Means for.* Tick *Compare simple main effects.* Choose Bonferroni for *Confidence interval adjustment.* Click *Continue.* Back in the "Univariable" pop-up dialog box, click *Options.* In the pop-up dialog box "Univariate: Options," tick *Descriptive statistics, Homogeneity tests* and *Estimates of effect size.* Click *Continue.* Click *OK.*

The result is in the output viewer. The results are shown in Figure 5.6. In the table "Descriptive Statistics," the mean value of time delayed for the combination of DC 2 and Store 3 is the highest: 20.44 minutes. The mean value of time

File: *Ch5_Supply_Chain_Data.sav*
Analyze > General Linear Model > Univariate

FIGURE 5.5
Two-Way ANOVA in SPSS (Steps)

delayed for the other combinations is between 3 and 6 minutes. The "Levene's Test of Equality of Error Variances" table shows that the time delayed "Based on Mean" is significant (p = 0.022). So, H_0 is rejected. In the "Test of Between-Subjects Effects" table, DC is not significant (p = 0.676), which means there is no significant influence of DC on the time delayed. So, H_1 is not supported. Store is significant (p = 0.011) with Partial Eta Squared equal to 0.114, meaning 11.4% of the variance in time delay can be accounted for by Store. So, H_2 is supported. The interactive effect of DC and Store (DC*Store) is significant (p = 0.039) with Partial Eta Squared equal to 0.086, meaning 8.6% of the variance in time delay can be explained by the interactive effect of DC and Store. So, H_3 is supported. Since Store is significant, we will look at the table "Pairwise Comparisons" for Store to find out the comparison of the time delayed for different stores. It shows that Store 3 has a significant 8.851 minutes more delayed time than Store 1 (p = 0.027) and a significant 8.893 minutes more delayed time than Store 2 (p = 0.030). But there is no significant difference in the delayed time when compared with Store 4. To read the result graphically, we can look at the graph "Estimated Marginal Means of Time Delayed (in minutes)." It shows that the combination of DC2 and Store 3 has the most time delayed, which aligns with the statistical results we have analyzed above.

File: *Ch5_Supply_Chain_Data.sav*
Analyze > General Linear Model > Univariate

Result

Descriptive Statistics

Dependent Variable: TimeDelayed

DC	Store	Mean	Std. Deviation	N
1 DC 1	1 Store 1	9.56	12.431	9
	2 Store 2	8.47	11.091	17
	3 Store 3	10.44	9.528	9
	4 Store 4	9.53	11.173	15
	Total	9.34	10.789	50
2 DC 2	1 Store 1	3.62	5.005	16
	2 Store 2	4.63	9.956	8
	3 Store 3	20.44	12.863	16
	4 Store 4	5.70	8.138	10
	Total	9.58	11.908	50
Total	1 Store 1	5.76	8.695	25
	2 Store 2	7.24	10.690	25
	3 Store 3	16.84	12.555	25
	4 Store 4	8.00	10.066	25
	Total	9.46	11.305	100

Pairwise Comparisons

Dependent Variable: TimeDelayed

(I) Store	(J) Store	Mean Difference (I-J)	Std. Error	Sig.[b]	95% Confidence Interval for Difference[b] Lower Bound	Upper Bound
1 Store 1	2 Store 2	.042	3.089	1.000	-8.288	8.373
	3 Store 3	-8.851*	3.045	.027	-17.061	-.640
	4 Store 4	-1.026	3.014	1.000	-9.154	7.102
2 Store 2	1 Store 1	-.042	3.089	1.000	-8.373	8.288
	3 Store 3	-8.893*	3.089	.030	-17.224	-.563
	4 Store 4	-1.069	3.059	1.000	-9.318	7.180
3 Store 3	1 Store 1	8.851*	3.045	.027	.640	17.061
	2 Store 2	8.893*	3.089	.030	.563	17.224
	4 Store 4	7.824	3.014	.066	-.304	15.952
4 Store 4	1 Store 1	1.026	3.014	1.000	-7.102	9.154
	2 Store 2	1.069	3.059	1.000	-7.180	9.318
	3 Store 3	-7.824	3.014	.066	-15.952	.304

Based on estimated marginal means

* The mean difference is significant at the .05 level.

b. Adjustment for multiple comparisons: Bonferroni.

Levene's Test of Equality of Error Variances[a,b]

		Levene Statistic	df1	df2	Sig.
TimeDelayed	Based on Mean	2.495	7	92	.022
	Based on Median	.979	7	92	.452
	Based on Median and with adjusted df	.979	7	74.339	.453
	Based on trimmed mean	2.333	7	92	.031

Tests the null hypothesis that the error variance of the dependent variable is equal across groups.

a. Dependent variable: TimeDelayed

b. Design: Intercept + DC + Store + DC * Store

Tests of Between-Subjects Effects

Dependent Variable: TimeDelayed

Source	Type III Sum of Squares	df	Mean Square	F	Sig.	Partial Eta Squared
Corrected Model	2826.764[a]	7	403.823	3.781	.001	.223
Intercept	7511.000	1	7511.000	70.324	<.001	.433
DC	18.745	1	18.745	.176	.676	.002
Store	1265.970	3	421.990	3.951	.011	.114
DC * Store	928.065	3	309.355	2.896	.039	.086
Error	9826.076	92	106.805			
Total	21602.000	100				
Corrected Total	12652.840	99				

a. R Squared = .223 (Adjusted R Squared = .164)

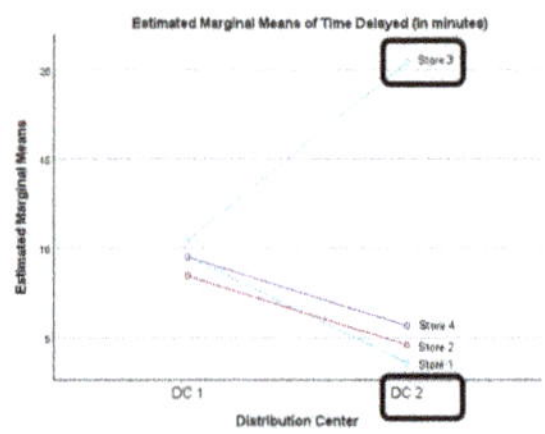

FIGURE 5.6
Two-Way ANOVA in SPSS (Results)

To do **two-way ANOVA in Excel**, open the file "*Ch5_Supply_Chain_Data.xlsx.*" Go to worksheet "Two-Way ANOVA." Columns B to D contain the variables *DC, Store* and *TimeDelayed.* The steps and results are in Figure 5.7. Go to *Add-ins > Real Statistics > Data Analysis Tools.* In the pop-up dialog box, click the tab page *Anova* and then click *Two Factor Anova* and *OK.* In the "Two Factor Anova" pop-up dialog box, select cells B1 to D101 as the *Input Range.* When we later interpret the result, column B (i.e., DC) means "Rows" in the result, while column C (i.e., Store) means "Columns." Click the radio-button *Standard format.* Choose *ANOVA – Regression* as the *Analysis Type.* Input H1 as *Output Range.* In the result, in the table "Descriptive Statistics," the mean value of the combination of DC 2 and Store 3 is the highest (i.e., 20.4375 minutes). In the "ANOVA" table, it shows that rows (i.e., DC) are not significant (p = 0.676), which means there is no significant influence on the time delayed by DC. So, H_1 is not supported. Columns (i.e., Store) are significant (p = 0.011). So, H_2 is supported. The interactive effect of DC and Store (DC*Store) is significant (p = 0.039). So, H_3 is supported.

The supply chain team now knows that the route of delivery from DC 2 to Store 3 has significant delays with a mean time of around 20 minutes, while

File: *Ch5_Suppy_Chain_Data.xlsx (Worksheet: Two-Way ANOVA)*
Add-ins > Real Statistics > Data Analysis Tools (Anova > Two Factor Anova)

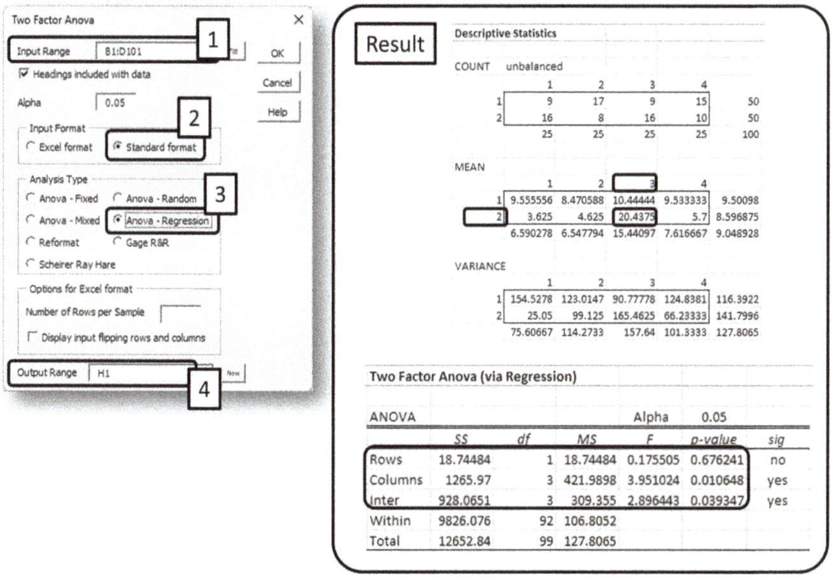

FIGURE 5.7
Two-Way ANOVA in Excel

the mean values of the time delayed for the other routes are between 3 and 6 minutes, which are considered acceptable. Therefore, they decide to focus on analyzing the route from DC 2 to Store 3 by supply chain mapping.

5.9 SUPPLY CHAIN MAPPING

Supply chain mapping is a process of using a graph to visualize the flow of products, money or information (Mubarik et al., 2021). First, the entities are identified, for example, the warehouses and the stores. Second, their relationships are analyzed, such as the route between two locations. This can help identify bottlenecks which are possible factors of delays.

In the example of our Best Toy Company, the supply chain team has identified that the route between DC 2 and Store 3 has significantly longer delays compared to other routes. Therefore, they drill down into details to figure out the bottlenecks by supply chain mapping. This route goes from DC 2, passes through the cross-harbor tunnel toll area and goes straight to the loading area of Store 3, which is located at City Central. They identify the main

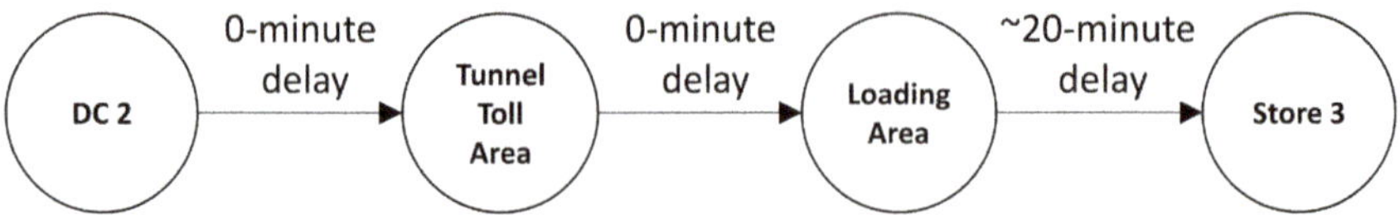

FIGURE 5.8
Supply Chain Mapping

locations this route passes: (1) DC 2, (2) tunnel toll area, (3) loading area and (4) Store 3. The locations are also connected by arrows indicating their transport directions, as shown in Figure 5.8. They track the time of arriving at these main locations with the Global Positioning System (GPS) on the trucks and compare it with the expected time. They figure out that, in fact, the transportation on this route has no delays up to the loading area of the building where Store 3 is located. They then study the videos from the truck cameras, which show that there is a long queue of trucks in the loading area, introducing the 20-minute delay. The supply chain team discusses with the facility management staff of the building where Store 3 is located and identifies the less congested hours. By adjusting the transporting hours, the delay issue is much resolved.

So far, in this chapter, different analytics tools, including metrics, statistical analysis, linear programming and supply chain mapping, have been discussed to solve supply chain problems. On top of these useful tools and skills, **real-time monitoring** is noteworthy. Let us read the case study from **Walmart** to learn how they actually operate with data.

5.10 CASE STUDY: WALMART'S REAL-TIME MONITORING

Walmart Inc. is an American multinational supermarket and grocery store chain. It was founded in 1962. It has been the world's largest company by revenue for many years, according to the Fortune Global 500 List (Collins, 2023; Marr, 2016).

Supermarkets compete on price, convenience and customer service. Customers like to shop the products in one shop at the best price with good customer service. They also expect the product to be in the shop when they need it. Walmart knows this well. Therefore, they have set up indicators to trigger alerts to the shops and monitor the indicators in real time. One Halloween, the highly popular cookies with high predicted sales were not selling at all in some stores. This triggered an alert to the responsible team in those stores. It was found that these cookies had simply not yet put on the shelves. This does not involve complicated logic, but if they were not monitored in real time, the sales period may have simply passed and the revenue been missed.

Therefore, on top of predicting the right products at the right price, at the right place and at the right time, monitoring the indicators in real time is of the same high value.

5.11 THE FUTURE OF SUPPLY CHAIN ANALYTICS

Supply chain management covers a network of processes within and across companies, comprising tiers of suppliers and customers (Bento et al., 2024; Wang et al., 2007).

Integrating sophisticated data analytics capabilities in Enterprise Resource Planning (ERP) systems is a future development. Most companies capture data in the supply chain process in ERP systems. With the advancement in technologies, like Global Positioning System (GPS) and the Internet of Things (IoT), the detailed location of the products and the exact time of deliveries can be tracked, providing an additional source of abundance data for companies (Kunrath et al., 2023; Souza, 2014). ERP systems have the strength of capturing data in one central database instead of having data located fragmentedly in different systems. If ERP systems can build on this strength, with the incorporation of sophisticated data analytics capabilities, these systems can bring company decision-making for supply chain management to new heights.

Analyzing the social network in supply chain management is also a next trend in the field (Bento et al., 2024; Wichmann & Kaufmann, 2016). Apart from managing the flow of products, money and information, the success of supply chain management also relies on the effective collaborating activities involving the elements of vendor relationship and customer relationship which deserve supply chain professionals' attention. In data analytics, **social network analysis (SNA)** can be applied to analyze relationships in this network of relationships. Understanding the mechanics of these relationships helps the supply chain team identify bottlenecks due to human conflicts, improve communication effectiveness and enable collaboration efficiency.

This chapter has covered different data analytics applications in supply chain management with real-world case studies. The future trends of data analytics in this field were also discussed.

The data analytics skills discussed in Chapters 3 to 5 can, in fact, can be applied in different business areas. With more practice, these analytics skills will enable you to solve different business problems in different organizations.

REFERENCES

Association for Supply Chain Management. (2022). *ASCM Supply Chain Operations Reference Model SCOR Digital Standard.* https://scor.ascm.org/

Bento, A. I., Cruz, C., Fernandes, G., & Ferreira, L. M. D. F. (2024). Social network analysis: applications and new metrics for supply chain management – a literature review. *Logistics, 8*(1), 15.

Bowers, M. R., Petrie, A., & Holcomb, M. C. (2017). Unleashing the potential of supply chain analytics. *MIT Sloan Management Review, 59*(1), 14.

Cheung, W., Leung, L. C., & Wong, Y. M. (2001). Strategic service network design for DHL Hong Kong. *Interfaces, 31*(4), 1–14.

Collins, G. (2023, June 23). *Walmart tops the Fortune 500 list with USD611.3bn revenue.* Business Chief. https://businesschief.com/articles/walmart-tops-the-fortune-500-list-with-us-611-3bn-revenue

Dhaigude, A. S., Chatterjee, D., & Chakrabarti, S. (2018). *Kamaths Ourtimes Ice Creams: Eliminating the Bottleneck Effect.* Ivey Publishing.

Hult, G. T. M., Ketchen, D. J., & Nichols, E. L. (2002). An examination of cultural competitiveness and order fulfillment cycle time within supply chains. *Academy of Management Journal, 45*(3), 577–586.

Kunrath, T. L., Dresch, A., & Veit, D. R. (2023). Supply chain management and industry 4.0: a theoretical approach. *Brazilian Journal of Operations & Production Management, 20*(1), 1263.

Marr, B. (2016). Walmart: how big data is used to drive supermarket performance. In B. Marr (Ed.), *Big Data in Practice: How 45 Successful Companies Used Big Data Analytics to Deliver Extraordinary Results* (pp. 5–10). West Sussex, United Kingdom: John Wiley and Sons Ltd.

Mubarik, M. S., Kusi-Sarpong, S., Govindan, K., Khan, S. A., & Oyedijo, A. (2021). Supply chain mapping: a proposed construct. *International Journal of Production Research, 61*(8), 2653–2669.

Nelson, R. D. (2002). John Deere optimizes operations with supply management efforts. *Journal of Organizational Excellence, 21*(2), 3–11.

Nguyen, T. T. H. (2024). Measuring supply chain performance using the SCOR model. *Operations Research Forum, 5*(2), 37.

Randall, W. S., & Farris, M. T. (2009). Supply chain financing: using cash-to-cash variables to strengthen the supply chain. *International Journal of Physical Distribution & Logistics Management, 39*(8), 669–689.

Robertson, P. W. (2021). *Supply Chain Analytics: Using Data to Optimise Supply Chain Processes.* Taylor & Francis Group.

Souza, G. C. (2014). Supply chain analytics. *Business Horizons, 57*(5), 595–605.

Stock, J. R., & Manrodt, K. B. (2020). *Supply Chain Management.* McGraw-Hill Education.

Wang, W. Y. C., Heng, M. S. H., & Chau, P. Y. K. (2007). *Supply Chain Management: Issues in the New Era of Collaboration and Competition.* Idea Group Publishing.

Wichmann, B. K., & Kaufmann, L. (2016). Social network analysis in supply chain management research. *International Journal of Physical Distribution & Logistics Management, 46*(8), 740–762.

6

Building Analytics Capabilities, Running Projects and Future Trends

A 2023 global survey of over 100 organizations in the Fortune 1000 has shown that 87.9% of them said that investments in data and analytics are a top organizational priority (Statista, 2024). This investment intention has resulted in a global data analytics market size valued at USD 64.99 billion in 2024 (Fortune Business Insights, 2025). This huge amount of investment in resources for data analytics is largely because of the fact that the sources and outcomes of data analytics bring competitive advantage (Cosic et al., 2015). According to the resource-based view (RBV) of the firm, organizations use their internal attributes and resources to generate outcomes, which help organizations outperform competitors by competitive advantages (Barney, 1991). These internal resources are likely *valuable*, *rare*, *inimitable* and *non-substitutable* (VRIN). The three main types of organizational resources include physical capital resources (e.g., infrastructure and computers), human capital resources (e.g., skillsets, experience, judgment, and relationships) and organizational capital resources (e.g., culture, organization governance, formal and informal planning and controlling systems). These resources, although not usually directly transferable to one another, complement and work together to enhance organizational capabilities, including technology, people and culture capabilities, which bring organizations competitive advantages (Cosic et al., 2015).

In this chapter, the three types of organizational resources leveraged during the journey in which organizations build the three types of analytics capabilities will be explored. Real-world case studies on how companies may grow analytics capabilities using their resources will be discussed. Though these distinctive resources may not be easily duplicated, their experience will likely be inspirational. The text will then discuss project objectives to be achieved

DOI: 10.1201/9781032642307-6

along the roadmap of an organization's analytics maturity (Davenport & Harris, 2017). The future of data analytics will also be explored.

6.1 ANALYTICS CAPABILITIES: THE RESOURCE-BASED VIEW

Organizations use their resources to exploit opportunities or neutralize threats through the capabilities these resources generate (Barney, 1991). According to the resource-based view (RBV) of the firm (Barney, 1991), there are three types of resources, namely physical capital resources, human capital resources and organizational capital resources. For data analytics, organizations use physical capital resources to build technology capabilities, human capital resources to develop people capabilities and organizational capital resources to establish culture capabilities (Cosic et al., 2015), as shown in Figure 6.1. The processes through which organizations build the linkage between the resources and the corresponding capabilities may vary. Whether the organizations can identify these processes and whether these processes can be replicated determine the *value, rareness, inimitability* and *non-substitutability* (VRIN) of these resources and capabilities. These capabilities integrate to contribute to competitive advantage. When the linkage between resources and capabilities is ambiguous, success is difficult to replicate, even within the same organization. Therefore, the following three sections intend to shed light on these linkages, demonstrating through discussions and real-world case studies.

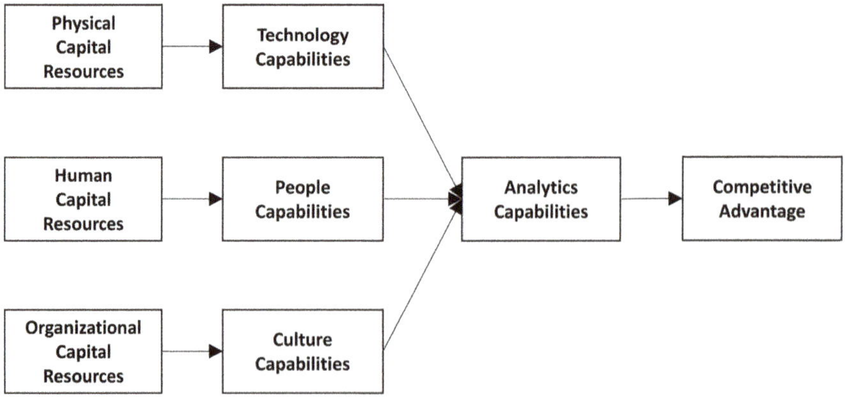

FIGURE 6.1
Organization Resources and Analytics Capabilities

6.1.1 Physical Capital Resources and Technology Capabilities

Physical capital resources in organizations are usually tangible and relatively easily quantifiable assets such as infrastructure, networks, computers and technology. These resources are generally highly commoditized and likely replicable. For example, if one organization implements a 5G network with an internet provider, other organizations can engage that provider to have the network available. However, how the organization makes use of this resource to provide technology capabilities can make a difference. If the organization builds computer systems running on the network to gather data, which provide insights for the organization to make better decisions via data analytics, this provides distinctive competitive advantages. Data are not easily imitable due to the unique historical conditions and the fact that they are socially complex to generate. Some data must be collected and gathered at a particular time and place, and these data cannot be easily gathered once the time has passed and the situations cannot be reproduced. Most may think that data analytics is only exclusively available for large organizations. In fact, small and medium-sized enterprises (SMEs) can also make use of data analytics to gain a competitive edge. Let us see a real-world case study from **XDel Singapore** to see how they turn technology resources into success (Kusnadi et al., 2021).

XDel Singapore was established in 1993. XDel is a short form for "Express Delivery." XDel provides express courier and delivery services, as well as international cross-border logistics activities. Starting from a two-man operation, XDel grows to be a company with about 100 staff in 2021. Revenue has risen to USD 5.4 million in 2020. The company has long invested in technology to support its business, cumulating to USD 1.5 million since the establishment of the company. They built and have kept enhancing their in-house HOMES Enterprise Resource Planning (ERP) system and LUKE mobile app to capture courier attendance, verify and authenticate secured delivery, advise the couriers on the best vehicle route, handle billing, analyze delivery quality and empower their customers to track the progress of the delivery. Apart from providing a single source of truth, the system provides a distinctive function, which is providing an application programming interface (API) to integrate with the systems of clients who offer the company a certain volume of business. This level of customized service can only be provided with an in-house IT team, not by any off-the-shelf IT package providers. The company believes that their tech-savviness provides them a competitive advantage comparable to large courier players like DHL by improving significantly in efficiency and productivity, making better decisions by data analytics like heat maps of delivery areas and route planning, enhancing security for confidential documents and empowering customers to track delivery progress.

You may find that in XDel Singapore's case study, the process of transforming their physical capital resources into technology capabilities largely depends on their in-house IT team. In the next section, let us look at how organizations may transform their human capital resources into people capabilities.

6.1.2 Human Capital Resources and People Capabilities

Literature has consistently suggested that human capital resources contribute to organizational competitive advantages (Barney & Wright, 1998; Das Gupta, 2020; Delery & Roumpi, 2017). To equip the human capital resources with analytics capabilities, apart from learning these skills, which were largely covered in the previous chapters of this book, some organizations also start by partnering with consultants, collaborating with academics, or acquiring resources with these skillsets from other organizations.

Engaging with consultants is a common industry practice, which provides instant specialized analytics knowledge and skills. In order to retain these skills within the organizations, some managers run analytics projects by seconding their employees to work with the consultants to gain hands-on analytics skills during the project and by arranging proper handover sessions when the project ends.

Scholar-practitioner collaboration is also increasingly common. A real-world case study from **Inditex** shows how they collaborate with academics to start building analytics capabilities in organizations (Simón & Ferreiro, 2018). Inditex is a Spanish multinational fashion retail company with brands like Zara and Pull&Bear. The company has invited the academics to join their analytics projects as academic advisors. Their academic research capabilities help the company gain pace in picking up analytics skills. Through the collaboration, the academics may discover new knowledge through real-world data, contributing to knowledge through journal publications. The company also increases its positive image through collaboration with academics.

Acquiring human resources with analytics skills is a direct way to build analytics capabilities in the workforce. The analytics skills in some industries like finance may be more common than in other industries. A real-world case study from **Chow Tai Fook Jewellery Group**, one of the world's largest jewelers, has acquired their analytics resources from the finance industry to improve their inventory management (Zhang & Chen, 2019). Some companies may be willing to offer very high salary packages to acquire scarce skillsets in the human resource market. For example, **Uber Technologies**, a multinational transportation company, lured scientists away from Carnegie Mellon University during a collaboration on driverless car research (Ramsey & MacMillan, 2015). This real-world case has shown that such human resource competitions can sometimes be fierce. However, the case did not further report if those scientists performed better or worse after joining Uber, as it is not difficult to understand that different organizations have different cultures, which provide different environments that may alter employee performance. In the next section, how organizations may transform their organizational capital resources into culture capabilities will be explored.

6.1.3 Organizational Capital Resources and Culture Capabilities

Organizational capital resources in organizations are processes or usually intangible characteristics such as culture, reputation and governance systems. These attributes or characteristics are complex, integrated and difficult to imitate. For example, the culture emerged in the early stage of an organization's history is unique. The reputation built along the development process of an organization may simply be inimitable. The governance systems also contribute to an organization's culture capabilities. These capabilities provide a foundation for the people working there to realize their potential and contribute to the organization. Imagine an organization having the culture capabilities to support evidence-based decision rather than decisions by gut feeling would be more likely to accept using data analytics to make decisions. Culture capabilities are usually built from organizational capital resources such as leadership practices, governance processes, reward systems, and training and development programs. Let us see a case study from **Agoda**, an online travel agency, on the journey they took to build their data analytics culture for managing human resources (Goh & Mark, 2017).

Agoda is a global online travel agency headquartered in Singapore founded in 2005. In 2007, Agoda was acquired by the Priceline Group (now Booking Holdings, an American travel technology company) with a focus on expanding in Asia. By 2016, Agoda had grown into a multinational company with 40 offices in 31 countries and over 2,500 employees. As an online travel agency, like other technology companies, Agoda is accustomed to using data to garner insights and make data-driven decisions in pricing and services provided to their customers. The company targeted extending this data-driven practice and making a fundamental change in the role of human resources (HR), from a policy-setting and compliance-monitoring department to one that develops data-driven insights to empower frontline managers, for example, to make decisions on bonuses to motivate their employees. The senior management team had this aligned vision for the change. To initiate it, the company recruited a new director to lead the analytics transformation process. The company first digitized the HR processes using information systems like Workday and Greenhouse. With the data ready, they built correlations between performance and bonuses in a user-friendly format shown to managers for their data-driven decision-making. Was this the end of implementing analytics in HR? In fact, not yet. There were more challenges the company was facing. For example, some frontline managers believed that they were already good at what they did and how they did it. If the correlation results presented evidence showing their shortcomings, some managers were defensive and resistant to change. Changing business processes and employee behaviors is usually the most difficult and time-consuming challenge of cultural change (Davenport & Harris, 2017).

This case study did not report how Agoda handled those challenges. However, as mentioned in Chapter 1, data analytics is not a one-off process, and the transformation journey will continue. Different companies pursuing this analytics journey are likely in different stages at a certain point in time. Davenport and Harris (2017) define this journey in the five stages of the analytics maturity roadmap.

6.2 PROJECTS ALONG THE ROADMAP OF ANALYTICS MATURITY

To become an analytically mature organization which makes the full use of analytics as a competitive advantage, Davenport and Harris (2017) identify the five stages of the analytics maturity roadmap. The objectives of the projects at each stage are also highlighted in the following paragraphs.

Stage 1 – *Prerequisites to Analytical Competition* – is a preparation stage. Organizations at this stage have little awareness of analytics, with poor-quality data and minimal analytical capabilities. A 2023 global survey from over 100 organizations in the Fortune 1000 has shown that, though the majority said that investments in data and analytics are a top organizational priority, only 37% said their efforts in improving data quality were successful (Statista, 2024). There is no fast track, only hard work, when facing data quality issues. The main objectives in this stage are to gain management support and obtain accurate data. After these objectives are achieved, some organizations choose to go full steam ahead to analytical competition, while other organizations choose to go step by step to stage 2.

Stage 2 – *Prove-It Detour* – is an experimental stage. Organizations at this stage implement some small-scale analytics tasks, document benefits and share news with key stakeholders. The objectives of the projects at this stage are to acquire analytics experience, gather successes and gain enough sponsorship to move to the next stage.

Stage 3 – *Analytical Aspirations* – is a visionary stage for analytics competition. Organizations at this stage have a vision to launch their first major project for competitive advantages. The objectives of this stage are to scope the project, secure committed resources, and have a timetable to implement an integrated enterprise-wide analytics platform for their first major project.

Stage 4 – *Analytical Companies* – is the implementation stage of the first enterprise-wide analytics project. At this stage, organizations acquire solid analytics capabilities mentioned in the previous sections of this chapter. The objective of the projects in this stage is to integrate analytics practices into different organizational processes. This may be a difficult part, as mentioned in the case study of Agoda in the previous section.

Stage 5 – *Analytical Competitors* – is the harvest stage. Organizations at this stage turn analytics capabilities into strategies and competitive advantages. They report their innovations and growth in performance driven by analytics. The key objective of this stage to continue gathering new data to ensure the models remain applicable as the business environment changes (Gray & Shellshear, 2025). Organizations are also advised to avoid complacency and stay vigilant to sustain their competitive advantage through data analytics.

6.3 FUTURE TRENDS OF DATA ANALYTICS

There is no doubt that data analytics will continue to flourish in different industries, with more and more organizations announcing successful stories of data analytics applications (Boulton, 2020). The recent technological advancements in machine learning (ML) and artificial intelligence (AI) also catalyze the applications of data analytics in business (Gartner, 2025). More developments in data analytics are foreseeable.

First, more autonomous analytics for some relatively straightforward analytics models are expected (Davenport & Harris, 2017). Second, the demand for integrating predictive analytics functions into organizations' information systems, such as Enterprise Resource Planning (ERP) systems, will increase

(Shi & Wang, 2018). Third, the presence of autonomous analytics allows more time for data analytics scientists to explore more complex models like those using SPSS process (Preacher & Hayes, 2004). Fourth, the increasing scale of analytics projects requires organizations to strengthen their governance of the analytics processes and professional trainings in data ethics (Baijens et al., 2022).

REFERENCES

Baijens, J., Huygh, T., & Helms, R. (2022). Establishing and theorising data analytics governance: a descriptive framework and a VSM-based view. *Journal of Business Analytics, 5*(1), 101–122.

Barney, J. (1991). Firm resources and sustained competitive advantage. *Journal of Management, 17*(1), 99–120.

Barney, J. B., & Wright, P. M. (1998). On becoming a strategic partner: the role of human resources in gaining competitive advantage. *Human Resource Management, 37*(1), 31.

Boulton, C. (2020, February 25). *5 data analytics success stories: an inside look*. CIO.com. https://www.cio.com/article/230618/6-data-analytics-success-stories-an-inside-look.html

Cosic, R., Shanks, G., & Maynard, S. B. (2015). A business analytics capability framework. *Australasian Journal of Information Systems, 19*, S5–S19.

Das Gupta, A. (2020). *Strategic Human Resource Management: Formulating and Implementing HR Strategies for a Competitive Advantage*. Productivity Press.

Davenport, T. H., & Harris, J. G. (2017). *Competing on Analytics, Updated, with a New Introduction: The New Science of Winning*. Harvard Business Review Press.

Delery, J. E., & Roumpi, D. (2017). Strategic human resource management, human capital and competitive advantage: is the field going in circles? *Human Resource Management Journal, 27*(1), 1–21.

Fortune Business Insights. (2025, May 19). *Data analytics market size, share & industry analysis*. https://www.fortunebusinessinsights.com/data-analytics-market-108882

Gartner. (2025, March 5). *Gartner identifies top trends in data and analytics for 2025*. https://www.gartner.com/en/newsroom/press-releases/2025-03-05-gartner-identifies-top-trends-in-data-and-analytics-for-2025

Goh, K., & Mark, K. (2017). *Agoda: People Analytics and Business Culture*. Ivey Publishing.

Gray, D., & Shellshear, E. (2025). *Why Data Science Projects Fail*. CRC Press.

Kusnadi, Y., Pan, G., & Lim, T. (2021). *XDel Singapore: Using Technology to Deliver Simplicity*. SMU Centre for Management Practice.

Preacher, K. J., & Hayes, A. F. (2004). SPSS and SAS procedures for estimating indirect effects in simple mediation models. *Behavior Research Methods, Instruments, & Computers, 36*(4), 717–731.

Ramsey, M., & MacMillan, D. (2015, May 31). *Carnegie Mellon reels after Uber lures away researchers*. The Wall Street Journal. https://www.wsj.com/articles/is-uber-a-friend-or-foe-of-carnegie-mellon-in-robotics-1433084582

Shi, Z., & Wang, G. (2018). Integration of big-data ERP and business analytics (BA). *Journal of High Technology Management Research, 29*(2), 141–150.

Simón, C., & Ferreiro, E. (2018). Workforce analytics: a case study of scholar-practitioner collaboration. *Human Resource Management*, *57*(3), 781–793.
Statista. (2024, March 14). *State of data and analytics investment at companies worldwide in 2023.* https://www.statista.com/statistics/1453262/global-state-of-data-analytics-investment/
Zhang, W., & Chen, J. (2019). *Digging for Gold with Data Analytics at Chow Tai Fook.* HKU Business School.

Index

For Product Safety Concerns and Information please contact our EU
representative GPSR@taylorandfrancis.com
Taylor & Francis Verlag GmbH, Kaufingerstraße 24, 80331 München, Germany

www.ingramcontent.com/pod-product-compliance
Ingram Content Group UK Ltd.
Pitfield, Milton Keynes, MK11 3LW, UK
UKHW022121190926
475702UK00013B/1582
* 9 7 8 1 0 3 2 6 1 9 9 9 6 *